BIDEN AND BEYOND
The United States Rethinks South Asia

BIDEN AND BEYOND
The United States Rethinks South Asia

Editors

C. Raja Mohan
Hernaikh Singh

Institute of South Asian Studies,
National University of Singapore, Singapore

World Scientific

NEW JERSEY · LONDON · SINGAPORE · BEIJING · SHANGHAI · HONG KONG · TAIPEI · CHENNAI · TOKYO

Published by

World Scientific Publishing Co. Pte. Ltd.
5 Toh Tuck Link, Singapore 596224
USA office: 27 Warren Street, Suite 401-402, Hackensack, NJ 07601
UK office: 57 Shelton Street, Covent Garden, London WC2H 9HE

Library of Congress Control Number: 2024938894

British Library Cataloguing-in-Publication Data
A catalogue record for this book is available from the British Library.

BIDEN AND BEYOND
The United States Rethinks South Asia

Copyright © 2024 by World Scientific Publishing Co. Pte. Ltd.

All rights reserved. This book, or parts thereof, may not be reproduced in any form or by any means, electronic or mechanical, including photocopying, recording or any information storage and retrieval system now known or to be invented, without written permission from the publisher.

For photocopying of material in this volume, please pay a copying fee through the Copyright Clearance Center, Inc., 222 Rosewood Drive, Danvers, MA 01923, USA. In this case permission to photocopy is not required from the publisher.

ISBN 978-981-12-7642-2 (hardcover)
ISBN 978-981-12-7643-9 (ebook for institutions)
ISBN 978-981-12-7644-6 (ebook for individuals)

For any available supplementary material, please visit
https://www.worldscientific.com/worldscibooks/10.1142/13412#t=suppl

Desk Editors: Claire Lum/Kura Sunaina

Typeset by Stallion Press
Email: enquiries@stallionpress.com

Printed in Singapore

© 2024 World Scientific Publishing Company Pte. Ltd.
https://doi.org/10.1142/9789811276439_fmatter

Preface

Although its interest and attention in South Asia has tended to be episodic, the United States (US) has remained the most important external power shaping the Indian subcontinent's trajectory since the region's independence in the middle of the 20th century. While Britain's influence as the former colonial power steadily declined, the Soviet Union emerged as the principal great power competitor to the US in South Asia. The 21st century has seen the steady rise of China as a critical external actor in the subcontinent even as the US remained somewhat narrowly focused on the great war on terror in Afghanistan. The first signs of a dramatic transformation in the US' policy towards the region came in 2017 when President Donald Trump signalled his impatience with the extended US military intervention in Afghanistan that began after the massive terror attack against New York and Washington on 11 September 2001. Trump ordered peace talks with the Taliban insurgents and his administration made it quite clear that the priority was to find a quick and safe exit for American troops from Afghanistan.

Equally important was the articulation of the Indo-Pacific strategy by the Trump administration at the end of 2017. The strategy, in essence, was about replacing the Asia-Pacific regional framework that dominated US thinking on the East with an Indo-Pacific construct. At the core of this new strategy were two significant decisions. The first was a recognition that an increasingly assertive China poses major challenges to American interests in Asia and that Washington needs to find a way to balance Beijing in the region. This complemented Trump's broader contestation with China on trade issues. The second significant element of the strategy was to bring India into the East Asian geopolitical calculus. The decision to put 'Indo' into the 'Pacific' befuddled most observers in Asia, but the Trump administration set about the task of intensifying strategic engagement with India and initiated deep structural changes in the way it dealt with Asia. For many observers of the US and Asia, it was by no means clear if Trump's policies had bipartisan domestic political support and would survive his defeat in the 2020 elections. After all, many leading lights of the Republican as well as Democratic parties had mounted serious criticism of Trump's China strategy and the Indo-Pacific framework.

The origins of this volume date back to the moment when Trump lost his bid for re-election and Joe Biden was yet to take charge. We at the Institute of South Asian Studies (ISAS) at the National University of Singapore (NUS) published a volume, *President Biden and South Asia*, under the South Asia Discussion Papers (SADP) series in January 2021. The objective was to review the Trump administration's policies towards the subcontinent and delineate the potential direction in which Biden might set out to take the US' South Asian policy. We were convinced at that point that Trump's approach marked an important turning point in the US' engagement with South Asia. The question was whether Biden would continue down that road. The first two and a half years of the Biden term have given us ample evidence that the US has doubled down on the course laid out by Trump. If anything, Biden has been more systematic and thorough in competing vigorously with China, lending greater substance to the Indo-Pacific framework, putting India at the very centre of the US' strategy for South Asia as well as the Indo-Pacific. This, in turn, is having a profound impact on intra-South Asian relations as well as the subcontinent's engagement with broader Asia and the major powers, including China, Japan, Russia and Europe.

This volume is an attempt to capture some of the structural changes in the subcontinent triggered by the US' regional policies initiated under Trump and reinforced under his successor, Biden. We invited some of the contributors to the SADP series in January 2021 as well as others to offer a comprehensive assessment of the new US approach to South Asia and its wider implications. We are grateful to all the scholars who contributed to this volume and have together offered some invaluable insights into the shifting terrain of South Asia's regional and international relations.

We would like to thank Ms Wini Fred Gurung, then at ISAS, for her valuable assistance in helping us put together this volume. We also thank Associate Professor Iqbal Singh Sevea, Director, ISAS, for his strong and consistent support for this project.

C. Raja Mohan
Hernaikh Singh
April 2024

© 2024 World Scientific Publishing Company Pte. Ltd.
https://doi.org/10.1142/9789811276439_fmatter

Contents

Preface		v
Chapter 1	The United States and South Asia: New Thinking *C. Raja Mohan and Hernaikh Singh*	1
Chapter 2	The Biden Reset: Implications for South Asia *Monish Tourangbam*	13
Chapter 3	India at the Centre, Small States In and Af-Pak Out: Understanding Biden's South Asia Policy *Yogesh Joshi and Devyani Chaturvedi*	33
Chapter 4	Carving a Relationship: The United States and the Taliban's Afghanistan *Javid Ahmad and Marvin G. Weinbaum*	53
Chapter 5	Reflections on United States–Pakistan Relations, Post-American Withdrawal from Afghanistan *Michael Kugelman*	79
Chapter 6	Nepal and Bhutan: The United States Returns to the Himalayas *Nishchal N. Pandey*	97

Chapter 7	United States–Bangladesh Relations since Joe Biden's Assumption of Office	113
	Farooq Sobhan	
Chapter 8	The United States and Sri Lanka: Winning Back Colombo	137
	Asanga Abeyagoonasekera	
Chapter 9	The United States and the Maldives: Setting Strategic Ties	159
	Amit Ranjan	
Chapter 10	Beyond Biden: India–United States Relations	177
	S. D. Muni	
Chapter 11	United States–India Trade Relations: The IPEF and Beyond	197
	Amitendu Palit	
Chapter 12	Indian Americans: Visibility and Influence	217
	Seema Sirohi	

About the Editors	235
About the Contributors	237
Index	243

© 2024 World Scientific Publishing Company Pte. Ltd.
https://doi.org/10.1142/9789811276439_0001

Chapter 1

The United States and South Asia: New Thinking

C. Raja Mohan and Hernaikh Singh

One of the many surprises from the United States (US) President Joe Biden, who took charge of the White House in January 2021 after the tumultuous Donald Trump era, has been the unprecedented attention his administration has been paying to India. India's Prime Minister Narendra Modi was only the third leader hosted for a state visit at the White House by Biden until June 2023. Exuding great personal bonhomie towards Modi, Biden promised to make the relationship with India "one of the most consequential partnerships" of the US.[1] The visit also saw the US announce significant liberalisation of US defence, advanced technology transfers to India and a beef up of the Indo-Pacific engagement. Historically, US–India relations have tended to oscillate between hostility and hesitant engagement, earning such descriptions as "estranged democracies"[2] and "impossible allies".[3]

The transformation of the US' policy towards India under the Biden administration can be summed up as putting India first in America's South Asia policy. This contingency was not something that any observers of US engagement with the subcontinent had bet on over the decades. Although the bilateral relationship has steadily moved in an upward direction since the visit of US President Bill Clinton to India in March 2000 — after a gap of nearly 22 years — it was only in the second decade of the 21st century that it generated much mutual trust and a robust agenda for strategic cooperation. With US–India relations poised for take-off, the US' policy towards the subcontinent has come a full circle — from the traditional focus on Pakistan to India as the new fulcrum of its regional policy.

This change is rooted as much in factors purely bilateral to India and the US as in more significant geopolitical and geoeconomic changes that have unfolded in the region and the world. The last decade has seen significant changes in the global environment and the US response to these changes. Meanwhile, the salience of the subcontinent has continued to rise in the region and beyond. This volume brings together perspectives on the dynamic interaction under the Biden administration between an altered global environment, new trends in US foreign policy and the structural changes in South Asia.

In this introductory essay, we briefly review the decline and rise of South Asia's strategic salience for Washington since the middle of the 20th century. We examine the discontinuities in America's regional policy that emerged under the Trump administration and a more deliberate recalibration of US policy towards the subcontinent under Biden. We conclude this chapter by highlighting the key themes of the chapters that follow.

Relative Decline

The Indian subcontinent had become steadily marginal to the US and the West during the Cold War. Although undivided India significantly contributed to the Allied victory in the First and Second World Wars, independent India distanced itself from the West in the security domains and drew closer to the Soviet Union. Pakistan, in contrast, became part of the US' Cold War alliances against Moscow. From a global perspective though, the subcontinent was on the sidelines of the Cold War confrontation, concentrated in Europe and Northeast Asia.

To be sure, India carried a strong global voice in the Cold War's early years. As it drifted towards the Soviet Union and closed its economy, India's salience diminished on the world stage. Pakistan was an important ally of the West in the Cold War and was widely seen as a moderate Islamic nation with a leadership role in the Muslim world. Pakistan, however, could not turn these strategic advantages into long-term economic gains. Its turn to Islamic politics at home and in the region eventually constrained its Asian global possibilities. More fundamentally, the partition of the subcontinent left a host of problems between India and Pakistan and turned their energies to dealing with prolonged bilateral conflicts that reduced the political weight of both countries on the regional and global stages. During the colonial era, India was at the centre of economic globalisation in Asia and the Indian Ocean. Post-colonial South Asia, however, turned inwards economically in the name of socialism. This led to the region's relative decline in Asia, parts of which were making significant economic advances.

The end of the Cold War seemed to witness a decline in the US' strategic interest in the subcontinent. The US, which had invested massively in Pakistan to defeat the Soviet occupation of Afghanistan during the 1980s, turned its back on the region once Moscow withdrew its troops at the end of the decade. After the Soviet Union collapsed, the US' focus was on broader issues rather than developing productive bilateral relations. At the top of the US' agenda was a commitment to end India–Pakistan tensions in Kashmir and roll back the nuclear and missile programmes of both countries. The US' pressures turned out counterproductive as New Delhi and Islamabad brought their nuclear programmes out of the closet and declared themselves nuclear weapon powers. The US' attempt at mediating the Kashmir question and dousing the India–Pakistan conflicts over it in the 1990s left both New Delhi and Islamabad unhappy and left America's Kashmir project unsuccessful.

Re-engagement

Several developments at the turn of the 21st century saw a resurgence of the US' interest in the subcontinent. The 9/11 terror attacks against New York and Washington saw the US return to Afghanistan, push the Taliban out of power, establish a substantive American and North Atlantic Treaty Organization (NATO) military presence, commit significant resources to drain the swamps of terror in the country and launch the economic and political reconstruction of the country. President George W. Bush's new effort in Afghanistan, declared as part of the "Great War on Terror",[4] relied heavily on geographic access to Pakistan. The Bush administration declared Pakistan as a "major non-NATO ally"[5] and offered significant military and economic assistance to Pakistan. Unlike in the past though, Washington managed to prevent the new engagement with Pakistan from derailing the emerging strategic possibilities with India. The Bush administration achieved this goal by "de-hyphenating' its relations with India and Pakistan. It also accepted the de-facto nuclear weapon status of India and Pakistan, amended the non-proliferation regime to facilitate renewed international civil nuclear cooperation with New Delhi and consciously eschewed activism on the Kashmir question. In declaring that Kashmir was a bilateral dispute, Washington formally set aside persistent Pakistani demands for American mediation. This generated trust in New Delhi about the US' intentions and created a space for productive engagement. Meanwhile, Pakistan enjoyed a special status as American forces stayed in Afghanistan to pursue the war on terror and stabilise Afghanistan.

Bush managed what none of his predecessors could do — develop good relations simultaneously with both India and Pakistan, pursue each on its own merit and avoid being drawn into the Indo-Pak disputes. If the engagement with Pakistan was driven by the US' commitment to Afghanistan, the new partnership with India was animated by a perceived need to ensure a stable balance of power in Asia. As China's rapid rise sharpened the US' concerns about Asian balance, India's strategic weight steadily increased. This broad orientation continued under President Barack Obama (2009–2017).

Two other factors contributed to the growing importance of the region in Washington. The first factor was India's faster economic growth in the new millennium and the impressive performance of Bangladesh, which produced a new commercial significance for the region. Until the slowdown of the late 2010s, the subcontinent was one of the fastest-growing regions of the world, just after China. India's two-way trade in goods and services with the US soared to US$191 billion in 2022,[6] making the US the most important trading partner for India. The expanding commercial engagement, despite persistent trade disputes, gave greater breadth and depth to Washington's interest in India. The second factor was the significant expansion of the Indian diaspora in the US. The Indian diaspora in the US is now estimated at around four million, of which nearly two million are said to be registered voters.[7] Their concentration in some of the deeply contested battleground states has seen both the Democratic and Republican parties vying for influence among the Indian community. Meanwhile, the population with origins in the rest of the subcontinent is also growing. The academic and professional success of the South Asian diaspora has seen its members occupy important positions in American businesses as well as in the executive and legislatures of the government at the federal, state and local levels. The expansion of the diaspora has also transposed political contestations within and among the South Asian nations into the public and political square in the US. Competitive mobilisation of the diaspora by India and Pakistan and protests by multiple dissident South Asian groups appear to have become part of the region's deepening ties with the US.

Trump Discontinuity

The subcontinent was one of the few regions that drew early policy attention from Trump in the summer of 2017 when he formally outlined a new policy framework for the region. Although branded as a South Asia policy, it was essentially about Afghanistan and Pakistan. Trump, who argued against America's endless wars in the Greater Middle East, announced a renewed effort to stabilise Afghanistan. That involved a small increase in military presence in Afghanistan and new pressure on Islamabad to help negotiate a peace settlement that would help Trump end America's military intervention in Afghanistan. The Trump administration signed a broad bilateral agreement with the Taliban in February 2020 after nearly 18 months of negotiations. It codified the US' commitment to withdraw its troops from Afghanistan, the Taliban's promise not to attack the US and its allied troops, intra-Afghan talks for a ceasefire and a new political compact to govern the nation. However, this agreement has been criticised as a withdrawal pact rather than a peace settlement. The Taliban, too, have proved the sceptics right by continuing to attack government troops and civilians while delaying talks with the government.

That did not deter Trump from making a decisive shift towards ending American occupation and state-building in Afghanistan. Pakistan, which claimed credit for facilitating talks between the US and the Taliban, was hopeful that its help in brokering the deal would persuade the Trump administration to take a more favourable approach to the issues between Islamabad and New Delhi. Those hopes did not materialise when the US signalled a clear tilt towards India in the two crises over Kashmir that unfolded in 2019. In the wake of a major terror attack in Pulwama in India in February 2019, Washington defended India's right to self-defence and compelled Islamabad to release an Indian Air Force pilot it had detained after a brief air skirmish between the two sides. When India changed the constitutional status of Kashmir in August 2019, a furious Pakistan, backed by China, sought to raise the issue in the United Nations Security Council, and the US helped block a discussion on it. The Trump administration's responses confirmed a distinct departure from the past on Kashmir and an unambiguous political tilt towards India. That tilt could be attributed to the growing convergence of the US and Indian perceptions of the Chinese challenge and the recognition of the need to strengthen their bilateral partnership. The US defined the China challenge by articulating a new strategy for the Indo-Pacific. Modi ended the ambivalence on the Indo-Pacific that he inherited from his predecessor, Manmohan Singh.

As the pressure from China mounted on a range of issues, including on India's Himalayan and maritime frontiers, Modi not only embraced the concept of the Indo-Pacific but also joined hands with the US in reviving the Quadrilateral Security Dialogue (Quad) — which brings together Canberra, New Delhi, Tokyo and Washington — that went into hibernation soon after its unveiling in 2007. India's strong critique in 2017 of China's Belt and Road Initiative resonated well with the Trump administration, and the two sides began discussions on coordinating their efforts in the Quad to offer credible alternatives to infrastructure development in the Indo-Pacific. As the US' strategic focus shifted from the Af-Pak region to the Indo-Pacific, the Trump administration not only sought a stronger security partnership with India but also with the other South Asian littorals like Bangladesh, Sri Lanka and the Maldives. The defence pact, signed in late 2020 by the Maldives and the US, pointed to the return of South Asian waters to renewed prominence. With China's naval power projection into the Indian Ocean, Washington adjusted the lens from which it viewed the subcontinent and its maritime domain.

However, the Trump disruption was broader than constructing a new strategic geography called the Indo-Pacific. Trump challenged many of the main post-War assumptions of the US on the benefits of military alliances, the virtues of free trade and the merits of open borders for immigration. While the doubts about alliances did not come in the way of building a stronger partnership with India, trade and immigration became contentious issues between Washington and New Delhi. Although the trade deficit with India was not among the largest facing the US, Trump never forgot to refer to India as the "tariff king"[8] and demanded greater market access for US products. Attempts by Washington and New Delhi to negotiate a mini-trade deal did not succeed. On the immigration front, Trump's effort to limit the H-1B visas was seen as a huge long-term challenge to the Indian information technology sector that depends on these visas to a considerable extent.

Biden's Recalibration

The Trump disruption was ultimately about the fundamental questions relating to the future of American engagement with the world. Trump's policies produced a strong backlash from the foreign policy establishment and the business elite, both of whom hoped that Biden's election as the president in November 2020 would help restore the status quo ante in Washington. If Trump shocked the US and the world with bold departures from past policies, Biden was equally surprising in his persistence with many of Trump's policies. Two of them are germane to the US' relations with South Asia.

The first was Biden's decision to complete Trump's plans to withdraw from Afghanistan and focus on the Indo-Pacific. Biden recognised the futility of continued military presence in Afghanistan and that it was better for the US to cut its losses and focus on the new challenges in the Indo-Pacific. Biden chose to elevate the Quad forum revived in 2017 by the Trump administration. He convened the first Quad summit virtually in March 2021, and by June 2023, there were five Quad summits. Biden also unveiled the AUKUS alliance with Australia and the United Kingdom — the objective was to boost Australian deterrent capabilities by providing Canberra with nuclear-powered submarines and other advanced technologies. The focus on the Quad and AUKUS was part of Biden's emphasis on rebuilding alliances and strengthening partnerships. Unlike Trump, who berated US allies in Europe and Asia as "free riders",[9] Biden recognised that alliances were at the heart of sustained US primacy in global affairs. Biden also appreciated the fact that strong allies with greater capabilities would ease the US' burden of managing the global order at a time of declining domestic support for expansive global commitments.

Second, the emphasis on alliances was rooted in the clear recognition that China posed the principal challenge to US security and prosperity. There was no retreat from this formulation after the Russian invasion of Ukraine in February 2022. While the US notes the near-term problem presented by Russia in Europe, Washington believes that China's ambition to replace the US-led global order remains the main long-term challenge. Unlike Trump, Biden has sought systematic and vigorous competition with China across the board — from military to economy and technology. He also focused on renewing America's domestic strengths to cope with the demands of competing with China. Biden brought greater clarity to Trump's argument that economic globalisation did not work for the working people in the US and rejected the pursuit of free trade as an end in itself. He sought to rework the global economic order and make it less centred on China by promoting resilient supply chains and deeper economic cooperation with "trusted geographies" like India. This, in turn, reduced the salience of trade disputes between Washington and New Delhi and laid an entirely new basis for commercial engagement between the US and India.

The shift in the US' policy from the war on terror to great power competition and land wars in the Greater Middle East to maritime contestation in the Indo-Pacific have had profound consequences for the US' relations with the South Asian subcontinent. Equally consequential was the emergence of the US–China rivalry as the principal factor shaping Asian geopolitics. For nearly five decades, Asia operated on the assumption of a reasonably cooperative relationship between the US and China. Today, the region is coping with the reality of an intense and all-out geopolitical and geoeconomic contest between Washington and Beijing. South Asia has to deal with other trends in American foreign policy under

Biden — the renewed emphasis on support for democracy and human rights, a renewed focus on multilateralism and a special emphasis on addressing the dangers of climate change.

The chapters in this volume explore the changing terrains of American engagement with South Asia. Monish Tourangbam delves into the sources and implications of the Biden administration's policy reset on South Asia. Yogesh Joshi and Devyani Chaturvedi parse the intersection between the changing geopolitical priorities of Washington's policy towards the subcontinent. Javid Ahmad and Marvin G. Weinbaum reflect on the US failure to stabilise Afghanistan and warn against the dangers of Washington abandoning the Afghan people to illiberal forces at home and regional rivalries. Michael Kugelman examines one of the most significant changes in American policy towards South Asia — the loss of a strategic anchor in the US–Pakistan relationship after the US' withdrawal from Afghanistan and its new focus on building the India partnership to balance China. Nishchal N. Pandey offers an assessment of the growing US engagement with the Himalayan states — Nepal and Bhutan — amidst the rivalry with China, the renewed focus on the Tibetan refugees and the Indo-Pacific framework. Farooq Sobhan notes the broad upward trajectory in Washington's relations with Dhaka but points to the tensions generated by the US' attention to human rights and political freedoms in Bangladesh. America's new interest in South Asia's maritime spaces has inevitably drawn Washington's attention to the two island nations — Sri Lanka and the Maldives. Asanga Abeyagoonasekera examines the inability of Colombo to build on the new US interest, given its authoritarian temptation at home and the Chinese embrace abroad. Amit Ranjan notes how the recent positive evolution of American ties with the Maldives is driven by the commitment of the current government to a strong partnership with India and the deepening India–US maritime partnership to balance Beijing's forays into the Indian Ocean.

S. D. Muni maps the deepening strategic bonds between Washington and New Delhi amidst shared perceptions of the Chinese challenge and the growing imperative of regional security cooperation that is likely to survive a change in governments in either capital. Amitendu Palit examines the multiple dimensions of the growing but complex trade relations between the US and India that have an impact not only on the nature of the bilateral relationship but also on the global and Indo-Pacific economic order. Finally, Seema Sirohi examines the rising salience of the Indian diaspora in the US and the challenges it confronts, including internal divisions and external challenges in American society.

For nearly half a century, the US and international academic and policy discourse on South Asia was dominated by the India–Pakistan conflict, the Kashmir and Afghan questions, and the dangers of nuclear weapons proliferation. Although many of these problems might remain important, new issues have come to the fore and are reshaping the subcontinent and its relations with the US. These include the rise of China and its growing conflicts with Washington and New Delhi, the emergence of India as a major power and the growing strategic importance of the smaller states in the subcontinent. Taken together, the contributions in this volume offer valuable insights into the rapidly changing American engagement with South Asia.

Endnotes

1. "India, US friendship among most consequential in world: Biden", *The Hindu*, 26 June 2023, https://www.thehindu.com/news/national/india-us-friendship-among-most-consequential-in-world-biden/article67009683.ece.
2. Dennis Kux, *India and the United States: Estranged Democracies, 1941–1991* (Pennsylvania: Diane Publishing, 1992).
3. C. Raja Mohan, *Impossible Allies: Nuclear India, the United States and the Global Order* (New Delhi: India Research Press, 2006).
4. George W. Bush Presidential Library, "Global war on terror", National Archives, United States, https://www.georgewbushlibrary.gov/research/topic-guides/global-war-terror.
5. David Rohde, "US will celebrate Pakistan as a 'Major Non-NATO Ally'", *The New York Times*, 19 March 2004, https://www.nytimes.com/2004/03/19/world/us-will-celebrate-pakistan-as-a-major-non-nato-ally.html.
6. Joint statement from the United States and India, The White House, 22 June 2023, https://www.whitehouse.gov/briefing-room/statements-releases/2023/06/22/joint-statement-from-the-united-states-and-india/#:~:text=The%20U.S.%2DIndia%20trade%20and,in%20March%20in%20New%20Delhi.
7. Sumitra Badrinathan, Devesh Kapur and Milan Vaishnav, "How will Indian Americans vote? Results from the 2020 Indian American attitudes survey",

Carnegie Endowment for International Peace, 14 October 2020, https://carnegieendowment.org/2020/10/14/how-will-indian-americans-vote-results-from-2020-indian-american-attitudes-survey-pub-82929.
8. Sanjeev Miglani, "Trump says working on a very big trade deal with India, but will take time", *Reuters*, 19 February 2020, https://www.reuters.com/article/uk-india-usa-trump-idUKKBN20D0FY.
9. Michael Moran, "What Trump gets right about alliances", *Foreign Policy*, 5 December 2019, https://foreignpolicy.com/2019/12/05/trump-right-alliances-free-riding-american-military-might-nato-japan-south-korea/.

© 2024 World Scientific Publishing Company Pte. Ltd.
https://doi.org/10.1142/9789811276439_0002

Chapter 2

The Biden Reset: Implications for South Asia

Monish Tourangbam

Introduction

After four disruptive years of the Donald Trump presidency, Joe Biden entered the Oval Office as the 46th President of the United States (US) with the promise to bring "America back" to the global stage as the primary exponent of multilateralism and to put an end to the unilateral call for "America First". Biden advocated putting diplomacy at the forefront of America's engagement with the world. The US had to win back allies and partners across the world who were apparently left disgruntled by Trump's presidential style. Amidst deepening political polarisation inside the US, an uncertain global balance of power and the disastrous consequences of the COVID-19 pandemic, Biden took office, vowing to reset the course of US foreign policy and restore faith in America's global leadership. Amidst the broader reorientation in US foreign and national security that recognises a new great power competition underway with China, it becomes imperative to assess the implications for South Asia, more particularly, India, Pakistan and Afghanistan, which remain the primary vectors of Washington's South Asia strategy.

This chapter attempts to first unpack the broader context of the US' foreign policy contours under the Biden administration. Thereafter, it analyses the implications of Biden's foreign policy outlook for South Asia following the fateful decision to withdraw from Afghanistan.

Biden's Foreign Policy for an Uncertain World

In his first foreign policy speech after assuming the US presidency, Biden was emphatic in saying:

> We will repair our alliances and engage with the world once again, not to meet yesterday's challenges, but today's and tomorrow's. American leadership must meet this new moment of advancing authoritarianism, including the growing ambitions of China to rival the United States and the determination of Russia to damage and disrupt our democracy.[1]

The US' foreign policy is at a crossroads in the face of an uncertain geopolitical and geoeconomic environment. While the rise of China and its assertive behaviour across the Indo-Pacific occupy the primary focus of the US' foreign policy and national security teams, Russia's invasion of Ukraine in February 2022 has upended the Euro-Atlantic security order, putting a greater onus on the Biden administration to confront the twin challenges of China and Russia.[2] Biden's National Security Strategy (NSS) and National Defense Strategy (NDS) categorically reflect the US' more immediate and long-term threat perceptions and challenges. The NSS contends that "The post-Cold War era is definitively over, and a competition is underway between the major powers to shape what comes next".[3] The four years of the Trump administration have significantly shaped the contours of the succeeding administration in terms of re-engaging the US with traditional allies and reorienting attention to the multilateral avatar of America's foreign policy.

The US had lost its credibility as a global leader during the Trump administration; restoring its rightful place in the world was Biden's call of duty.[4] To turn Washington's attention on the American people and nation-building at home while battling global challenges has been a constant theme in Biden's foreign policy agenda, and long-drawn foreign wars have been as unpopular as ever among the American electorate.[5] Therefore, ending the war in Afghanistan and bringing American forces back home remained high on the priority list of the Biden administration. Moreover, there is a shift in America's strategic priority from battling violent extremist organisations to new long-term great power competition with China and responding to the current aggression from Russia in the Atlantic theatre. Although the policy pronouncement of the rebalancing strategy during the Barack Obama administration heralded such a shift from costly wars in Afghanistan and Iraq, the final withdrawal from Afghanistan marked a distinct departure towards handling the vagaries of a new great power competition with China, which is more comprehensive and global in nature.

Starting in 2001, for more than two decades, the US' strategy in South Asia was identified with its costly war on terror in Afghanistan. The "Operation Enduring Freedom" to hunt those responsible for the 9/11 attacks finally ended up in a campaign to oust the Taliban who were harbouring them. With the Taliban leadership shifting base to Pakistan and the Al-Qaeda leader, Osama Bin Laden, untraceable until 2011 (when he was tracked down in Abbottabad and killed), Washington went into the business of erecting an interim administration in Kabul. The US' military and civilian involvement in the reconstruction of Afghanistan, in concert with its partners and allies, largely defined the contours of the US' strategy in South Asia in the subsequent two decades. Amidst its foreign policy commitments in Afghanistan, the George W. Bush administration also launched its misadventure in Iraq in 2003 that not only diverted resources from the Afghan theatre but also led to the US being sucked into the Middle East quicksand, diverting America's strategic attention from a rising China.

The new focus on inter-state strategic competition and the threats from near-peer competitors was made apparent in the NSS, NDS and National Military Strategy of the Trump administration, which found broad continuity in the Interim National Security Strategic Guidance (INSSG) of the Biden administration.[6] Before the release of Biden's NSS and NDS, Biden's INSSG argued that the US "must also contend with the reality that the distribution of power across the world is changing, creating new threats" and pointed to China rapidly becoming more assertive.[7] The same document contended that the US "should not, and will not, engage in "forever wars" that have cost thousands of lives and trillions of dollars", and that the US "will work to responsibly end America's longest war in Afghanistan while ensuring that Afghanistan does not again become a safe haven for terrorist attacks against the United States".[8]

Ending the Afghanistan Era in the US Strategy

Even as all hell broke loose in Afghanistan when American forces withdrew and Kabul fell to the Taliban in August 2021, Biden remained steadfast in his decision to withdraw, contending that a delayed pull-out would have done nothing to make things better in Afghanistan. That the US was going to pull out from Afghanistan was a foregone conclusion. When Biden took over as president, a withdrawal was imminent, but the manner in which it played out certainly led to an unbridgeable security gap. The way in which the Kabul government and the US-trained Afghan security collapsed raised an avalanche of concerns and speculations. Biden rationalised his decision and contended that terrorist groups such as Al-Qaeda stood relatively decimated and that Afghanistan, in the near future, would not be used to launch attacks against the American homeland.

Speaking about the end of the war in Afghanistan, Biden expressed surprise at the inability of the Afghan security forces to hold on as expected and at the fleeing of President Ashraf Ghani from his country. Yet, he firmly argued that his administration was ready for the exigency which was "to safely extract American citizens before August 31, as well as embassy personnel, allies and partners and those Afghans who had worked with us and fought alongside us for 20 years".[9]

For Biden, the rationale for pulling out of Afghanistan, despite all the criticism, seemed quite clear. The US succeeded in what it primarily set out to do in Afghanistan with the killing of Bin Laden in 2011, but it stayed on for another decade and, hence, it was time to end the war. Biden's promise to "restore America" was clearly predicated on revitalising its economy for the benefit of the American "middle class"[10] and such a commitment did not sit well with continuing the costly war in Afghanistan. In foreign policy parlance, it meant making the controversial exit from the foreign war and putting American resources where they were required. Also, at this point, nothing is more present and clearer a danger than the threat that China's rise poses to America's primacy in the international system. The primary thrust, as Biden contended, was to deal with the "threats of 2021 and tomorrow" and not the "threats of 2001".[11] The decision to pull back from Afghanistan was clearly in line with doing externally what was required for doing more at home, even though the way the American withdrawal took place and the Taliban took over Kabul made voices across the world echo American retrenchment and question its role as a security guarantor in other geopolitical regions. The NSS says, "In an interconnected world, there is no bright line between foreign and domestic policy".[12]

The fall of Kabul to the Taliban in August 2021, and the complete chaos that ensued in the airport in Kabul, turned many against Biden's foreign policy choice.[13] Watching the Taliban takeover on television screens and social media, many around the world, particularly Afghans, furiously expressed their anguish at being left in the lurch. However, Biden stood firm, justifying his decision as being hard and controversial, but the right one to make. Biden reiterated his intention to not bequeath a 20-year-old war to another presidency and concentrate more on the clear and present dangers to America's national security. "I'm now the fourth United States President to preside over American troop presence in Afghanistan: two Republicans, two Democrats. I will not pass this responsibility on to a fifth", Biden said.[14] Biden pronounced in his speech confirming the withdrawal: "…to those asking for a third decade of war in Afghanistan, I ask: What is the vital national interest? In my view, we only have one: to make sure Afghanistan can never be used again to launch an attack on our homeland".[15] The US withdrawal from Afghanistan was playing out when the Biden presidency was promising the return of "American leadership and engagement". US Secretary of State, Antony J. Blinken, in laying out the essence of Biden's "foreign policy for the American people", contended that the US pulling back from the global landscape either meant "another country tries to take our place, but not in a way that advances our interests and values; or, maybe just as bad, no one steps up, and then we get chaos and all the dangers it creates. Either way, that's not good for America".[16]

The primary question following the Taliban takeover in 2021 has been about the continuity and change in the resources that could be and should be deployed to safeguard America's interest, which remains to prevent any future attacks on the American homeland. The end of the military campaign in Afghanistan is also seen as the culmination of a long-drawn debate on redirecting the resources and strategy of the US' military forces towards greater and imminent threats, and not on nation-building efforts. The NSS emphasised, "We ended America's longest war in Afghanistan, and with it an era of major military operations to remake other societies, even as we have maintained the capacity to address terrorist threats to the American people as they emerge".[17]

Since the Taliban took over the levers of power in Kabul, the terms of engagement with Washington have shifted dramatically. This did not come as a surprise as the Trump administration had already negotiated a peace deal with the Taliban in Doha, Qatar, sans the Afghan government. Therefore, the Taliban entering into a power arrangement in Afghanistan in some form or the other was a foregone conclusion. The Biden administration has been propagating an approach towards peace and security in Afghanistan that is not US-led, but one with great involvement from the regional powers. The NSS highlighted Washington's intention to "increase cooperation and support to trusted partners" and shift from a "US-led, partner-enabled" strategy to one that is "partner-led, US-enabled".[18]

The national security approach of the Biden administration reflects one that aspires to be cognisant of the evolving full spectrum of terrorism threats in the 21st century to reorient capability and strategy effectively. Washington believes that its true objective in Afghanistan had been fulfilled almost a decade ago with the killing of Bin Laden and other key leaders of Al-Qaeda, and the recent assassination of Ayman al-Zawahiri reaffirmed America's "ability to maintain the fight against al-Qa'ida, ISIS, and associated forces from over the horizon".[19]

While focusing attention on evacuation exercises and other humanitarian efforts, the US, in concert with other like-minded partners, geared its approach towards using all forms of leverage to make the Taliban uphold "[their] counterterrorism commitments; demonstrating respect for human rights, particularly those of women and girls; and establishing an inclusive and representative political system".[20] As the US reassesses the level of its involvement and engagement in a

Taliban-run Afghanistan, the emerging dynamics of its relationship with Pakistan will be highly consequential. Even as Washington prepares for the threats of tomorrow, it remains to be seen whether Afghanistan will prove to be a threat of yesteryears or a threat that will still need American policy attention despite the growing shift to great power competition with China.

US–Pakistan Ties: A New Phase of Low

The US–Pakistan relationship has been passing through choppy waters and an uncertain path. However, in the more circumscribed objective of preventing future terrorist attacks emanating from Afghanistan and developing what is being termed as "over the horizon capabilities",[21] Washington might still find it difficult to completely untangle from its complex relationship with Islamabad. That the US military views the rapid fall of Kabul as unprecedented, which might still pose security threats to the American homeland, was made clear during a US Senate hearing in 2021 with top US military leaders.[22] One of the stronger statements coming out of the hearing was that "a reconstituted Al-Qaeda or ISIS [Islamic State] with aspirations to attack the United States is a very real possibility, and those conditions to include activity in ungoverned spaces could present themselves in the next 12 to 36 months".[23] In recent years, the US–Pakistan relationship has largely revolved around each side trying to extract the best out of a highly transactional relationship premised on what Pakistan could do for the US in Afghanistan and what the US could offer in return.

Wendy Sherman, US Deputy Secretary of State, captured the uncertain path ahead for US–Pakistan ties when she commented, "We [the US] don't see ourselves building our broad relationship with Pakistan and we have no interest in returning to the days of a hyphenated India, Pakistan. That's not where we are, that's not where we are going to be".[24] During the 20 years of the war on terror in Afghanistan, Pakistan's relationship with the US came under much scrutiny. While Pakistan remained a major non-North Atlantic Treaty Organization ally of the US in Afghanistan, several instances raised questions over the sincerity with which Pakistan was fighting the war on terrorism. The most spectacular of these was

America's primary target, Bin Laden, being in Abbottabad, a stone's throw away from Pakistan's military academy. A prevalent view regarding Pakistan has often been of an ally that is inevitable, but not necessarily desired. The Obama administration, in fact, after an assessment of the security environment, came to designate a separate Afghanistan–Pakistan desk, with a Special Representative, calling it the epicentre of terrorism. The assessment not only saw the Pakistan military, and particularly its intelligence wing, the Inter-Services Intelligence, as tolerating the Taliban in Quetta, but also intently propping up the group as a means to unsettle the Afghan government and prevent a stronger India–Afghanistan alignment. The bottom line was that America's efforts to bring long-term peace and stability in Afghanistan were doomed to fail unless its key ally, Pakistan, stopped providing safe havens and other forms of assistance to the Taliban.[25]

Just as Pakistan, during the Cold War, was roped in for a transactional alliance to help the US fight communism in Asia, Pakistan, after becoming an ally of America's war on terror, was expected to help in return for economic and military assistance flowing from the US. However, like during the Cold War, Pakistan, as an American ally in the war on terror, had its own axe to grind. Much of Pakistan's strategy, whether it is playing ball with the Chinese while being allied with the US or sheltering the Taliban while on an official task to help the Americans fight them, has been premised on strengthening its position vis-à-vis India. Over the years, despite the power asymmetry between the US and Pakistan, the former's ability to extract commitments and concessions from the latter has always been suspect and a matter of debate rather than fact.[26] Whether during the Cold War alliance against communism or the post-9/11 alliance against terrorism, the scorecard of US–Pakistan mutual expectations and outcomes has always been a chequered one.

While America expected Pakistan to do more in its fight against terrorism, Pakistan has constantly complained that the US did not appreciate its sacrifices and efforts in the global war on terror. Moeed Yusuf, Pakistan's National Security Adviser, accused the now deposed US-supported Afghan government of using Pakistan as a scapegoat to distract from its own inefficiencies. He called on the US to engage diplomatically with the Taliban and not to "isolate Afghanistan to punish its new rulers".[27] Writing for *Foreign Affairs* in October 2021, Yusuf also emphatically argued:

> Apart from the Afghan people, Pakistan has been the greatest victim of the wars in Afghanistan. The Soviet invasion in 1979 and the subsequent US-led military campaign after 9/11 were not of Pakistan's making. Yet, our society, polity and economy have borne the brunt of the conflict over the last four decades.[28]

Yusuf contented that "Pakistan does not wield any extraordinary influence over the new rulers in Kabul, as both monetary assistance and legitimacy for the Taliban can come (or not) only from the world's major powers".[29] Top Pakistani officials sounded optimistic for a Taliban-ruled Afghanistan, contending that the Taliban were "not insensitive to what is being said by neighbours and the international community".[30] Washington went ahead with a policy of engaging without any immediate plan for recognition. While in Pakistan, Sherman said, "We will not, however, judge the Taliban on their words, but on their actions. And, so far, their actions have fallen far short of those public commitments".[31] The absence of trust between the two countries, however, is not likely to bring about a complete halt in the sort of security cooperation that Washington might still seek from Islamabad, and the diplomatic, economic and military support that Islamabad will desire from Washington despite the growing scope of Sino-Pakistan alliance.[32]

Despite Pakistan's central role in the US' Afghanistan strategy since 2001, either Washington has accused Islamabad of not being committed to fighting terrorism wholeheartedly or Islamabad has called out Washington's failure to recognise Pakistan's sacrifices. The seesawing of geopolitics from the Cold War to the present times has led to either the upgrading or downgrading of Pakistan's role in the US' strategy towards South Asia. American retrenchment from Afghanistan has, yet again, brought about a phase of the US–Pakistan relationship devoid of any grand strategic purpose; hence, vulnerable to a downturn and US lawmakers losing interest in Pakistan. When geopolitics is favourable, any shortcoming in the relationship tends to be overlooked and the larger purpose of the partnership seems to override all other cases.[33]

In the absence of an imminent concern for America's interest and with the spectre of a rising China engulfing American strategic thinking and implementation, the glaring gaps in the relationship are more prominent. The domestic churning in Pakistan, leading to the ousting of Prime Minister Imran Khan in April 2022, who also accused Washington of the outcome of his fate, almost brought the US–Pakistan relationship to a standstill. Even as the new administration in Pakistan and the Biden team attempt to create some traction to bring a new sense of purpose to the relationship, Biden publicly called Pakistan "one of the most dangerous nations in the world" possessing "nuclear weapons without any cohesion", which sparked another round of verbal volleys. Pakistan's Foreign Minister Bilawal Bhutto-Zardari retorted, "I believe this is exactly the sort of misunderstanding that is created when there is a lack of engagement".[34]

Islamabad's strategic value in Washington is intertwined largely with the developments in Afghanistan. The extent of American involvement post-withdrawal and the nature of Washington's relationship with the Taliban regime will largely determine the terms of engagement between the US and Pakistan. Biden's national security outlook and the NDS clearly envision a future of competition, contestation and cooperation with China, most particularly in the mega geopolitical region of the Indo-Pacific, which has subsumed other sub-regional theatres, including South Asia. As a result, Washington's engagement with Islamabad is circumscribed, less strategic and more tactical, although still relevant. It seems merely focused on a transactional negotiation of what Pakistan can offer in America's counterterrorism efforts and the quid pro quo towards Pakistan's need for military and civilian assistance.[35]

US–India Partnership: The Indo-Pacific Shift

The blooming strategic bonhomie between the US and India around this time was a product of the structural compulsions resulting from China's rise. Washington's approach to New Delhi is clearly strategic, reflecting a broader frame of reference: the Indo-Pacific's security and stability. Geopolitics resulting from China's assertive rise favours a closer embrace between the US and India. The strategic convergence has withstood the change of administrations at both ends and any conflict of interest emerging out of divergent threat perceptions. Although India's close defence partnership with Russia and relations with countries like Iran that remain at the top tier of America's adversaries have often come in the way of the growing US–India bonhomie, policymakers on both sides have managed to leverage the broader strategic purpose and positive arc to tide over such differences. For instance, more recently, Russia's invasion of Ukraine and India's response to the same sparked some concerns. However, high-level meetings between Indian and American leaders, the Quadrilateral Security Dialogue (Quad) summit and the 2+2 dialogue between the foreign and defence ministries of the two countries testify to the strong structural convergence in joint management of the Indo-Pacific.[36]

At the heart of the US–India partnership has been the shifting balance of power in the Indo-Pacific and the inherent uncertainties because of China's comprehensive rise and power projection. India had started featuring in the US' grand strategy of counteracting China's rise at the onset of the 21st century and, given India's challenge of dealing with a proximate power like China, it serves India's strategic imperative as well.[37] The rise in India's material capabilities and its more overt aspirations to become a power of global consequence made the US reorient its strategy to accommodate India's own concerns and align expectations. In the last two decades and more, both Washington and New Delhi have invested time and energy to impart more clarity into the strategic partnership, which will become even more important in the coming times when the global order is at a point of unmistakable geopolitical, geoeconomic and technological transition.

The US–India relationship has come to enjoy enviable bipartisan support in the US and has equally witnessed enthusiasm from the two major political parties in India. As Indian Prime Minister Narendra Modi emphasised during his speech to the joint session of the US Congress in 2016, "Today, our relationship has overcome the hesitations of history. Comfort, candour and convergence define our conversations. Through the cycle of elections and transitions of administrations, the intensity of our engagements has only grown".[38] The burgeoning defence partnership between the two countries through the Defense Technology and Trade Initiative has been the mainstay of the relationship. The growing sophistication and regularity in defence purchases, the growing linkages between the defence industrial conclaves and prospects for co-production and co-development reflect an undeniable dimension of cooperation. The partnership between the American defence industries and India's defence industrial ecosystem is instrumental to India's goal of self-reliance. Moreover, the military-to-military exercises between all the armed forces increase the level of interoperability. The foundational agreements, signed after long negotiations, have put the two countries on a higher level of coordination. Rear Admiral Michael L. Baker, US Defence Attaché in India, commented:

> India has the ability to choose its partners. It has made a conscious decision to diversify over the last decade. It has made a conscious decision to continue to diversify going forward. And it has made a conscious decision to partner with the US in a host of areas. My focus is on how to take that forward.[39]

Beyond the bilateral ties, the US and India are equally motivated to engage in multilateral platforms, most prominently, the Quad summit that brings these two countries together with Japan and Australia for a coordinated and increasingly multi-faceted agenda to shape the rules of the road in the Indo-Pacific. The Quad, at its core, shows a shared interest among the four democracies to manage the strategic ramifications of China's rise in the Indo-Pacific. However, it has developed a more multifaceted outlook, covering diverse aspects of non-military issues that are of common concern and will need a coordinated strategy.[40]

Given the long years of the US' influence on the geopolitics of South Asia, the withdrawal of American forces from Afghanistan will lead to a reimagining and reorienting of the pivot around which regional countries fashion their strategies.[41] India had invested heavily in building a comprehensive relationship with the Afghan government in the previous 20 years, and, hence, a complete and rapid fall of that political dispensation and the return of the Taliban was bound to throw New Delhi off balance. After the fall of Kabul to the Taliban, discussions between Washington and New Delhi revolved around growing security concerns in Afghanistan and a shared approach to Afghanistan, particularly in terms of not being in a hurry to give "recognition, let alone giving legitimacy" to the Taliban regime. In bilateral understanding, as well as in a multilateral approach with like-minded partners, the effort has been geared towards strengthening "counterterrorism and humanitarian cooperation" and opening channels of communications with the Taliban with an intent to move the new leadership towards an inclusive government and society.[42]

Nevertheless, the focus of the US–India partnership and that of the Quad is largely premised on shaping the contours of a free, open, inclusive and rules-based order in the Indo-Pacific. The South Asian countries in India's immediate neighbourhood have become heavy recipients of Chinese investments, infrastructure building and financing, and are important nodes in China's Belt and Road Initiative. Therefore, one of the significant ways in which the US Indo-Pacific strategy could feature South Asian geopolitics and geoeconomics post-American Afghan withdrawal will be in creating convergence with India and other like-minded partners to ramp up regional infrastructure building and financing efforts, thus providing alternatives to Chinese designs in South Asia.[43] More recently, Washington and New Delhi have made a conscious move towards jointly embracing and leveraging the ongoing technological transition. Both sides announced the US–India initiative on Critical and Emerging Technology (iCET) last year "to elevate and expand our strategic technology partnership and defense industrial cooperation between the governments, businesses and academic institutions of our two countries", leading to the inaugural meeting of the iCET in Washington in early 2022.[44]

Conclusion

While the Afghan withdrawal conjures up images of a retreating America and raises questions over the future of its power, Biden's America is not an isolationist America. Washington's strategic designs are aimed at coming to terms with a strategic reality that stands at an inflection point. There is a weakening of the old world order; yet, there is a lack of clarity on the emergence of a new one. During such an era of transition and transformation, Washington intends to choose its fights wisely and aims to double down on its alliances and like-minded partnerships to counter the destabilising impact of China's rise. In the coming times, Washington will have to locate South Asia in its Indo-Pacific strategy. Given this new prism of the US' strategy, its ties with India feature most prominently in bilateral as well as multilateral ways.

That the US was going to withdraw from Afghanistan was a foregone conclusion as Obama entered the White House and initiated the surge and exit policy. Even as the Trump administration, in its South Asia policy of 2017, called for a condition and not a timeline-based strategy, the real goal was the withdrawal and in what way it was to be eventually executed. However, the march of the Taliban to Kabul, the complete and rapid collapse of the Afghan security forces, and an absconding Afghan president created a confusing image of the limits of American power and strategy in South Asia and in the world. The fundamental shift in Washington's South Asia strategy during the Biden administration has been the withdrawal of the US forces from Afghanistan. While there is broader continuity in Washington's strategic embrace with New Delhi, the US–Pakistan dynamics and maintaining America's retracted presence in Afghanistan have been more volatile.

Washington certainly sees new strategic challenges from a rising and assertive China across the spectrum. To confront the same, it intends to cement old alliances and build new partnerships like the one with India. Therefore, the US, under the Biden presidency, views India in the broader scheme of strategic balance in the Indo-Pacific. At the same time, Pakistan and Afghanistan remain more circumscribed in Washington's security and defence calculations.

Even as the US raises questions about the Taliban's failure to adhere to human rights and counterterrorism commitments, Afghanistan is no longer on the priority radar screen of American policymaking and strategy. This means a definite reduction in the geostrategic value of Pakistan for American strategy and a larger room for criticism of Pakistan's democratic deficit. Moreover, it also means a stronger shift of focus to the partnership with India in the context of the evolving geopolitical challenges in the Indo-Pacific. At a time when the prevailing security and financial order, spearheaded by the US, is under scrutiny more than ever before, and with China's growing ability to influence outcomes in regions beyond its own, the withdrawal from Afghanistan portends a new era in the US' South Asia strategy. This new era, in which Washington addresses the three major vectors of its South Asian strategy — India, Afghanistan and Pakistan — will be determined by the US Indo-Pacific strategy and how these countries feature in that larger picture.

Endnotes

1. "Remarks by President Biden on America's place in the world", The White House, 4 February 2021, https://www.whitehouse.gov/briefing-room/speeches-remarks/2021/02/04/remarks-by-president-biden-on-americas-place-in-the-world/.
2. Ravi Agrawal, "Is there a Biden Doctrine?", *Foreign Policy*, 2 February 2023, https://foreignpolicy.com/2023/02/02/biden-doctrine-russia-china-defense-policy/.
3. "The national security strategy", The White House, October 2022, p. 6, https://www.whitehouse.gov/wp-content/uploads/2022/10/Biden-Harris-Administrations-National-Security-Strategy-10.2022.pdf; and "National Defense Strategy of the United States of America", US Department of Defense, 27 October 2022, https://media.defense.gov/2022/Oct/27/2003103845/-1/-1/1/2022-NATIONAL-DEFENSE-STRATEGY-NPR-MDR.PDF.
4. "Inaugural address by President Joseph R. Biden, Jr", The White House, 20 January 2021, https://www.whitehouse.gov/briefing-room/speeches-remarks/2021/01/20/inaugural-address-by-president-joseph-r-biden-jr/.
5. Antony J. Blinken, "A foreign policy for the American People", US Department of State, 3 March 2021, https://www.state.gov/a-foreign-policy-for-the-american-people/.
6. "National security strategy of the United States of America", The White House, December 2017, https://trumpwhitehouse.archives.gov/wp-content/uploads/2017/12/NSS-Final-12-18-2017-0905.pdf; "Summary of the 2018 national defense strategy of the United States of America", U.S. Department of Defense, 2018, https://dod.defense.gov/Portals/1/Documents/pubs/2018-National-Defense-Strategy-Summary.pdf; and "Description of the national military strategy 2018", US Joint Chiefs of Staff, 2018, https://www.jcs.mil/Portals/36/Documents/Publications/UNCLASS_2018_National_Military_Strategy_Description.pdf.
7. "Interim national security strategic guidance", The White House, March 2021, https://www.whitehouse.gov/wp-content/uploads/2021/03/NSC-1v2.pdf.

8. Susanna George, Adam Taylor, Dan Lamothe, and Jennifer Hassan, "Scenes of deadly Chaos unfold at Kabul Airport after Taliban's return", *The Washington Post*, 16 August 2021, https://www.washingtonpost.com/world/2021/08/16/afghan-kabul-airport/.
9. "Remarks by President Biden on the end of the war in Afghanistan", The White House, 31 August 2021, https://www.whitehouse.gov/briefing-room/speeches-remarks/2021/08/31/remarks-by-president-biden-on-the-end-of-the-war-in-afghanistan/.
10. Antony J. Blinken, *op. cit.*
11. "Remarks by President Biden on the end of the war in Afghanistan", The White House, 31 August 2021, https://www.whitehouse.gov/briefing-room/speeches-remarks/2021/08/31/remarks-by-president-biden-on-the-end-of-the-war-in-afghanistan/.
12. "The national security strategy", The White House, October 2022, p. 14, https://www.whitehouse.gov/wp-content/uploads/2022/10/Biden-Harris-Administrations-National-Security-Strategy-10.2022.pdf.
13. "Biden's Withdrawal from Afghanistan: The reality of an unmitigated disaster", *Forbes,* 17 August 2021, https://www.forbes.com/sites/steveforbes/2021/08/17/bidens-withdrawal-from-afghanistan-the-reality-of-an-unmitigated-disaster/?sh=410877b02f2c.
14. "Remarks by President Biden on Afghanistan," The White House, 16 August 2021, https://www.whitehouse.gov/briefing-room/speeches-remarks/2021/08/16/remarks-by-president-biden-on-afghanistan/.
15. *Ibid.*
16. Antony J. Blinken, *op. cit.*
17. "The national security strategy", The White House, October 2022, p. 20, https://www.whitehouse.gov/wp-content/uploads/2022/10/Biden-Harris-Administrations-National-Security-Strategy-10.2022.pdf.
18. *Ibid.*, p. 30.
19. The White House, "National security strategy", The White House, October 2022, p. 30, https://www.whitehouse.gov/wp-content/uploads/2022/10/Biden-Harris-Administrations-National-Security-Strategy-10.2022.pdf.
20. Kate Bateman, "A year after the Taliban Takeover: What's next for the U.S. in Afghanistan?", United States Institute of Peace, 11 August 2022, https://www.usip.org/publications/2022/08/year-after-taliban-takeover-whats-next-us-afghanistan.
21. The White House, *op. cit.*

22. Barbara Sprunt, "Generals say they recommended keeping US troops in Afghanistan", *NPR,* 28 September 2021, https://www.npr.org/2021/09/28/1040877300/austin-milley-mckenzie-senate-hearing-afghanistan.
23. Eric Schmitt, "McKenzie suggests the US may not be able to prevent Al Qaeda and ISIS from rebuilding in Afghanistan", *The New York Times*, 28 September 2021, https://www.nytimes.com/2021/09/28/us/politics/isis-al-qaeda-afghanistan.html.
24. Nayanima Basu, "No interest in returning to days of a hyphenated India & Pakistan, US Deputy Secy of State says", *The Print*, 7 October 2021, https://theprint.in/diplomacy/no-interest-in-returning-to-days-of-a-hyphenated-india-pakistan-us-deputy-secy-of-state-says/747064/.
25. Barack Obama, *Promised Land* (New York: Crown Publishing, 2020), pp. 320–321.
26. Robert M. Hathaway, *The Leverage Paradox: Pakistan and the United States* (Washington DC: Woodrow Wilson International Center for Scholars, 2017).
27. News Desk, "'Treat Pakistan like an ally, not a scapegoat', NSA tells US", *The Express Tribune*, 10 October 2021, https://tribune.com.pk/story/2317124/treat-pakistan-like-an-ally-not-a-scapegoat-nsa-tells-us.
28. Moeed Yusuf, "How Pakistan Sees Afghanistan: Peace Is Possible Only If the World Engages With the Taliban", *Foreign Affairs*, 7 October 2021, https://www.foreignaffairs.com/articles/afghanistan/2021-10-07/how-pakistan-sees-afghanistan.
29. *Ibid.*
30. Edith M. Lederer, "The AP interview: Don't isolate the Taliban, Pakistan urges", *AP News*, 24 September 2021, https://apnews.com/article/pakistan-afghanistan-united-nations-taliban-shah-mehmood-qureshi-258c17303271aa440cf60f5a9444e143.
31. Kamran Yousaf, "Sherman hails 'longstanding ties' with Pakistan", *The Express Tribune*, 9 October 2021, https://tribune.com.pk/story/2323957/sherman-hails-longstanding-ties-with-pakistan.
32. "Talks with Pakistan on counterterrorism measures to continue, says US' Wendy Sherman", *WION*, 9 October 2021, https://www.wionews.com/south-asia/talks-with-pakistan-on-counterterrorism-measures-to-continue-says-us-wendy-sherman-419349.
33. Naeem Salik, *Learning to live with the Bomb Pakistan: 1998–2016* (Oxford: Oxford University Press, 2017).
34. World News, "Antony Blinken's Call to Bilawal Bhutto-Zardari Hints at US-Pak Ties Reset", *Hindustan Times*, 8 May 2022, https://www.

hindustantimes.com/world-news/blinkens-call-to-bilawal-hints-to-possible-reset-in-us-pak-ties-101651928835678.html; "Dismiss US Ambassador over Biden Remark, says Pak's Islamist Party", *ANI*, 17 October 2022, https://www.aninews.in/news/world/asia/dismiss-us-ambassador-over-biden-remark-says-paks-islamist-party20221017201300/; and Sayantani Biswas, "Pakistan to Summon US Ambassador Donald Blome over Biden's 'Most Dangerous Nation Remark", *Mint*, 15 October 2022, https://www.livemint.com/news/world/pakistan-to-summon-us-ambassador-donald-blome-over-biden-s-most-dangerous-nation-remark-11665835534525.html.
35. Monish Tourangbam, "The hype and reality of Pakistan Factor in India–US relationship", *IndiaTimes.com*, 25 September 2022, https://www.indiatimes.com/explainers/news/the-hype-and-reality-of-pakistan-factor-in-india-us-relationship-580475.html.
36. US Department of State, "Fourth Annual US–India 2+2 Ministerial Dialogue", US Department of State, 11 April 2022, https://www.state.gov/fourth-annual-u-s-india-22-ministerial-dialogue/.
37. Condoleezza Rice, "Promoting the national interest", *Foreign Affairs*, 2000, 79(1), 45–62.
38. Press Information Bureau, 2016, "Government of India, Prime Minister's Office, text of the Prime Minister's address to the joint session of US Congress", 8 June 2016, https://archive.pib.gov.in/newsite/PrintRelease.aspx?relid=146076.
39. Dinakar Peri, "We want to be the partner of choice for India: US defence official", *The Hindu*, 2 November 2022, https://www.thehindu.com/news/national/we-want-to-be-the-partner-of-choice-for-india-us-defence-official/article66087413.ece?homepage=true.
40. Ministry of external affairs, government of India, Quad Joint Leaders' Statement, 24 May 2022, https://www.mea.gov.in/bilateral-documents.htm?dtl/35357/Quad_Joint_Leaders_Statement.
41. C. Raja Mohan, "What does US departure from Afghanistan mean for South Asia?", *The Indian Express*, 11 May 2021, https://indianexpress.com/article/opinion/columns/india-pakistan-relations-us-in-middle-east-afghanistan-7309907/.
42. Stuti Bhatnagar, "Afghanistan's collapse shifts strategic dynamics in South Asia", *The Interpreter*, 18 August 2021, https://www.lowyinstitute.org/the-interpreter/afghanistan-s-collapse-shift-strategic-dynamics-south-asia; Nayanima Basu, "India raises concerns over Haqqanis, ISI in Afghanistan with visiting US Deputy Secy of State", *The Print*, 6 October 2021, https://

theprint.in/diplomacy/india-raises-concerns-over-haqqanis-isi-in-afghanistan-with-visiting-us-deputy-secy-of-state/746487/; and "Joint statement from Quad Leaders", *The White House*, 24 September 2021, https://www.whitehouse.gov/briefing-room/statements-releases/2021/09/24/joint-statement-from-quad-leaders/.
43. Mercy A. Kuo, "US South Asia Policy: The fallout from Afghanistan: Insights from Michael Kugelman", *The Diplomat*, 6 September 2021, https://thediplomat.com/2021/09/us-south-asia-policy-the-fallout-from-afghanistan/.
44. "Fact sheet: United States and India elevate strategic partnership with the initiative on Critical and Emerging Technology (iCET)", The White House, 31 January 2023, https://www.whitehouse.gov/briefing-room/statements-releases/2023/01/31/fact-sheet-united-states-and-india-elevate-strategic-partnership-with-the-initiative-on-critical-and-emerging-technology-icet/#:~:text=President%20Biden%20and%20Prime%20Minister,institutions%20of%20our%20two%20countries.

© 2024 World Scientific Publishing Company Pte. Ltd.
https://doi.org/10.1142/9789811276439_0003

Chapter 3

India at the Centre, Small States In and Af-Pak Out: Understanding Biden's South Asia Policy

Yogesh Joshi and Devyani Chaturvedi

Introduction

South Asia's position in the strategic priorities of the United States (US) has transformed significantly since the Cold War. From a peripheral region, South Asia is now among the top contenders in the US' strategic priorities. America's engagement with South Asia in the first two decades after the collapse of the Soviet Union was driven by both its promise and perils. If nuclear weaponisation in South Asia, particularly the arms race between India and Pakistan, imperilled the US' non-proliferation agenda, the global proliferation of terrorism from Pakistan and Afghanistan endangered American interests at home and abroad. On the other hand, India's economic rise offered the US a liberal, democratic partner in the Global South. Engagement with this rising power in South Asia served American economic and political interests.

In the last decade, particularly with the coming of the Donald Trump administration in the US, Sino-US competition has driven the US' South Asia policy. The competition between the US and China has resulted in three distinct trends in America's South Asia policy. The first is the strengthening of the India–US strategic partnership. American decision-makers increasingly view India as a critical node in their strategy to contain China's rise in Asia. The US' interests in New Delhi today are not simply driven by the promise of India's economic and political rise but also by its inherent utility in balancing China, whether economically, militarily or politically. Second, after almost two decades of investing in low-intensity counterterrorism and counter-insurgency missions in Pakistan and Afghanistan, Washington has decided to end such distractions, exemplified by its withdrawal from Afghanistan and its dwindling interests and engagement in Pakistan. Lastly, the US is increasingly engaging with other smaller South Asian states such as Bangladesh, the Maldives and Sri Lanka. Yet, these engagements are being facilitated by India. Much of this transformation in America's South Asia policy is happening under the auspices of its Indo-Pacific strategy. US President Joe Biden has continued and further intensified this shift in the US' approach to South Asia.

This chapter examines the impact of intensifying Sino-US competition and how that has resulted in the prioritisation of the South Asian region, accelerated solidification of ties with India, extraction of the US from distractions in the region and engagement with the other South Asian states via India. The first section underlines the trends in the US' approach towards South Asia in the post-Cold War period. It argues that the perils of non-proliferation and terrorism and the promise of a strategic partnership with India primarily drove the US' South Asia policy. The second section highlights how the intensifying Sino-US competition influenced America's South Asia policy under the Trump administration. The third section details how Biden's White House has continued with the shifts obtained in the US' foreign policy under the Trump administration.

The US South Asia Policy Post the Cold War

The inherent value of South Asia in the US' foreign policy was highly limited to the containment of the Soviet Union during the Cold War.[1] The end of the Cold War significantly reduced the geopolitical value of South Asia insofar as the Soviet collapse eliminated the requirements for frontline states in its containment strategy against global communism. As the global hegemon, with no comparable great power peer, the need for temporary allies vanished as was the case with Pakistan. The US had no long-term security commitments and treaty allies in the region. Unlike East and Southeast Asia, South Asia remained economically backward and insulated from global commerce and, unlike the Middle East, it lacked the strategic resources relevant to the US' economy. Washington had hardly any teeth in the South Asian region.

Yet, two factors contributed to continuous American involvement in South Asia.[2] The first was the subcontinental rivalry between India and Pakistan. Their pursuit of nuclear weapons and the intensifying sub-conventional war over Kashmir created severe concerns in Washington as a potential nuclear flashpoint. The conflict over Kashmir and the subcontinental atomic weapons arms race threatened global stability and imperilled the US' non-proliferation agenda. Second, the success of the Taliban in Afghanistan and the mushrooming of Islamic terrorism in the northwest region of South Asia seriously threatened American interests globally. The US' foreign policy in South Asia, at least in the last decade of the 20th century, was fundamentally driven by the need to contain nuclear proliferation and address the issue of terrorism emanating from the region. On both issues, the US failed miserably. The US underestimated India's motivation to pursue a nuclear weapons programme; it also overestimated its influence in stopping Pakistan from following the Indian lead. The May 1998 tests in the subcontinent were a significant setback to the global nuclear order held together by American power and interests. The US also failed to contain Islamic terrorism within South Asia. The Taliban became the incubators and facilitators of a global Islamic terrorist network in the form of Al-Qaeda, with strong links with local terrorist organisations operating in Kashmir and sheltered in Pakistan such as the Lashkar-e-Taiba and Jaish-e-Mohammed.

The growing relationship with India was one silver lining in this failed engagement with South Asia. India and the US were on opposite sides of the Cold War, at least ideologically and diplomatically. The collapse of the Soviet Union eliminated the central friction between them.[3] India's democracy and demography always rendered it an attractive partner, but New Delhi's post-Cold War economic liberalisation also made it a promising prospect for American markets. However, in the initial period of US unipolarity, India needed the US much more than the US needed India. New Delhi needed American markets and technology for its economic growth but, more importantly, the US' political and diplomatic support for its regional and global ambitions as a rising power.[4] In the regional context, India's rise required de-hyphenation with Pakistan and hyphenation with China; internationally, it necessitated India's accommodation in the global nuclear order as a nuclear weapon state. The process began with US President Bill Clinton's unconditional support for India during the Kargil War, which many analysts argue laid the foundation for an Indo-US strategic partnership.[5] The coming of neo-conservatives into power in the White House with the presidency of George W. Bush catapulted New Delhi as a long-term bet in the US' grand strategy against China's rise in Asia.[6] The Indo-US defence partnership kickstarted with the signing of the 2004 Next Steps in Strategic Partnership. The 2005 Civilian Nuclear Agreement attested to the US' support for India's rise in the international system, primarily through its accommodation in the global nuclear order.

The potential of the Indo-US strategic relationship remained underexploited for three reasons. First, the war against terror initiated in the aftermath of the 9/11 attacks on American soil catapulted Pakistan to prominence in the US' immediate security concerns. The campaign against the Taliban in Afghanistan and the subsequent nation-building process absorbed the US into its longest war, with Pakistan as its primary ally. For New Delhi, rather than the solution, Pakistan was indeed the source of all terrorism in the region. The war in Afghanistan and the campaign against Al-Qaeda allowed Islamabad to extract billions of dollars from the US in economic and military aid while continuing its support for terrorism inside India's body politic. Second, even when the Bush administration came to the White House explicitly intending to counter China's rise, Afghanistan and Iraq created a significant distraction. Washington was busy fighting ideological wars of choice in the Islamic world rather than preparing for the eventual war of necessity with China, its only potential great power rival. Lastly, New Delhi practised a conservative foreign policy as it remained wedded to non-alignment, strategic autonomy and multipolarity.[7] It refused to accelerate its budding defence relationship with the US and was sceptical of the US' commitment to counter China's rise.

The Barack Obama administration came at the heels of the US imperial overreach in the Middle East and a severe financial crisis, leading to a global perception of American decline. Obama's mandate was to extract Washington from the costly Middle East and Afghanistan wars and rebuild its economic prosperity. It also aimed to re-establish the US' global leadership by actively using international institutions and creating a remarkable power consensus in dealing with the pressing economic and political turmoil. In this quest, China was a critical partner. The Obama administration, therefore, proposed to work with Beijing. This compendium of the world's extant superpower and its rising challenger became a Group of 2 or G-2.[8] However, the initial China–US bonhomie fell through the cracks of Beijing's newfound power and ambition. An America in decline was not only a weak partner but also allowed Beijing to assert its hegemonic ambitions in Asia and beyond. China's maritime and territorial claims in the South China Sea and East Asia waters ruffled the US and its allies and challenged its primacy in the region.

Conversely, the Belt and Road Initiative (BRI) aimed to monopolise global economic development and position China at the centre of international trade and technological and connectivity networks. Obama's White House tried to check China's assertiveness by pivoting to what US Secretary of State Hillary Clinton had called the Indo-Pacific, but the policy lacked both vision and specifics. For Washington, getting out of Iraq and Afghanistan was the primary challenge.[9] Obama had succeeded in withdrawing from Iraq and reduced, to a considerable extent, the American footprint in Afghanistan. However, it had failed miserably in countering China's assertion in the region. In South Asia too, China's imprint was firmly established. All the South Asian states except India supported the BRI and were closely integrated with the Chinese economy. Yet, the Obama administration could not resolve the foreign policy dilemmas confronting the US' South Asia policy.[10] First, even when the US' counter-insurgency campaign successfully targeted its leadership, the Taliban remained ascendant on the battlefield. Second, Pakistan's loyalties in the war on terror remained divided between its interests in securing American largesse and its commitment to establishing strategic depth in Afghanistan by supporting the Taliban. Third, the preponderance of attention to the Af-Pak theatre diverted focus from the other smaller South Asian states, allowing China to expand its regional influence. The only saving grace in the US' foreign policy was the secular trend of the growing strategic partnership with India.[11] Obama was the first US president to attend India's Republic Day parade as a chief guest in 2015. He supported India's accommodation in the Cold War technology denial regimes such as the Nuclear Suppliers Group, Australia Group and the Missile Technology Control Regime. He openly declared the US support for India's permanent United Nations Security Council membership candidature. However, as Obama's tenure neared its end, the US–China rivalry had become the overriding factor in the US' grand strategy. The US' foreign policy would, henceforth, be driven by its looming hegemonic competition with Beijing. South Asia would emerge as the new battleground for great power competition.

China Drives the US' Policy in South Asia

Trump's presidency was a critical inflection point in US–South Asia relations. Trump exhibited remarkable clarity in the US' foreign policy objective of confronting China's rise, which no previous administration could do.[12] For Trump, China was not only the primary source of America's economic decline but also the most potent challenger of the US' hegemony in Asia and beyond. Confronting China required a punishing trade war, forcing American allies in Asia to take up the burden of deterrence and rebuilding American military capability. More importantly, it necessitated extraction from Afghanistan, calling out Pakistan's duplicity and roping India into a tighter strategic embrace. Trump's South Asia strategy document of August 2017 underlined the need to withdraw from Afghanistan.[13] For two reasons, ending America's war on terror in Afghanistan was easier for Trump. First, it supported his primary claim that the US was wasting its taxpayer's money on unnecessary wars in regions of no vital importance to the US' grand strategy. Second, unlike Bush and Obama, he had no prior investment in the policy of continuing American military presence in Afghanistan. Trump's outsider status in Washington's politics was a great asset. He also had little patience to tolerate Pakistan's continued support for the Taliban. He openly called out Islamabad for providing "safe havens" to "agents of chaos, violence and terror".[14] He also walked the talk; by 2018, Washington suspended most of its military aid to Pakistan.

Trump put India at the centre stage, calling its relationship with New Delhi a "key component in any strategy in the region".[15] If India wanted American recognition of its leadership in South Asia, Trump was more than willing to grant India its wish. This privileging of India over the other South Asian states was further reinforced with the announcement of the "Free and Open Indo-Pacific Strategy" in November 2019, which hailed India as being "vital" for the US' Indo-Pacific vision. Trump's presidency witnessed a deepening of trade ties as trade in goods and services doubled from US$60 billion in 2009 to US$146 billion in 2019.[16] The India–US defence relationship flourished with the signing of the Bilateral Communications Compatibility and the Security Agreement (BECA) and the Communications Compatibility and Security Agreement, the last of the four foundational defence agreements. Under Trump, the US cleared the sale of top-end military platforms such as Apache and Seahawk helicopters, AGM-84L Harpoon Block II missiles, MK 54 All Up Round Lightweight Torpedoes, Integrated Air Defense Weapon System and Related Equipment and Support, MK 45 5 inch/62 calibre (MOD 4) naval guns and related equipment, additional P8I Poseidon Long Range Maritime Patrol and Anti-Submarine aircraft, support packages worthy of India's fleet of C-17 Globemaster heavy-lift transport aircraft and 777 Large Aircraft Infrared Countermeasures Self-Protection Suites.[17] It also overruled the earlier ban on the transfers of unmanned aerial reconnaissance systems such as Reaper drones. Trump's support for India's punitive measures against Pakistan during the February 2019 Balakot strikes and the 2020 Galwan crisis engendered greater bilateral trust in the Indo-US military and diplomatic partnership.[18]

India became the bridgehead for the US' outreach to the smaller South Asian states. Countering Chinese influence and penetration in South Asia required greater synergy between the US and India. The US followed India's lead in responding to the political turmoil in the Maldives and Sri Lanka. The Quadrilateral Security Dialogue (Quad) group of countries focused on developmental and connectivity aid to counter China's BRI.[19] Challenging China's "debt-trap" diplomacy was a key component. India was the preferred partner in South Asia, whether it concerned the US' initiative on the Coalition for Disaster Resilient Infrastructure or leveraging the Blue Dot Network to create sustainable investment in the region.[20]

During the COVID-19 pandemic, the US supported India's medical and vaccine aid to the South Asian region through the Quad Vaccine Partnership.

Biden's Presidency

By the time Biden replaced Trump at the White House, the broad trajectory of the US' South Asia policy was firmly entrenched. First, the US' policy in South Asia had de-hyphenated India and Pakistan and firmly hyphenated India and China. In policy terms, it underscored the decreasing marginal utility of Pakistan and the increasing salience of India in the US' foreign policy. Sino-US competition has only aggravated these trends, with growing patterns of alignments between India and the US vis-à-vis the Sino-Pak axis. Second, with the prospect of the US' withdrawal from Afghanistan, the salience of non-traditional threats such as terrorism has significantly declined in the US' security engagements with the region. Conversely, its focus on China has increased the importance of New Delhi as a major offshore balancer in the Indo-Pacific. Third, China is the principal motivator for the growing Indo-US strategic partnership. The defence relationship is hardly restricted to a buyer–seller relationship; the US is a crucial enabler of India's deterrence capability along its Himalayan frontier. Lastly, to paraphrase C. Raja Mohan, India has emerged as a critical partner for the US' foreign policy in South Asia.[21] Having acknowledged India's leadership of the region, New Delhi is far more welcoming of American presence in South Asia than ever in its history.

However, even when there is bipartisan consensus in the US on the need to counter China's revisionist aims and assertive behaviour in the Indo-Pacific and South Asia, the intensity of its engagement and commitment has not escaped the vagaries of domestic politics and leadership styles. Irrespective of Trump's partisan domestic politics, the US adopted a more assertive attitude towards Beijing's intransigence in the region. In both words and deeds, the Trump administration realigned American foreign policy towards competing with China, lock, stock and barrel. In South Asia, Biden faced an enormous task: completing the withdrawal of US troops from Afghanistan, building on the strategic relationship with India, countering Chinese influence, penetrating the smaller South Asian states, and finally, scripting a Pakistan policy in the aftermath of the US' withdrawal from Afghanistan. However, rather than demonstrating any significant break from the Trump administration, Biden's South Asia policy showed remarkable similarity with its predecessor.

Primacy of India

Taking over from Trump, the Biden administration faced three major roadblocks vis-à-vis the burgeoning strategic partnership with India.[22] First, Trump's domestic "America First" rhetoric failed to complement his foreign policy. The fundamental assumption underlying Trump's populist political gimmick of "America First" was that the US had been robbed economically not only by China but also by its allies and partners. Trump even targeted preferential commercial treatment to regional partners like India. This severely strained the relations between New Delhi and Washington. Second, the Russian factor was one of the major irritants in the Indo-US relationship. Under Trump, India had escaped the punitive sanctions enacted by the US Senate under the Countering America's Adversaries Through Sanctions Act (CAATSA).[23] However, a democratic administration, given the Russian support for Trump's presidency and its involvement in the 2016 presidential elections, was expected to pursue a far more aggressive posture vis-à-vis Moscow. India's defence and political relationship with Russia could be severely threatened if Biden operationalised the CAATSA. The third was the growing influence of right-wing Hindu nationalism in Indian politics under Prime Minister Narendra Modi. Under Trump, Modi's Hindu nationalism received a free pass. The democratic transition at the White House portended ideological tensions between the two democracies.[24]

Notwithstanding such potential problems, it became apparent that the trajectory of the Indo-US strategic relationship would continue unabated under the new administration. In March 2021, the Biden administration published the Interim National Security Strategy (NSS) guidance. To counter the "distribution of power" in the international system accompanied by China's growing assertiveness, the US asserted the need to "reinvigorate and modernize" its "alliances and strategic partners". "Deepening of partnership with India" was central to this posture.[25] Second, soon after the announcement of the interim guidelines, the two strategic partners stared at a diplomatic crisis over a freedom of navigation operation conducted by ships from the Pacific fleet in India's exclusive economic zone. However, rather than a crisis in bilateral relations, the episode served as a reminder of the trust the two sides had developed over the last 30 years.[26] Notwithstanding the criticism from the country's strategic community, India's Ministry of External Affairs merely conveyed concerns "regarding this passage through our EEZ [Exclusive Economic Zone] to the government of [the] US through diplomatic channels."[27] At the same time, however, Admiral Kadambir Singh, Chief of Naval Staff, declared the capability and intentions of the Indian Navy to coordinate and interoperate with the navies of the other Quad countries.[28] Modi later argued that during a meeting with Biden, the India–US relationship had transitioned into a "partnership of trust".[29]

The Indo-US strategic partnership has only intensified. There appears to be far greater synergy in military cooperation between India and the US. The foundational defence agreements have helped India's operational preparedness on the China border. New Delhi enjoyed significant intelligence inputs from the US after the Galwan crisis of June 2020 that helped New Delhi prepare against any further grey zone operations by the People's Liberation Army (PLA). Such military coordination under the BECA has continued since then. In December 2022, prior intelligence inputs from the US were primarily responsible for India's successful prevention of the PLA's encroachment on Indian territory in Arunachal Pradesh. The operationalisation of foundational defence agreements is a success story of the Biden administration. The Sino-US and Sino-Indian economic competition has created greater synergy in the Indo-US trade relationship. Sanctioned under the Trump administration for unfair trade practices, the Indo-US economic partnership has turned a corner under the Biden administration. In April 2023, the US replaced China as India's biggest trading partner. The free trade agreement is still under consideration, but negotiations are in an advanced stage. However, supply chain resilience and technological cooperation drive the strategic partnership. As the Sino-US techno-economic war heats up, and advanced economies worldwide have strived to diversify their supply chain dependence on

China, New Delhi has positioned itself as a possible alternative. US support is critical in this regard. New Delhi is targeting niche industries such as semiconductor technology and foundries. The Vedanta–Foxconn deal to establish a semiconductor foundry in Gujarat may help kickstart this critical sector in the country. In May 2022, the two sides signed the initiative on Critical and Emerging Technologies, which may kickstart a new cooperation cycle on technologies such as quantum computing, semiconductor research and artificial intelligence.[30]

Biden's foreign policy vis-à-vis India has only accelerated the trajectory of the strategic partnership. It has also entered new domains such as supply chain resilience, cooperation in advanced and emerging technologies and climate change. The Russian war on Ukraine had the potential to derail the relationship. However, both the US and India have shown a remarkable understanding of each other's relationship with Russia.[31] The lowest common denominator in the Indo-US relationship remains China. Until the China threat continues to hurt US and Indian interests, extraneous factors can hardly affect the trajectory of the bilateral relationship.

Afghanistan and Pakistan

By the time Biden came to power, the trajectory of America's disenchantment with both Afghanistan and Pakistan had reached its apogee. The impending withdrawal from Afghanistan, spearheaded by the Trump administration, was a strategic requirement. Biden acknowledged so in the March 2021 interim NSS, which underlined the need for "disciplined choices" in US national defence and "responsible use" of its military power.[32] Disengaging from the "forever wars that have cost thousands of lives and trillions of dollars" was critical for domestic politics but more so to concentrate American energies on China.[33] Withdrawal would also automatically reduce Pakistan's remaining leverage with Washington. Not surprisingly, Pakistan did not figure in the new administration's NSS. The only question confronting the Biden administration was the withdrawal process: could it be managed with some understanding and power-sharing agreement with the Taliban?

However, the Taliban forced Biden's hands. Their movement towards Kabul was so swift that the Biden administration was left unprepared for a systematic withdrawal.[34] The messy exit was both a national and a human tragedy. The Taliban also backtracked from its commitments to act against potential havens for terrorists and human rights. America's longest war ended in dismal failure. The US was too fatigued and disinterested in pushing the Taliban to honour the promises made during the Doha negotiations. The only policy tools available to the Biden administration were economic sanctions and the Taliban's quest for international recognition.[35] However, these measures have had no visible impact on the Taliban. Their regressive politics have only intensified in the last two years.

Pakistan, however, suffered far more. Even before the withdrawal, the US–Pakistan relationship was highly transactional.[36] Pakistan's leverage over the US would significantly reduce after the latter's exit from Afghanistan. The Trump administration had cornered Islamabad on its support for terrorism, threatened economic sanctions and even cut off American aid to the region. Yet, Trump's personality-driven politics ensured a cosy relationship with Pakistan's Prime Minister Imran Khan. The Biden administration, however, viewed Khan with much greater scepticism. The Pakistani prime minister did not even receive a phone call from Biden when the latter assumed office. The chaos of Afghanistan not only underlined Pakistan's duplicity in the war on terror but Khan's celebratory rhetoric on the Taliban victory was also highly distasteful. The Biden–Khan equation ended up being the worst between any two leaders in the US and Pakistan. Within six months of American withdrawal from Afghanistan, Khan's erstwhile supporters in the powerful Pakistan military started plotting his removal. General Qamar Javed Bajwa, chief of the most powerful institution in Pakistan, was miffed by Khan's economic policies and fearful of his foreign policy choices, particularly regarding China and Russia. Whereas Khan aimed to push Islamabad firmly in the corner of China and Russia, the army wanted to strike a balance with the US from where it obtained its premium defence hardware.

The parliamentary coup orchestrated by the military created a significant crisis in US–Pakistan relations as Khan accused the opposition parties of working in cahoots with the US administration under a foreign conspiracy. Since then, Pakistan has been in a perpetual economic, institutional and political crisis.[37] The principal interlocuter of Pakistan's foreign policy — the military — has taken over the foreign policy agenda. The US continues to work with the Pakistan military, especially in continuing its over-the-horizon counterterrorism strategy, as illustrated by the successful targeting of Ayman al-Zawahiri near Kabul using American drones.[38] However, today, the equation between the US and Pakistan has completely flipped, compared to when the former was still engaged in Afghanistan. Pakistan is highly dependent on the US for its economic bailout; Washington, however, has no comparable interest in Pakistan. The US' disengagement with Af-Pak is complete.

Smaller States in South Asia

The third primary vector of the US' foreign policy in South Asia is its increasing focus on the smaller South Asian states.[39] As Raja Mohan perceptively observes, "The US is now paying serious attention to the subcontinent's smaller countries."[40] The Trump administration had started this transition from the excessive focus on Afghanistan and Pakistan to the South Asian states. China's influence and penetration in South Asia were principally responsible for such a shift, which also gelled well with the US' focus on the Indo-Pacific. Bangladesh, Sri Lanka, the Maldives and Nepal have garnered greater attention in American foreign policy. Trump's Indo-Pacific strategy underlined the need for "emerging partnerships" with the South Asian states;[41] Biden's Indo-Pacific strategy explicitly acknowledged India's "regional leadership" of the South Asian region. It also underlined the need for the countries "to work together and through regional groupings to promote stability in South Asia".[42] Countering China's "coercive behaviour" is the primary motivation behind the US' engagement of the smaller South Asian states.[43]

India was instrumental in brokering a defence pact between the US and the Maldives. Signed in September 2020, the Framework for the US Department of Defense–Maldives Ministry of Defense and Security Relationship was impossible without New Delhi's active encouragement, given the close strategic ties between New Delhi and Malé.[44] In 2013,

India scuttled a "status of forces" agreement between the Maldives and the US.[45] During the negotiating process, both the Maldives and the US kept New Delhi constantly engaged to the extent that the draft agreement was shown to Indian leadership before its final signing. The Biden administration continued this transition in US–Maldives relations with the inaugural bilateral defence and security dialogue between US Under Secretary Colin Kahl and Deputy Foreign Minister Abdullah Shahid of the Maldives in January 2021.

India has also promoted greater American engagement with Sri Lanka. Sri Lankan military operations against the Liberation Tigers of Tamil Eelam and the US' insistence on the ruling Rajapaksa family to account for perpetrated human rights abuses severely impacted the bilateral ties. Sri Lanka also looked increasingly towards China as its economic and political saviour. Under the Indo-Pacific strategy, the Trump administration began cultivating ties with the island state. In 2017, a US aircraft carrier docked at the Colombo port, the first in three decades. The US–Sri Lanka partnership dialogue began in 2019, and the Biden administration has continued to engage Colombo. Maritime security and disaster response in the Indian Ocean region is the primary vector of the US–Sri Lanka security cooperation. A decade of Chinese economic and political influence entrapped Sri Lanka into a severe "debt trap". It catalysed an economic downturn, resulting in a balance-of-payment crisis in early 2022. The Biden administration also took India's lead during the island state's economic and political turmoil. India helped by sanctioning loans and providing critical life-saving drugs and fossil fuel supplies. More importantly, India encouraged Sri Lanka to approach the International Monetary Fund rather than rely on China to seek debt relief and resolve the balance of payment crisis.[46] Indo-US cooperation helped stabilise the Sri Lankan economy.

In February 2023, Bangladesh finalised its Indo-Pacific Strategic Outlook, signalling some willingness to embrace the US-led Indo-Pacific strategy. Given India and Bangladesh's strategic proximity, it is believed that New Delhi has encouraged Bangladesh to become a part of the Indo-Pacific partnerships.[47] Gowher Rizvi, Advisor to Bangladesh's Prime Minister Sheikh Hasina, publicly expressed Bangladesh's interest in the

Indo-Pacific relationship and emphasised India's role to be of most importance.[48] Dhaka's proximity to South and Southeast Asia through the Bay of Bengal provides it significant traction in the region's emerging geopolitics. Therefore, both China and the US have strengthened their partnership with Bangladesh. However, Dhaka's gradual embrace of the Indo-Pacific Strategic Outlook, encouraged by India, provides a strategic advantage to the US.

Interactions between the US, India and Nepal are on the rise. Both the US and India are supporting each other's engagements with Nepal. The recent election of the Nepalese Congress to the parliament portends a reorientation in Nepal's strategic outlook.[49] It has embarked on new energy and infrastructure partnerships with the US and India. This sharply contrasts with the previously elected communist regimes that supported Chinese infrastructural projects under the BRI.

In February 2022, the Nepalese parliament finally approved the long-pending US Millennium Challenge Corporation's (MCC) Nepal Compact US$500 million development grant. The MCC grant aims to modernise Nepal's electricity and road infrastructure to improve its export supply capabilities to India. Since the MCC grant was seen to compete with China's BRI, pro-China voices in Nepal disapproved of the MCC. However, its parliamentary approval indicates some rebalancing away from Nepal's China-tilt.[50]

Conclusion

Post the Cold War, the US' strategic priorities in South Asia were driven by promises of India's economic potential and democratic credibility. It was, however, even more motivated by the perils of a nuclear arms race between Pakistan and India and the incubating terrorism in the Af-Pak region. The US' strategy failed on many fronts. Neither was the US able to contain nuclear proliferation in the region nor was it able to address the issue of rising terrorism. However, it did succeed in forging a strong diplomatic partnership, and eventually a defence partnership, with India. Relations between India and the US, over the years, have become the mainstay of the US strategy in South Asia. However, the strategy overall has witnessed a reorientation. China's newfound economic power, militaristic might and hegemonic ambitions in Asia catalysed such a change.

Trump's presidency punished China through a trade war, forced American allies in Asia to take the burden of deterrence, initiated the rebuilding of the American military and focused on extracting the US out of resource-draining distractions like Afghanistan. In the meantime, Trump's presidency placed India at the centrestage by recognising India's leadership in South Asia and its key role in the US' Indo-Pacific vision; deepening Indo-US economic and defence ties and facilitating the US outreach to the other South Asian states via India.

The Biden administration's US–South Asia strategy is also entrenched in similar trends, only aggravated by growing patterns of alignments caused by heightened Sino-US competition. The first is the strengthening of the Indo-US partnership through diplomacy, defence and economic ties — all of which are driven by New Delhi's critical role in cooperating with the US to counterbalance China in South Asia. The second is the withdrawal of American troops from Afghanistan. The extraction from the Af-Pak distraction had ripple effects on American engagement with Pakistan. Given Pakistan's proximity to China and Russia, the US' disengagement with the country seems to be conclusive, at least for the moment. Lastly, the US has broadened its focus to include engagements with the other smaller South Asian states such as the Maldives, Sri Lanka, Bangladesh and Nepal. This shift in the US' policy is an effort to counter China's influence and presence in the region. Given the relevance of these states in the US Indo-Pacific strategy, Biden, through India's "leadership" in the region, strives to build deeper engagement with the rest of the South Asia region.

Endnotes

1. Dennis Kux, *India and the United States: Estranged Democracies, 1941–1991* (Pennsylvania: Diane Publishing, 1992).
2. Srinath Raghavan, *Fierce Enigmas: A History of the United States in South Asia* (New York: Basic Books, 2018).
3. Sumit Ganguly and Manjeet S. Pardesi, "Explaining sixty years of Indian foreign policy", *India Review*, 2009, 8(1), 4–19.

4. Yogesh Joshi, "Can bandwagon no more: India's imperative for external balancing", *The Washington Quarterly*, 2022, 45(4), 133–156.
5. Strobe Talbott, *Engaging India: Diplomacy, Democracy and the Bomb* (Washington DC: Brookings Institution Press, 2004); and Bruce Reidel, "Kargil redefined Delhi-Washington ties", *The Hindustan Times*, 23 July 2019, https://www.hindustantimes.com/analysis/kargil-redefined-delhi-washington-ties/story-voZBERcKdRahw1RvH3ntjJ.html.
6. Ashley J. Tellis, "The evolution of US–Indian ties: Missile defense in an emerging strategic relationship", *International Security*, 2006, 30(4), 113–151.
7. Sunil Khilnani, Rajiv Kumar, Pratap Bhanu Mehta, Prakash Menon, Srinath Raghavan, Shyam Saran, Nandan Nilekani and Siddharth Varadarajan, "Non-alignment 2.0: A foreign and strategic policy for India in the twenty first century", Center for Policy Research, 2012, https://cprindia.org/wp-content/uploads/2021/12/NonAlignment-2.pdf.
8. C. Raja Mohan, "The G-2 Dilemma", *The Indian Express*, 11 June 2013, http://www.indianexpress.com/news/the-g2-dilemma/1127572/0.
9. Harsh V. Pant and Yogesh Joshi, *The US Pivot and Indian Foreign Policy: Asia's Evolving Balance of Power* (Basingstoke: Palgrave Macmillan, 2015).
10. John Ford, "The Pivot to Asia was Obama's biggest mistake", *The Diplomat*, 21 January 2017, https://thediplomat.com/2017/01/the-pivot-to-asia-was-obamas-biggest-mistake/; and Stephen M. Walt, "Barack Obama was a foreign-policy failure", *Foreign Policy*, 18 January 2017, https://foreignpolicy.com/2017/01/18/barack-obama-was-a-foreign-policy-failure/.
11. Frederic Grare, "Decades of India–US Relationship", Carnegie endowment for international peace, 27 July 2019, https://carnegieendowment.org/2019/07/27/looking-back-at-three-decades-of-india-u.s.-relationship-pub-79779.
12. Stephen M. Walt, "Trump's final foreign-policy report card", *Foreign Policy*, 5 January 2021, https://foreignpolicy.com/2021/01/05/trumps-final-foreign-policy-report-card/.
13. Jim Garamone, "President Unveils New Afghanistan, South Asia strategy, US Department of Defense", 21 August 2017, https://www.defense.gov/News/News-Stories/Article/Article/1284964/president-unveils-new-afghanistan-south-asia-strategy/.
14. *Ibid.*
15. *Ibid.*
16. Malancha Chakrabarty and Navdeep Suri (eds.), "A 2030 vision for India's economic diplomacy", Observer Research Foundation and *Global Policy*

Journal, 2021, https://www.orfonline.org/wp-content/uploads/2021/04/A_2030_Vision_for_Indias_Economic_Diplomacy.pdf.
17. Kashish Parpiani, "India–US defence trade continuity under Trump", Observer Research Foundation, *Brief No. 376*, July 2020, https://www.orfonline.org/research/india-us-defence-trade-continuity-under-trump-68919/.
18. Ashley J. Tellis, "A Smoldering Volcano: Pakistan and Terrorism after Balakot", Carnegie Endowment for International Peace, 14 March 2019, https://carnegieendowment.org/2019/03/14/smoldering-volcano-pakistan-and-terrorism-after-balakot-pub-78593; and Dipanjan Roy Chaudhary, "Global support for India on LAC clash gains momentum", *The Economic Times*, 20 June 2020, https://economictimes.indiatimes.com/news/defence/global-support-for-india-on-lac-clash-gains-in-momentum/articleshow/76476103.cms.
19. Zaheena Rasheed, "At Tokyo summit, Quad offers 'tangible benefits' to counter China", *Aljazeera*, 24 May 2022, https://www.aljazeera.com/news/2022/5/24/quad-leaders-meet-in-japan-to-discuss-china-russia-tensions.
20. "Fact sheet: The United States and India — Global leadership in action", The White House, 24 September 2021, https://www.whitehouse.gov/briefing-room/statements-releases/2021/09/24/fact-sheet-the-united-states-and-india-global-leadership-in-action/.
21. C. Raja Mohan, "The US role in South Asia", in *America's Role in Asia: Asian and American Views* (San Francisco: Asia Foundation, 2008), p. 56.
22. Michael Kugelman, "How May US–India Relations under Biden Differ from the Trump era?", *Asia Dispatches*, Wilson Center, 16 February 2021, https://www.wilsoncenter.org/blog-post/how-may-us-india-relations-under-biden-differ-trump-era.
23. Jeff Smith, "US CAATSA Sanctions and India: Waivers and geopolitical considerations", The Heritage Foundation, 7 April 2022, https://www.heritage.org/asia/report/us-caatsa-sanctions-and-india-waivers-and-geopolitical-considerations.
24. Mohamed Zeeshan, "Biden's problem with India", *The Diplomat*, 19 April 2022, https://thediplomat.com/2022/04/bidens-problem-with-india/.
25. "Interim National security strategic guidance", The White House, United States, March 2021, https://www.whitehouse.gov/wp-content/uploads/2021/03/NSC-1v2.pdf.
26. Yogesh Joshi, "The imperative of political navigation: India's strategy in the Indian Ocean and the logic of Indo-US strategic partnership", *US Naval War College Review*, 2022, 75(3), 1–29.

27. "Passage of USS John Paul Jones through India's EEZ," *Press Releases*, Ministry of External Affairs, India, 9 April 2021, https://www.mea.gov.in/press-releases.htm?dtl/33787/Passage_of_USS_John_Paul_Jones_through_Indias_EEZ.
28. Snehesh Alex Philips, "Quad navies can come together if needed in almost 'plug and play' manner, Navy chief says", *The Print*, 14 April 2021, https://theprint.in/defence/quad-navies-can-come-together-if-needed-in-almost-plug-and-play-manner-navy-chief-says/639988/.
29. "India-US relations a 'partnership of trust': PM Modi in meeting with Biden", *The Economic Times*, 24 May 2022, https://economictimes.indiatimes.com/news/india/india-us-relations-a-partnership-of-trust-pm-modi-in-meeting-with-biden/articleshow/91760722.cms.
30. "Fact sheet: United States and India elevate strategic partnership with the initiative on Critical and Emerging Technologies (iCET)", The White House, 31 January 2023, https://www.whitehouse.gov/briefing-room/statements-releases/2023/01/31/fact-sheet-united-states-and-india-elevate-strategic-partnership-with-the-initiative-on-critical-and-emerging-technology-icet/.
31. Yogesh Joshi, "Power of norms — or norms of power?: India's response to the Ukraine crisis", *AsiaGlobal Online*, Asia Global Institute, University of Hong Kong, 3 March 2022, https://www.asiaglobalonline.hku.hk/power-norms-or-norms-power-indias-response-ukraine-crisis.
32. "Interim national security strategic guidance", The White House, March 2021, https://www.whitehouse.gov/wp-content/uploads/2021/03/NSC-1v2.pdf.
33. *Ibid.*
34. "Afghanistan: Joe Biden defends US pull-out as Taliban claim victory", *BBC*, 1 September 2021, https://www.bbc.com/news/world-asia-58403735.
35. Madiha Afzal, "Has US policy towards Taliban-ruled Afghanistan failed Afghans?", *Brookings*, 29 September 2022, https://www.brookings.edu/blog/order-from-chaos/2022/09/29/has-us-policy-toward-taliban-ruled-afghanistan-failed-afghans/.
36. Madiha Afzal, "Post Afghanistan, US–Pakistan relationship stands on the edge of a precipice", *Brookings*, 13 October 2021, https://www.brookings.edu/blog/order-from-chaos/2021/10/13/post-afghanistan-us-pakistan-relations-stand-on-the-edge-of-a-precipice/.
37. Haroon Janjua, "Why is Khan blaming the West for his downfall?", *Deutsche Welle*, 31 March 2022, https://www.dw.com/en/pakistan-why-is-imran-khan-blaming-the-west-for-his-downfall/a-61316499.
38. Ayesha Siddiqa, "US interests in Af-Pak now just 'transactional'. People can fight their own battles", *The Print*, 8 August 2022, https://theprint.in/opinion/

us-interests-in-af-pak-now-just-transactional-people-can-fight-their-own-battles/1073294/.
39. Michael Kugelman, "Is Biden building a broader South Asia policy?", *Foreign Policy*, 2 June 2022, https://foreignpolicy.com/2022/06/02/south-asia-policy-biden-engagement-nepal-bangladesh/.
40. C. Raja Mohan, "Across South Asia, US and India push back against China", *Foreign Policy*, 6 April 2022, https://foreignpolicy.com/2022/04/06/us-india-china-sri-lanka-south-asia-geopolitics/.
41. "Indo-Pacific strategy report — Preparedness, partnerships, and promoting a networked region", US Department of Defense, 1 June 2019.
42. "Indo-Pacific strategy", Washington DC, The White House, February 2022, https://www.whitehouse.gov/wp-content/uploads/2022/02/U.S.-Indo-Pacific-Strategy.pdf.
43. *Ibid.*
44. Abhijnen Rej, "India welcomes US–Maldives Defense cooperation agreement in a sign of times", *The Diplomat*, 15 September 2020, https://thediplomat.com/2020/09/india-welcomes-us-maldives-defense-cooperation-agreement-in-a-sign-of-times/.
45. Devirupa Mitra, "Seven years on, India now backs a defence pact between the US and Maldives", *The Wire*, 13 September 2020, https://thewire.in/south-asia/seven-years-on-india-now-backs-a-defence-pact-between-the-us-and-maldives.
46. C. Raja Mohan, *op. cit.*
47. Michael Kugelman, "Bangladesh tilts towards the US in the Indo-Pacific", *Foreign Policy*, 30 March 2023, https://foreignpolicy.com/2023/03/30/bangladesh-us-indo-pacific-strategy-china/.
48. "Bangladesh moves closer to a full embrace of Indo-Pacific Strategy", *The Business Standard*, 23 April 2023, https://www.tbsnews.net/bangladesh/bangladesh-moves-closer-full-embrace-indo-pacific-strategy-608462.
49. C. Raja Mohan, *op. cit.*
50. Sujeev Shakya, "Nepal in the first half of 2022: Balancing act in geopolitics", *ISAS Insights No. 720*, Institute of South Asian Studies, National University of Singapore, 27 May 2022, https://www.isas.nus.edu.sg/papers/nepal-in-the-first-half-of-2022-balancing-act-in-geopolitics/.

Chapter 4

Carving a Relationship: The United States and the Taliban's Afghanistan

Javid Ahmad and Marvin G. Weinbaum

Introduction

With the harrowing scenes in mid-August 2021 of the last American military and diplomatic personnel hurriedly departing Kabul, along with Afghan citizens, the curtains closed on a two-decade-long United States (US) engagement in Afghanistan. The decision to cut Afghanistan loose had been set in motion by the Donald Trump administration's February 2020 agreement with the Taliban in Doha, Qatar, committing the US to a full military withdrawal. This commitment was sealed by President Joe Biden's decision in April 2021 that triggered the collapse of Afghan security forces and paved the way for the Taliban's overrunning of the country. The bungled American exit cast considerable doubt on the US' skills at crisis management and the quality of intelligence, tarnishing America's reputation as a responsible strategic partner. However, for most Americans, these outcomes were eclipsed by the sense of relief in seeing an end to a long-touted "forever war".[1]

With its exit, the US had finally been relieved of the heavy military and financial burden acquired from failed efforts to secure and nurture a flawed Afghan constitutional democratic order. The US was now seen as free to refocus its attention and resources on those global theatres thought to hold greater strategic value. As for Afghanistan, it was conceded that the Taliban would soon emerge ascendant and be able to consolidate power, made possible by the group's significant religious and tactical staying power in the country. However, finding it a vastly different country than existed in the 1990s, the Taliban movement might, as was argued by many, feel impelled to adopt more enlightened political, social and economic policies than had existed during their first emirate in the 1990s. It was also hoped that the region's powers, all with strong stakes and competing agendas in Afghanistan's future, would be compelled to aid the country in achieving a semblance of political and macroeconomic stability.

There were reasons, however, to question the wisdom of a complete US military withdrawal, certainly of so rapid a disengagement. Many American military and civilian analysts feared a regional power vacuum and that the very threats to American security that brought its intervention in 2001 could reemerge. The Taliban's quick, decisive victory may have spared Afghanistan from immediately being embroiled in a protracted civil war but could also make more remote any willingness to share power with other Afghan political stakeholders or to put the brakes on a wide mix of terrorist organisations. It was of concern that under a Taliban-governed Afghanistan, such groups as Al-Qaeda and Islamic State-Khorasan Province (ISIS-K) and their various ideological partners could find fertile soil on which to plan and mount attacks against the US and its allies. Importantly, without an on-the-ground presence, however small, successful counterterrorism operations would be difficult, if not impossible. With militant groups still active in Pakistan, there were additional worries expressed about nuclear theft and proliferation. It was also thought shortsighted to expect that Afghanistan — the hub of global terrorism, having Iran and China as neighbours, its borders abutting a Russian sphere of influence in Central Asia and with nuclear-armed Pakistan and India on its East — could fade as a US concern.

As it has turned out, developments in Afghanistan have made it difficult for Washington to make the clean break many thought possible. To date, neither the US nor any other country has granted the Taliban government diplomatic recognition. Yet, while some of the worst fears have, thus far, not materialised, it has become abundantly clear that in most respects, the Taliban's rule closely resembles the group's regressive

1996–2001 period. It has also become apparent that the Taliban are again largely impervious to international criticism and pressure concerning their domestic policies. Just as during the insurgency when expectations about successful peace talks with the Taliban were unrealistic, most of the global community's expectations to meaningfully influence the Taliban behaviour have, thus far, proven unproductive.

It can thus be asked how the US can shape its policies towards a Taliban-controlled Afghanistan to both safeguard American security and support the well-being of the Afghan people. After its years-long intensive involvement in Afghanistan and the manner of its departure, the US bears some responsibility for the difficult issues currently faced in Afghanistan. The country's humanitarian crisis and America's broader security interests would seem to rule out the option of treating Afghanistan and the region with benign neglect.

Above all, America's post-withdrawal Afghanistan policy has featured selective efforts to steer and moderate the Taliban's regime behaviour. In concert with most of the partner community, Washington has denied the Taliban government political recognition and direct financial and development assistance in hopes of convincing it to form a more politically acceptable and inclusive government. Variously motivated, the US and other countries have pressed the regime to share political power with a broad range of ethnic, factional, sectarian and regional interests. The regime has also been pressed to live up to promises not to provide a safe harbour to terrorist organisations bent on mounting regional and global operations. The Taliban have also been pushed to soften their harsh social restrictions, notably those affecting the treatment of Afghan women and their education and employment. In all these areas, the Taliban's actions have remained frustratingly disappointing, and the regime's competing rulers have cared less to salvage it.

This chapter, which reflects the authors' analysis and first-hand observations of the region, argues that the realisation of America's redefined objectives in Afghanistan are not advanced by isolating the Taliban government but are better served by carefully broadening and regularising engagement with the regime. Sanction-driven strategies have, to date, done truly little to alter the Taliban's behaviour, which, at times, has been counter-productive to important efforts to address the needs of the Afghan people. There should certainly be no illusions about what can be accomplished in broadening and deepening the US' engagement with a regime whose policies are wholly antithetical to American values and interests. However, a more targeted and tactful diplomatic relationship — one particularly focused on the Taliban's ideological power centres in Kandahar and Kabul — may help to clarify differences and identify areas of possible convergence. It may also point the way to how the US can find ways to work cooperatively, albeit transactionally, with the Taliban rulers on issues involving counterterrorism.

The Taliban's Ideological Promise, on Steroids

Since the group's founding in September 1994, the Taliban have impressively maintained their ideological promise — to take over Afghanistan and remould it. The broad contours of their ideological promise were simple: we are devout Muslims who fight for God and oppose corrupt leaders — whether they are former Afghan communists, jihadi leaders or educated technocrats — and we have an alternative vision for a new Afghanistan. The Taliban's brilliance has been found in refusing to veer off their promise, weathering all kinds of pressures and avoiding ideological compromise. The Taliban's founders understood from the outset that unless their basic promise was preserved, their movement would become irrelevant. They recognised the indispensable role religion plays in forcing fundamental political changes in Afghanistan. In doing so, the Taliban increasingly customised their ideology as a social and political project to bring back "original" Islam to purify and reorganise Afghan society.

The Taliban's current government — an uneasy coalition of ideological and business-driven governing partners — has kept firm to the group's sacred ideological agenda. In doing so, the new rulers have engaged in an organised campaign to solidify their rule and make their interim government permanent, principally through enacting three closely intertwined initiatives: fleshing out a state religious ideology, burnishing their "originalist" religious credentials and channelling Afghan nationalism into religious nationalism. A deeper look into these three initiatives provides important insights into how the Taliban interact with temporal political realities, including managing internal political and militant competitions.

In their first initiative, the Taliban rulers have laid the ground to effectively transform their religious movement into a permanent ideology that these authors would describe as "Talibanism". This hybrid code dictates the Taliban's worldview, which views society as a competition between godliness and worldliness. Historically, as Sunni Muslims, the Taliban's main reference point has been the Deobandi school, a variant of Hanafi Islam founded in the mid-19th century. While most Afghans follow Sunni Hanafi Islam, Talibanism is a shift away from traditional Deobandism and towards a more tailored and unwritten mixture of puritanical beliefs wrapped in Islamic *Sharia*.

Today, Talibanism commands that Islam dictate every aspect of daily life that is to be lived and preached. It considers the Afghan society insufficiently Islamic and in need of urgent re-Islamisation — either by invitation or coercion. It rejects all forms of republican rule because it follows human perversion. Talibanism also makes a marked distinction between Islamic law[2] and man-made laws, deeming the latter immoral because they follow the whims of corrupt humans. By reorganising Afghan society consistently with their Islamic rules,[3] Talibanism aspires to make Afghanistan a great nation again, in which the new rulers will lead without competition. A vast majority of the Afghan population rejects such forced Talibanism, posing an existential governance challenge for the Taliban regime.

In their second initiative, the Taliban rulers have revalidated themselves as the vanguard for a true Islamic leadership of Afghanistan. While there are many Taliban variants, a powerful cluster of religious clerics serves as the movement's nerve centre.[4] Unlike the Taliban's pragmatists, these clerics are originalists in their interpretation of Islam and view the Quran as their constitution. They believe that the recognition of a Taliban state springs from their own community of followers and not foreign states. They operate through a loose set of policy action documents, known as Dastur,[5] and consider a clerics-approved unitary Islamic Emirate as a model state. It is this select cast of characters that makes sensitive Taliban decisions through an inner religious *Shura,* including all ideological appointments that go unchallenged.[6]

In their third initiative, the regime has engaged in efforts to re-engineer the principles of Afghan nationalism to comport with Islamic nationalism. Historically, pan-Afghan nationalism had often emerged as a form of resistance against foreign incursions, bringing together a cross-section of Afghans bound by a common identity, history and threats. Over the years, however, the principal underpinnings of that nationalism have either weakened or have taken other forms. Amid the complex of a divided nation, Afghan nationalism today mainly centres around ethnic nationalism that emphasises the decentralisation of state power and resources.

This vacuum has provided the Taliban an opportunity to spearhead a return to the past by merging Afghan nationalism with Islamic nationalism. They envision creating a new narrative of Afghan Islam to include imposing a singular Islamic identity in Afghanistan.[7] It is also along these lines that the Taliban intend to develop a national security force, including a special unit of martyrdom soldiers that can fight and win.[8] This re-Islamisation also involves reforming the education system, including establishing a single national curriculum to knit religious education with regular schooling.

These efforts have enabled the Taliban to extend their minoritarian tyranny and consolidate power, acquire resources and remove competition. This power consolidation is pursued through a mixture of the Taliban's politics of vice and virtue, rewards and punishments, political alienation and patronage, including through appointments, shares in revenue collection and land distribution. *Sharia* courts now proliferate the country and civilian bureaucracy has become largely militarised. In this process, the Taliban rulers have presented their forced takeover as a grand referendum on their current rule, refusing to start a national dialogue process to establish an acceptable government, even if they end up leading it.

Old Terrorism, New Taliban

By any measure, the Taliban's return has morphed the terrorism landscape across the volatile region. Various competing jihadist forces have begun to engage one another, with some negotiating their own separate peace, while others realign to establish tactical partnerships. This militant reconciliation has enabled many groups to combine their battlefield tactics with technology, which has expanded their tactical staying power. Scores of foreign and unaffiliated jihadists now roam freely across the region. The Taliban have quietly cemented or adjusted their own arrangements with various jihadists, a deadly constellation involving Pakistani, Uzbek, Tajik, Uyghur, Arab and Baloch groups. They are reportedly registering foreign fighters and issuing them weapon permits and travel documents.

Troublingly, a tangled web of jihadists has romanticised the Taliban's victory. In a statement, Al-Qaeda glorified the Taliban for "breaking America's back",[9] showering it with praise for not abandoning the way of "jihad and martyrdom". The Taliban's takeover has also presented an impressive victory template to a raft of jihadi groups. Most are proudly using Taliban monikers such as al-Emirati, Haqqani, al-Omari, al-Afghani and al-Mansoori. One former senior aide to Osama Bin Laden publicly paraded his return to Afghanistan.[10] Jihadists have also used the Taliban's allure to expand their propaganda in social media spaces, including on Telegram, Twitter and Facebook.[11]

Furthermore, ISIS-K, the terror group's Afghan chapter rivalling the Taliban, has locked horns with the Taliban and has become the most kinetically active Salafist group in the country. ISIS-K considers the Taliban opportunistic nationalists and not pan-Islamists and has violently opposed them for imposing an exclusive Sunni Hanafi state.[12] On the ground, the group has replicated the Taliban's battlefield playbook, including organising hit-and-run operations, ambushes, roadside bombs and assassinations. One ISIS-K-claimed attack in November 2021 killed a senior Taliban leader who commanded the central military corps in Kabul. The group has also increased attacks on civilian targets to sow chaos, create sectarian tensions and erode confidence in the Taliban's assurance of security. It has also encouraged defections from the Taliban's ranks, while also expanding its recruitment among non-Pashtun groups opposed to the Taliban.

Beyond Afghanistan, ISIS-K has expanded its regional appeal by establishing a presence in Pakistan and Central Asia. In Pakistan, it has become closer to various groups, particularly the Pakistani Taliban. In Central Asia, ISIS-K's network has found important partners in militant Uyghurs, Uzbek jihadists like the Islamic Movement of Uzbekistan (IMU) and Katibat Imam al-Bukhari (KiB), as well as Tajikistan's Jamaat Ansarullah.

Yet, the Taliban have largely downplayed the ISIS-K threat despite adopting a brutal approach towards the group's members and offering them a choice: stay in Islam but leave ISIS-K or stay with ISIS-K but leave Islam. The second-order effect of the Taliban's approach, especially its apprehension or targeting of Salafist civilians, has increased the dangers of ISIS-K recruiting from the disgruntled Salafist population inside Afghanistan. As ISIS-K expands its role, possibly to achieve territorial gains, this shared threat could well serve to bring the Taliban and Al-Qaeda even closer and spell dangers of increased violence.

Arenas of the US' Policy

The US has found itself drawn into five major policy areas with the Taliban. These have confronted Washington with often tough policy choices made more difficult by political constraints at home and those confronted inside Afghanistan.

Evacuation and resettlement

This policy priority has grown out of America's moral obligations stemming from its previous engagement and involves facilitating the evacuation of American citizens and Afghans who supported the US' military operations and civilian programmes. This effort requires the processing of Afghans seeking resettlement in the US or another country. Although the US extracted over 120,000 Afghans following the Taliban's takeover, there remain an estimated 80,000 eligible Afghans and their families who are unprocessed for the Special Immigrant Visa (SIV) programme. A great many of those evacuated to locations outside of Afghanistan have encountered resettlement difficulties. Those outside the US, who are ineligible for the SIV programme, can apply for temporary permission through the "humanitarian parole" programme to enter the US, though even, if granted, leaves them in legal limbo.

In FY2022, the US set aside US$2.7 billion for the Department of Defense to transport, house and feed Afghan evacuees. However, much remains to be done to make the backlogged and complicated asylum and time-bound SIV processes for Afghans faster, smoother and fairer. With direct support from the US Congress, the Biden administration needs to make additional SIV and other visa categories available, expedite the gruelling security vetting process, appropriate more funds, expedite the hearing of appeals and negotiate the safe passage of Afghans to leave Afghanistan. The US Congress is required to relax the immigrant laws, specifically the introduced Afghan Adjustment Act that would establish a legal pathway for Afghans to secure US residency and citizenship.[13]

The physical evacuation of Afghans offers a clear example of the intersection between US and the Taliban interests. At least, for a time, the Taliban's interest in allowing the evacuation of Afghans to proceed coincided with those of the US and other countries. Although the Taliban created numerous obstacles to the evacuations, limited dialogue with the Taliban officials facilitated the departure of those many individuals opposed to the regime. By the close of 2021, however, this mutuality of interests faded, nearly stopping all US-facilitated evacuations.

Humanitarian

A second policy area — Afghanistan's severe food and health crises — has dominated America's post-withdrawal involvement in the country.[14] The Western exit set in motion conditions that worsened the circumstances for Afghanistan's chronically malnourished population, leaving two-thirds in need of life-saving humanitarian assistance. The Taliban's failure to pay salaries and provide security has led many skilled and educated Afghans to quit. Amid the financial meltdown, unemployment has sharply increased, consumer buying power reduced and many supply networks dried up. With millions of Afghans internally displaced, healthcare facilities are short of medicines and equipment.

If the worst-case predictions of widespread famine in Afghanistan have thus far been avoided, it has been because of the timely intervention of the international aid community. Aid organisations have sustained at least minimal levels of food security for millions of Afghans. Despite their suspicion of foreign influences and jealous guarding of their regained sovereignty, the Taliban have largely welcomed foreign humanitarian assistance. In the 1990s, a hapless Taliban were known to have given foreign aid agencies almost free reign in providing assistance. Today, a more assertive Taliban seek a larger and more direct role. The US and other donors have sought to guard themselves against the Taliban's interference in relief efforts and prevent the Taliban from financially profiting from the assistance. In some cases, the Taliban have created obstacles for relief operations by extracting revenues involving various licences, taxes and administrative fees applied on humanitarian organisations.[15] In other cases, local Taliban authorities have worked alongside international agencies in delivering food and medical supplies to the affected population.

Despite its disengagement, the US has continued to serve as the largest aid donor to Afghanistan. Between August 2021 and December 2022, Washington committed more than US$1.1 billion to humanitarian assistance.[16] In January 2022, the United Nations (UN) launched its largest humanitarian funding appeal for US$5 billion to shore up collapsed basic services. More financial pledges were attracted from a broad number of countries in a March 2022 pledging event but fell short of meeting the US$5 billion funding appeal. Nearly all US relief support has been channelled through UN agencies and US Agency for International Development-partnered non-government organisations. The World Food Programme and the UN Children's Fund have also launched essential funding programmes to prevent starvation as have such groups as the International Rescue Committee, CARE, Roots of Peace and Save the Children, many of them active in Afghanistan for more than 30 years.

Unfortunately, UN efforts at coordination, as well as supervision and verification of the various aid delivery at both the national and local levels, leave much to be desired. Despite its limitations to closely monitor aid delivery and its effectiveness, Washington could work to influence the priorities of the relief organisations and assist in building a consensus among them. Nevertheless, any gains achieved in overcoming Afghanistan's food and health insecurity may not be sustainable without an investment in development and increased economic stabilisation. Washington has, thus far, refused to seriously consider widening the scope of its bilateral aid programme beyond the humanitarian assistance even though the line drawn to deny the Taliban development financing is already blurred.

However, much remains in Afghanistan with regard to establishing a modus operandi with the Taliban on the provision of future assistance. It offers Washington an important area of opportunity to carve out a sphere of shared interests with the Taliban. The regime's willingness to allow aid flows and operational freedom to aid workers is unlikely to come about through its surrender to outside pressures but rather as a result of building a multi-layered relationship with the Taliban. Such a relationship is needed to have even the most hardliners among the Taliban realise how their grip on power could be threatened by mass hunger and the suspension of foreign assistance. For this, sustained diplomatic presence is probably essential.

Financial

The fastest and most effective way of addressing Afghanistan's economic crisis is by putting money in the hands of the people. The withdrawal of foreign financial assistance and freezing of financial reserves in the wake of the Taliban's takeover crippled an economy that had grown accustomed to having three-quarters of the government budget covered by foreign donors.[17] The cut-off also brought the financial system to its knees. What the Taliban seek is the injection of liquidity into the economy to strengthen the currency and prevent hyperinflation. Recapitalisation of the banking system is crucial to any hopes of reviving the economy and could be given a substantial boost by injecting a portion of the previous regime's frozen US$3.5 billion foreign reserves now managed through the newly established Afghanistan trust fund in Switzerland. The remainder of the estimated US$5.5 billion in frozen assets remains held in banks in the US, the United Arab Emirates (UAE) and Europe.

Washington has been reluctant to release these funds without assurance that they will not serve to enrich the Taliban coffers. Several meetings have been held in Doha with Taliban representatives to discuss potential mechanisms for an off-budget, condition-based and incremental release of these funds guaranteed by multiple parties.[18] The expectation is that if provided with technical assistance, a recapitalised central bank could be managed by career professionals independent of the Taliban's influence. Discussions with the Taliban government settling the dispute over the frozen reserves provide a good example of the value of constructive engagement with the regime. They may provide the opportunity to open other fruitful areas of engagement with the regime, including cooperation on counter-narcotics, disaster response preparedness and border security.

What is indisputable is that US' sanctions have deepened Afghanistan's financial crisis. While nothing would have a greater impact than the transfer of the frozen funds, other measures that soften economic sanctions could help in reviving the shattered economy. Since December 2021, the US Treasury Department has facilitated UN-delivered cash shipments to Afghanistan, averaging US$40 million a week.[19] This cash support, deposited directly into a private Afghan commercial bank rather than the Taliban-controlled central bank, has largely ensured currency stability and controlled inflation. The cash liquidity has helped cover the salary payments of civil servants, as well as the costs of food and other basic imports. Similarly, in March 2022, the US Treasury Department issued a sweeping general licence to expand the authorisation for commercial and financial transactions.[20] Given the other difficulties in conducting business in Afghanistan, the move was not expected to have a great impact, but it points the way towards the regularisation of relations with the regime.

Human Rights

A fourth policy arena tests the US government's stated pledge to "put human rights at the centre of its domestic and foreign policy".[21] No issues have elicited more attention for Americans than the Taliban's restrictions on women's schooling, domestic travel and employment. The economic hardships in removing women from the workforce have been profound. The Taliban's decision in December 2022 to ban women from employment with foreign relief organisations has led to many groups suspending vital operations. There have additionally been psychological effects of gender suppression that have seen the ambitions of a generation of urban women crushed by the Taliban's decisions, reversing gains achieved over 20 years.

In pressing the Taliban to alter their human rights practices, Washington is typically accused of interfering in Afghanistan's domestic affairs.

Taliban leaders insist that Islamic law provides women all the liberties and protections they require. In an interview, the Taliban's acting prime minister, Mullah Mohammad Hassan Akhund, declared that women's "rights [are] set by almighty Allah for humanity" and follow a "divinely defined path".[22] Unsurprisingly, the linking of the Taliban's reversal of policies on women's issues to securing diplomatic recognition by the US and others has proven largely ineffective, perhaps even counterproductive. While expanded US engagement cannot simply be expected to improve the Taliban's policies towards women, it could conceivably strengthen the hand of those among the Talibani rulers who are inclined to modify the regime's worst gender practices.

Counterterrorism

A fifth policy sector — counterterrorism — exists even though the US capacity to undertake operations has been greatly curtailed. The bulk of American military and intelligence resources in Afghanistan aimed at preventing the planning and execution of US-directed terrorist attacks have been lost. The remaining few counterterrorism tools are poor substitutes for what was possible when US troops and intelligence operatives were present on the ground and worked in collaboration with various Afghan security partners. Hopes that at least a small contingent of US Special Forces and intelligence personnel would remain for counterterrorism purposes after the US' withdrawal were dashed when the Taliban refused to agree to such a presence. Two US administrations saw forcing the issue as jeopardising the peace agreement with the Taliban. Although ambitions for an effective and wholesale "over the horizon" counterterrorism capacity have so far survived, the US' ability to monitor threats and launch operations has largely diminished.

On the face of it, the Taliban should be able to find a common cause with the US and collaborate against such organisations as ISIS-K, the Taliban's principal rival. The Taliban's rivalry with ISIS-K can now serve their interests in conveying to the international community that the regime takes seriously its repeated assurance that no group will be allowed to use Afghan soil to attack a third country. Yet, the Taliban government has refused to explore establishing a working relationship with the US on counterterrorism issues. Building the trust needed to develop cooperation, if not collaboration, with the Taliban on counterterrorism may only be achievable through more regular bilateral engagement.

With counterterrorism occupying much of Washington's thinking about Afghanistan, there is a priority placed on exploiting opportunities for intelligence gathering on ISIS-K and evidence of whether or how Al-Qaeda and other organisations are strengthening themselves. The absence of cooperation with the Taliban and the difficulty in cultivating intelligence sources without a presence in the country require greater reliance on intelligence sharing with Pakistan, India and the Central Asian republics. Having its own counterterrorism liaison office in Kabul, however limited, could also improve Washington's ability to gauge growing Chinese economic activities more closely and Russia's expanding ties in Afghanistan.

Regional Stakes and Realignments

Like in the past, virtually every neighbouring and regional country has found it difficult to find common ground with Afghanistan, much less with the Taliban regime. Three sets of regional actors are presently involved in Afghanistan. The first includes those with dedicated militant and militia networks operating in the country in support of their extraterritorial ambitions or political overreach, like Pakistan and Iran. The second includes those who are merely dangling the promise of financial and political support to the Taliban but are either unwilling or unable to out-invest the US, like China and Russia. The third set involves those who desire a neutral Afghanistan and have adopted a cautious approach to meaningfully engage the Taliban, like India and the Central Asian republics.

Most of the regional players have, so far, pursued largely uncoordinated efforts to both balance off their engagements with the Taliban and manage relationships with their historic non-Taliban factional partners. The Taliban's own regional approach is that their cooperation depends upon the degree to which each regional country supports the anti-Taliban resistance groups — now or in the future. In doing so, the Taliban have shrewdly exploited the sprawling network of Afghanistan-based militant groups as a form of extortion to extract concessions, including diplomatic recognition and normalising commercial ties. Yet, no regional country could offer the Taliban enough to walk away from non-Afghan jihadist groups that threaten regional security. However, despite the absence of shared regional understanding on the way forward, each regional country has engaged the Taliban as a short-term insurance policy.

Pakistan

During the peace talks in Doha, the now defunct Afghan republic desired national sovereignty as part of a negotiated settlement, and Pakistan wanted a piece of that sovereignty. In so doing, Pakistan kept its historic relationship with the Taliban open-ended and provided the Taliban a longer-term predictability in their partnership. After the Taliban made important territorial gains while negotiations were still underway in Doha, Pakistan saw an opportunity to push for a military settlement instead of a political deal. It was no surprise that Pakistani leaders and extremist religious parties alike later celebrated the Taliban's takeover.

For two decades, a crucial misjudgment of multiple American–Afghan policies was ignoring Pakistan's nefarious role as business as usual. One folly of the US Pakistan policy was that Washington often enraged Pakistan with strong statements, but it failed to follow through on them. Over four successive US administrations, Pakistan skillfully weathered American pressures and stood firmly by the Taliban.

However, the Taliban's return has begun to turn the tables against Pakistan — a cruel irony in which Pakistan's stability has been threatened by the Pakistani Taliban who are supported by their friends in the Taliban government. In recent months, the Pakistani Taliban have staged an alarming number of attacks against Pakistan's security services, brazenly broken into prisons to release their fighters, breached military checkpoints, attacked mosques and undermined Pakistanis' confidence in their government's assurance of security. This cross-border threat from the Pakistani Taliban has stoked tensions between Pakistan and the Taliban government. While Pakistan has conducted cross-border operations against the Pakistani Taliban camps in Afghanistan, they have demanded that the Taliban regime restrain the threat inside Afghan geography. The Taliban rulers helped broker a ceasefire agreement between the two sides, but it quickly failed. Beneath these tensions remains a broader perception of Pakistan to function as the gatekeeper to Afghanistan. Pakistani leaders have done little to clear this perception, fuelling mistrust among the Afghan people and select Taliban factions about Pakistan's objectives.

Iran

For Tehran, the Taliban problem is a complex issue. Most Iranian leaders distrust the Taliban, but they cannot afford to ignore them. Before the Taliban's takeover, Tehran enjoyed a strong relationship with select Taliban factions and even allowed them to operate the Mashhad Shura inside Iran. With its Afghanistan portfolio managed by Iran's Revolutionary Guard Corps, Iran was reportedly the second-largest source of support to the Taliban after Pakistan. At one point, the relationship was so strong that fighters from Lebanon's Hezbollah trained Taliban snipers. Outside the Taliban, Tehran leveraged other important elements as part of its Axis of Resistance, particularly the Fatemiyoun Brigade. Recruited from Afghanistan's Shia community, this expendable militia group fought for Tehran's interests in Syria. Iran also enjoyed greater coordination with Pakistan and Russia on the way forward in Afghanistan.

Tehran will continue to exploit these assets when necessary, but its immediate priority now concerns dealing with the unpredictable Taliban government. In recent months, Tehran's ties with the Taliban have become strained over violent border skirmishes, increased cross-border trafficking and flow of refugees, management of Afghan water flowing into Iran and Iran's brutal treatment of Afghans. The relationship has been further strained by Iran's public calls on the Taliban to establish an inclusive government. For now, despite its history of supporting anti-Taliban factions, Tehran also fears that any support to anti-Taliban resistance would weaken the Taliban's ability or willingness to fight a shared enemy — ISIS-K. Ultimately, Tehran seems to operate under the belief that its policy vis-à-vis the Taliban depends on how the Taliban's own relationship with Washington evolves.

Russia

For many years, Russia was the third-largest source of support to the Taliban after Pakistan and Iran. During the Doha peace talks, all three countries supported the Taliban in return for vague political guarantees, including, for the Taliban, the assurance to accommodate several non-Taliban Afghan political factions in a future government. Those promises did not materialise when the new rulers went on to form a Taliban-only government after assuming power.

Though not an immediate neighbour to Afghanistan, Russia is concerned about the indirect militant threat from Afghanistan which includes ISIS-K. In September 2022, ISIS-K targeted Russia's diplomatic mission in Kabul, killing two Russian personnel. Moscow is also concerned about ISIS-K's growing appeal among the Central Asian jihadists and its expanding ties with the IMU, KiB and Jamaat Ansarullah. So far, Moscow has focused on uniting the five Central Asian states, each of which has separately engaged the Taliban regime to establish a joint buffer zone against the shared threat from Afghanistan. In doing so, Russia has convened several regional dialogues through its Moscow Format Consultations on Afghanistan, involving representatives from Pakistan, Iran, India and China. While the grouping also includes Afghanistan, Moscow's exclusion of the Taliban has left the process weak.

India

The Taliban's return has upended India's historically positive role in Afghanistan. Although New Delhi did not play an active role in Afghanistan's peace talks in Doha, it was troubled by the resulting US–Taliban agreement. India's terrorism concerns had generally been both Pakistan-centric and those directly involving the Taliban. Many in New Delhi favoured a no-deal scenario with the Taliban over one that favoured expanding Pakistan's role in a Taliban-controlled Afghanistan.

Importantly, the counterterrorism guarantees promised in the Doha agreement did not specify important anti-India groups and the Taliban's relationship with them, including Al-Qaeda, in the Indian subcontinent. For years, this Al-Qaeda affiliate has maintained a strong presence in the

Taliban ranks. Today, the group also leverages significant operational capabilities inside India. While New Delhi requires security guarantees to safeguard its personnel and interests in Afghanistan, the presence of reliably anti-India elements within the Taliban ranks has made the prospects of wholesale Indian engagement with the regime increasingly challenging.

Nevertheless, India has cautiously taken incremental steps to explore pathways to deal with the Taliban. It has deployed a small technical team to staff its diplomatic mission in Kabul and has provided important humanitarian assistance to Afghanistan. It has also quietly instrumentalised its strong relationship with Qatar and the UAE, on which the Taliban rulers depend, to open additional communication channels with the Taliban regime. However, despite its weak hand and the fact that it is constantly tested by the sceptical Taliban wary of India's possible future support to anti-Taliban resistance, New Delhi cannot afford to stand as a mere spectator.

China

For years, China has viewed Afghanistan as uncharted territory. Despite leveraging important ties with the Taliban in the 1990s, much of Beijing's Afghan policy depended on Pakistan's support to ensure the security of Chinese interests and personnel in Afghanistan. However, the Taliban's return has changed Beijing's calculations, forcing it to keep its diplomatic mission open in Kabul and to engage directly with the regime, particularly the Haqqani Taliban.

In general, China's Afghan policy had been motivated less by economic interests and more by its security concerns. In its economic engagement, Beijing has often overpromised Afghanistan but underdelivered. Since 2007, Chinese state-owned companies held prime contracts for the Amu Darya hydropower plant and the Aynak copper mine in Afghanistan, a lucrative copper deposit valued at US$50 billion that Beijing managed on a 30-year lease. To date, the agreements have neither generated revenues nor created employment opportunities for Afghanistan.

Today, Beijing has renewed similar pledges to the Taliban regime, including a promise to integrate Afghanistan into China's signature Belt and Road Initiative, build a US$200 million industrial park and scrap tariffs on all imported Afghan goods. In April 2022, Beijing launched the Tunxi Initiative — a regional platform involving all of Afghanistan's six neighbours and Russia — to support humanitarian efforts in Afghanistan. To date, no large-scale assistance has been delivered. Instead, China has signed lucrative oil and gas contracts with the Taliban government, where Chinese companies will drill three oil fields worth US$400 million for 25 years.[23] Crucially, the agreement involves an unequal revenue-sharing arrangement, enabling the Chinese companies to contractually receive 80 percent of the generated revenues. Should these engagements proceed, Beijing is likely to push the Taliban to allow Chinese private security companies to deploy in Afghanistan to protect its interests.

For now, Beijing's primary concern revolves around threats from militant Uyghurs operating under the Taliban's protective umbrella. This concern includes possible arms sales to the Uyghurs and the dangers of them reorganising and expanding their partnerships with other jihadist groups. So far, Beijing has traded off certain support to the Haqqani Taliban in return for their cooperation and intelligence sharing against the group. Some reports indicate that Beijing has agreed to supply border surveillance systems to the Taliban to track cross-border movements of the Uyghurs.

However, Uyghur fighters have generally maintained a unified front against China. They also now leverage important operational alliances with groups such as the Pakistani Taliban, Al-Qaeda affiliates and the Islamic State. In December 2022, an ISIS-K-claimed attack on a hotel in Kabul frequented by Chinese nationals left several Chinese dead. The attack, likely to be supported by ISIS-K's Uyghur partners, undermined Beijing's confidence in the Taliban's security and forced Beijing to advise its nationals to leave Afghanistan.

For their part, the Taliban view the Chinese model of cooperation in the form of mutual non-interference in domestic affairs. No Taliban leader has commented about Beijing's treatment of the Uyghur population, a tacit endorsement of anti-Uyghur measures being China's internal anti-terrorism policy. Beijing has reciprocated by extending the Taliban with political cover, including by accusing the US of creating a humanitarian catastrophe in Afghanistan, holding hostage the country's frozen foreign reserves and stealing them. Beijing has further urged Washington to release those assets to the Taliban government. Beijing also accused Washington of "double standards" in its counterterrorism operations after the US strike killed Al-Qaeda leader Ayman al-Zawahiri in Kabul, stressing that such strikes should not violate other countries' sovereignty.[24]

America's Redefined Objectives and Policy Constraints

At present, four strategic objectives are ordinarily cited as arguing for continuing American involvement in Afghanistan. The most readily appreciated is that terrorist organisations be prevented from regrouping on Afghan soil to plan attacks on the US and its allies. This is made very real by the refusal of the Taliban to sever their long-held ties to Al-Qaeda and the resilience of ISIS-K. The second is that a humanitarian crisis over scarce food and healthcare be alleviated both for its own sake and to prevent a refugee surge that could destabilise the region and impact Europe politically. The third is that the Taliban regime be induced to improve gender and other basic rights, including for religious minorities. The fourth is to temper any strategic advantage that Russia, China and Iran can gain militarily, economically and politically from America's diminished presence in the region.

For now, the US has concluded that it cannot change the ideological dynamics of today's Afghanistan. In July 2021, Biden declared that "no nation has ever unified Afghanistan", emphasising the prospects of "one unified government" as "highly unlikely".[25] In this context, several factors complicate the formulation of the US' policy towards the Taliban regime. Along with a mutual lack of trust, uppermost are the deep differences in visions of a preferred Afghan end state. This stands clearest in the clashing views on the role of women in society but also broadly applies to differences in beliefs about the purposes served by the government and the requirements of a functioning economy. These differences do not require resolution to form a practical relationship with the Taliban, but its scope is bound to remain limited by the seeming inability of the Taliban to act transactionally. Neither threats nor incentives have, to date, induced the Taliban to make meaningful concessions that would deny them a monopoly of power or compromise what they believe is Islamic doctrine.

Simply put, why after succeeding in a lengthy, hard-won victory, should the Taliban see a reason to share power with individuals associated with a detested previous regime? The Taliban's inflexibility on religious grounds has been made clear by the directive of the group's supreme leader, Mullah Haibatullah Akhundzada, to officials of his regime that they review all past policies and laws that might prevent the institution of a "pure Islamic system".[26]

To be sure, no Afghan group has emerged to credibly challenge the Taliban nor does any command the Taliban-like longer-term tactical or religious staying power. Due to the Taliban's exclusionary policies, some Afghan ethnic factions have called for a softer partition of Afghanistan to splinter the country into a loose confederacy of statelets. Other Afghan resistance groups have called for the establishment of an interim military republic. To date, Washington has shown little appetite to muddy the already toxic waters by supporting any of the fledgling and politically problematic resistance organisations. Regardless, a stable Afghan state and viable economy are very much in the US interest even though many of the needed elements are in short supply in Afghanistan. The country is in the hands of rulers who have few administrative skills for governance in a highly diverse country of roughly 40 million. The regime's bureaucracy has been depleted by the fleeing or firing of those with the necessary managerial or technical skills, further limiting the Taliban's hope of reviving the economy.

As Washington decides on charting a direction with the Taliban regime, it finds itself burdened in shaping policy by the legacy of its past engagement with Afghanistan's previous republic. The US carries the weight of an unfulfilled military mission and an uncompleted exercise of state building, as well as the experience of a failed peace process. Many periodicals and books have dwelled on the faulty assessments and misleading statements of military and civilian leaders over the course of the Afghan conflict. The publicity given to a long series of reports issued by Afghanistan's watchdog, the Special Inspector General for Afghanistan Reconstruction, for its cataloguing of the waste and misappropriations of funds over two decades of aid policy has been instrumental in shaping popular opinion.[27] Plainly, the US Congress, the media and much of America's public, while sympathetic to the plight of the Afghan people, still look suspiciously at any normalising of relations with the Taliban. Placing a mission or a liaison office in Kabul is further complicated by Washington's heavy diplomatic security requirements.

Formulating a broad post-withdrawal US policy on Afghanistan is also affected by having to compete with compelling domestic and international issues dominating the news cycle, all of which keep Afghanistan policy on the back burner. In general, policies towards Afghanistan are often seen as having been short-term and shortsighted and on a single track. Complaints about the lack of long-term strategic thinking about Afghanistan that were apparent for two decades are now no less valid. They are likely to remain as a consequence of a US national security establishment that now has little time for Afghanistan and is disinclined to acknowledge the full significance of its region.

Nevertheless, America's present approach towards the Taliban dabbles between necessary engagement and condemning the regime's vile actions. Make no mistake, while no Taliban action, thus far, is redeemable, their staying power requires Washington to readjust its approach and specifically engage the regime's powerful clerical rulers in Kandahar, potentially by developing new sources of pressure and leverage. Tribalised, it is these men who wield real power and command greater legitimacy. While it is unclear what place pragmatic politics occupy in these clerics' worldview, there is little credible information about their personalised styles of leadership, how they deliberate, how they compromise and how they arrive at decisions. This dearth of political intelligence worsened by Washington's negligible contacts with these individuals has seriously reduced the practicality of US options.

More direct and low-visibility contact with the Taliban rulers in Kandahar could prove useful to better understand their ideological priorities and explore areas for accommodation and compromise. Direct contact could also help Washington integrate necessary regional collaborators and enforcers whose common interest is mitigating the Taliban's inclination to facilitate destabilising extremist factions residing within their borders. A useful start could be helping these clerics interpret their religious priorities within which they might be nudged towards acceptable engagement, requiring them to counter terrorist groups, ease social restrictions and start an inclusive national dialogue process to establish an acceptable national government.

Until then, it is imperative for Washington to remedy the limits of its current "over the horizon" counterterrorism engagement in Afghanistan. This includes operationally defining the horizon, finding local security partners and improving intelligence collection and threat monitoring capabilities on the ground. Parallel to this is a requirement for a redefined US counterterrorism strategy and its rules of engagement for the region. Dealing with offshore threats over multiple horizons also requires regional middlemen for necessary airspace access and intelligence sharing, which, in Afghanistan's case, largely revolves around Pakistan. However, Pakistan's role as a sincere US counterterrorism partner too is problematic for reasons including tense bilateral relations and divergence of interests as well as troubling trends in Pakistan's internal rhetoric stoked by growing anti-Americanism.

In the end, there is no risk-free approach to dealing with the Taliban, which contains all the ingredients for its own destruction — one that might put Afghanistan's neighbours at risk and force US involvement. However, getting America's Taliban policy right could spare the US from circumstances that again force its return.

Endnotes

1. "Remarks by President Biden on the end of the war in Afghanistan", The White House, 31 August 2021, https://www.whitehouse.gov/briefing-room/speeches-remarks/2021/08/31/remarks-by-president-biden-on-the-end-of-the-war-in-afghanistan/.
2. "Interview with spokesman of the Taliban's Ministry of Foreign Affairs", *DW News*, n.d., *Twitter*, https://twitter.com/dwnews/status/1478478286477004801.
3. Steve Coll, "Looking for Mullah Omar", *The New Yorker*, 15 January 2012, https://www.newyorker.com/magazine/2012/01/23/looking-for-mullah-omar.
4. "Audio statement of Mullah Mohammad Hassan Akhund, Acting Prime Minister of the Islamic Emirate", *Ariana News*, 17 November 2021, https://www.facebook.com/ariananews/videos/867197190659078.
5. Muhammad Amir Rana, "A big test for the Taliban", *Dawn*, 21 August 2021, https://www.dawn.com/news/1641951/a-big-test-for-the-taliban.

6. "Taliban appoint members as 44 governors, police chiefs around Afghanistan", *Reuters*, 7 November 2021, https://www.reuters.com/world/asia-pacific/taliban-appoint-members-44-governors-police-chiefs-around-afghanistan-2021-11-07/.
7. "Exclusive interview with Sher Mohammad Abbas Stanikzai", *Youtube*, https://www.youtube.com/watch?v=nuwil-5-hY0.
8. Abubakar Siddique, "As Taliban attempts to transform from insurgency to government, suicide bombers remain key to its strategy", *Radio Free Europe/Radio Liberty*, 4 November 2021, https://www.rferl.org/a/taliban-suicide-bombings-afghanistan/31546216.html.
9. "Al Qaeda Praises Taliban's 'historic victory' in Afghanistan", *FDD's Long War Journal, 2021*, 31 August 2021, https://www.longwarjournal.org/archives/2021/08/al-qaeda-praises-talibans-historic-victory-in-afghanistan.php.
10. "Osama Bin Laden's Aide Amin Ul Haq returns to Afghanistan, Al-Qaeda commander returns", *Republic TV*, https://www.youtube.com/watch?v=1-dlh8KEsrc.
11. "Racists and Taliban supporters have flocked to Twitter's new audio service after executives ignored warnings", *Washington Post*, 10 December 2021, https://www.washingtonpost.com/technology/2021/12/10/twitter-turmoil-spaces/.
12. Kamran Bokhari, "The long shadow of deobandism in South Asia", *New Lines Magazine*, 23 November 2021, https://newlinesmag.com/essays/the-long-shadow-of-deobandism-in-south-asia/.
13. Doris Meissner and Julia Gelatt, "Straight path to legal permanent residence for Afghan evacuees would build on strong US precedent", *Migration Policy*, 10 March 2022, https://www.migrationpolicy.org/news/afghan-adjustment-commentary.
14. "Afghanistan: Economic crisis underlies mass hunger", *Human Rights Watch*, 4 August 2022, https://www.hrw.org/news/2022/08/04/afghanistan-economic-crisis-underlies-mass-hunger.
15. "SIGAR 58th quarterly report to US congress", Special Inspector General for Afghanistan Reconstruction, 30 January 2023, https://www.sigar.mil/pdf/quarterlyreports/2023-01-30qr.pdf.
16. "Remarks by Ambassador Robert Wood at a UN Security Council briefing on the humanitarian situation in Afghanistan", United States Mission to the United Nations, 20 December 2022, https://usun.usmission.gov/remarks-by-ambassador-robert-wood-at-a-un-security-council-briefing-on-the-humanitarian-situation-in-afghanistan/.

17. Bobby Ghosh, "What will the Taliban do with a $22 billion economy?", *Bloomberg*, 20 August 2021, https://www.bloomberg.com/opinion/articles/2021-08-20/taliban-now-have-a-22-billion-economy-where-will-afghanistan-s-money-go.
18. "US delegation meeting with Taliban representatives", US Department of State, 2022, https://www.state.gov/u-s-delegation-meeting-with-taliban-representatives-2/.
19. "Cash shipments to the UN in Afghanistan — Info sheet", *UNAMA*, 9 January 2023, https://unama.unmissions.org/cash-shipments-un-afghanistan-%E2%80%93-info-sheet.
20. "Issuance of Afghanistan-related general license", Department of the Treasury, 25 February 2022, https://home.treasury.gov/policy-issues/financial-sanctions/recent-actions/20220225.
21. "2021 country reports on human rights practices — Afghanistan", US Department of State, https://www.state.gov/reports/2021-country-reports-on-human-rights-practices/afghanistan/.
22. "Taliban PM: Government, nor anyone can dare amend human rights set by god", *Voice of America*, 9 July 2022, https://www.voanews.com/a/6652117.html.
23. "A Chinese company has signed an oil extraction deal with Afghanistan's Taliban", *CNN Business*, 6 January 2023, https://edition.cnn.com/2023/01/06/business/china-company-taliban-oil-deal-hnk-intl/index.html.
24. "Zawahiri Killing: China calls out US 'double standards on terror'", *Hindustan Times*, 4 August 2022, https://www.hindustantimes.com/videos/world-news/zawahiri-killing-china-calls-out-u-s-double-standards-on-terror-101659596661281.html.
25. "Remarks by President Biden on the drawdown of US forces in Afghanistan", The White House, 8 July 2021, https://www.whitehouse.gov/briefing-room/speeches-remarks/2021/07/08/remarks-by-president-biden-on-the-drawdown-of-u-s-forces-in-afghanistan/.
26. "Afghan supreme leader orders full implementation of Sharia law", *The Guardian*, 14 November 2022, https://www.theguardian.com/world/2022/nov/14/-afghanistan-supreme-leader-orders-full-implementation-of-sharia-law-taliban.
27. "SIGAR Afghanistan Reports", Special inspector general for Afghanistan reconstruction, https://www.sigar.mil/allreports/.

Chapter 5

Reflections on United States–Pakistan Relations, Post-American Withdrawal from Afghanistan

Michael Kugelman

In recent months, some analysts have spoken of a reset in the relations between the United States (US) and Pakistan.[1] This assertion is likely informed by several key developments since August 2021. They include the departure of American forces from Afghanistan, which means the Afghan lens through which Washington has long viewed relations with Islamabad no longer applies, the emergence of a new and more pro-US government in Islamabad, and an upsurge in high-level US engagement with Pakistan.

Certainly, prospects for US–Pakistan relations have brightened since April 2022 when Pakistani Prime Minister Imran Khan — a sharp, strident critic of US policy — lost a parliamentary no-confidence vote and accused the Joe Biden administration of being complicit in his ouster. Additionally, a new type of US–Pakistan relationship, one mainly driven in Washington by the US State Department and largely framed around non-security cooperation, is beginning to take shape.[2]

However, talk of a broader and better relationship should not be overstated. Insufficient bandwidth, mistrust and, above all, geopolitical constraints limit the possibilities for an expanded partnership. The first two factors tend to be more pronounced in Washington than in Islamabad, and that is unsurprising given that, broadly speaking, there is more receptivity within the Pakistani government to expand the partnership than there is within the Biden administration.

Brighter Prospects for Partnership

The relationship between the US and Pakistan has long been awkward, yet enduring. It is often described as a bad marriage — despite fundamental differences, the two sides grudgingly stay together. Soon after Pakistan's independence, the two countries established a Cold War alliance even though Washington was initially hesitant because it did not view South Asia as a major battleground for the US' rivalry with the Soviet Union. The 9/11 attacks, which came during a difficult moment in US–Pakistan bilateral relations, several years after Washington sanctioned Islamabad for becoming a nuclear weapons state, resulted in a new counterterrorism alliance. And yet, Pakistan would back the very Haqqani network terrorists that US forces were fighting in Afghanistan, as well as additional militant groups — especially Lashkar-e-Taiba and Jaish-e-Mohammed — that threatened and, in the case of the 2008 Mumbai terror attacks, targeted Americans. Today, Washington's relationship with Islamabad is its most volatile partnership in South Asia, and yet, Pakistan remains America's only ally in the region.[3]

Accordingly, there was good reason to believe that following the US' withdrawal from Afghanistan, a fragile partnership would somehow remain intact despite finding itself at risk of being set adrift after being deprived of its strategic anchor. Sure enough, the relationship has experienced a surge in momentum. Several factors help explain this resilience.

Drivers of the Relationship's Resurgence

First, relations were not actually that bad in the period before the current momentum surge. There were no crises over nuclear weapons, terrorism, military operations or spy craft — all sharp tension points in the decades past. In the months after the US' withdrawal from Afghanistan, the two sides signed new accords in areas ranging from clean water to educational exchanges — areas in the broader development sphere that have long been consistent, albeit unheralded, sources of cooperation for US–Pakistan relations.

Second, it is important to separate the symbolic dimensions of the relationship from its more substantive components. One reason for the increased high-level engagement in 2022 was that the year marked the 75-year anniversary of US–Pakistan relations.[4] Commemorating that milestone was a core incentive for much of that top-echelon diplomatic engagement, and it was often highlighted explicitly in official post-meeting readouts.[5] In effect, those engagements were, in many cases, simply meant to mark a milestone in relations and not to focus on substantive negotiations towards new agreements.

Third, in May 2022, a new US ambassador, Donald Blome, arrived in Islamabad. He came four years after the departure of his predecessor, David Hale. Bilateral diplomacy, especially in delicate relationships, is easier to coordinate and pursue when a formal ambassador is on the ground in both capitals. Blome's brand of public diplomacy has helped smooth US–Pakistan relations. His statements have been positive and supportive, with little, if any, public criticism of Islamabad. He has also been physically visible and active, travelling frequently around Pakistan and uninterested in staying behind embassy walls despite a resurgence in terrorist attacks in Pakistan. A visit he made in October 2022 to the disputed region of Pakistan-administered Kashmir, which prompted a statement of protest from New Delhi, was especially well received in Pakistan. That visit, which focused on trade ties, was not meant to be provocative; it was meant to demonstrate that with a formal ambassador back in place, Washington was committed to pursuing commercial relations with Pakistan, including with interlocutors in Pakistan-administered Kashmir.[6]

Fourth, while the US' withdrawal from Afghanistan may have deprived the US–Pakistan relationship of its core strategic anchor, it has also removed a major bone of contention. During the nearly 20-year war in Afghanistan, Washington and Islamabad were allied with opposing parties to the conflict, making the war a long-running tension point for bilateral relations.[7] With Washington having ended its war in Afghanistan, there is now more alignment between the two countries' interests — both support the delivery of humanitarian assistance to the Afghan people and both worry about terrorism risks emanating from Afghanistan (Islamabad may be more inclined than Washington to consider recognising the Taliban regime, but this is not a point of tension). Bilateral conversations on Afghanistan no longer get bogged down in acrimonious exchanges about Pakistan's support for terrorists that target US forces.

Additionally, the post-Afghanistan withdrawal era has provided the two sides with more policy space to explore new areas for partnership. These include climate change, clean energy, trade and investment. Humanitarian assistance — long a key focus of bilateral cooperation — re-emerged as another core sphere for collaboration after Pakistan's 2022 floods and amid the COVID-19 pandemic. Washington has donated more pandemic vaccines to Pakistan than to any other country, other than Bangladesh.[8] Additionally, the two sides launched a new bilateral health dialogue in July 2022.

However, while the US' withdrawal from Afghanistan provided the relationship with the necessary policy space to explore a broader partnership, the new government in Pakistan, which took office in April 2022, provided it with the necessary diplomatic space to do so. Khan's allegation — wholly lacking in evidence — that the Biden administration helped remove him from power had made diplomatic relations prohibitively toxic. Even before he levelled that accusation, Khan was skating on thin ice with Washington where many had long resented his strong rhetoric against the US' policy in Pakistan. Also, Khan's comment, after the Taliban seized power in Afghanistan in 2021 that Afghans had "broken the shackles of slavery",[9] went down very poorly in Washington. For many US officials, it validated the long-simmering frustration over Pakistan's support for the Taliban during the war in Afghanistan.

Pakistan's governing coalition, while weak, divided and — thanks to its failure to ease a rapidly worsening economic crisis — unpopular at home, has telegraphed its intention for warm relations with Washington. While the current government's shelf life is likely to be short — national elections are scheduled to happen by the end of 2023 — it is one with which Washington is comfortable working.

These factors help explain the surge in bilateral engagement throughout much of 2022 and early 2023. There were multiple minister-level meetings, including between US Secretary of State Antony J. Blinken and his counterpart, Bilawal Bhutto, and between US Trade Representative Catherine Tai and Pakistani Commerce Minister Syed Naveed Qamar. Top US officials, including US State Department Counselor Derek Chollet, have made visits to Islamabad. During the summer of 2022, Dilawar Syed, the State Department's Special Representative for Commercial and Business Affairs, made a week-long visit to Pakistan. That is a strikingly long visit for a senior official without Pakistan in his portfolio — an indication that Washington was serious about engaging Islamabad. High-level security engagement has been less frequent, though in early 2023, a senior Pakistani military delegation travelled to Washington for a defence dialogue, and senior US officials travelled to Islamabad for a counterterrorism dialogue.

The largely non-security focus of current relations points to another achievement for US–Pakistan relations. For years, the relationship was plagued by a sequencing problem that fuelled tensions: Islamabad wanted to expand the partnership beyond security. Washington resisted, instead preferring to focus first on making progress with issues related to the war in Afghanistan, counterterrorism and security, more broadly. Today, the two appear to be more on the same page, with Washington now willing to engage on issues beyond security.

Limits of US–Pakistan Relations

It is notable, however, that most of this high-level engagement has been purely exploratory; it has produced few deals or other substantive outcomes. That speaks to how the relationship is still feeling its way post-Afghanistan withdrawal, but it likely also reflects the relationship's limits, which are considerable.

Bandwidth, Geopolitics and Mistrust

First, bandwidth is a major obstacle. This is not the case in Pakistan where relations with Washington are always a priority no matter how good or bad a state the partnership is in. That is especially true now, with the current government, for political reasons, wanting to assert its desire for strong relations with Washington in order to contrast its position with that of Khan, its bitter political rival. Additionally, Pakistan's severe economic crisis makes partnership with Washington — Pakistan's top export destination and a country with considerable influence over the International Monetary Fund and other financial institutions important for Islamabad's immediate economic interests — even more essential.

The calculus is quite different in Washington. Quite simply, the Biden administration does not have much time to dedicate to US–Pakistan relations. Its foreign policy space is consumed by the war in Ukraine and the US–China competition. Its bandwidth on external policy will soon be further constrained as it goes into election campaign mode, with presidential polls scheduled for November 2024. Not surprisingly, the administration has not undertaken a policy review on Pakistan, and it is unlikely to do so prior to the end of its term. If Pakistan were a more high-priority relationship for Washington, the administration would give it more time. However, Pakistan, while formally a non-North Atlantic Treaty Organization (NATO) ally of Washington, does not get the front-burner priority status of NATO, Middle East and East Asian treaty allies; of core rivals like China, Russia and Iran; or of major flashpoint states like North Korea and Syria.

Second, geopolitical guardrails constrain the partnership. Critically, each country has close relations with the other's top rival. Pakistan is a close ally of China. Despite recent bumps in relations — from reduced Chinese investments in Pakistan to Beijing's concerns about security risks in Pakistan — Pakistan–China relations remain strong, in great part because India is their shared rival. Meanwhile, competition with China is the centre-point of Washington's foreign policy. There is a strong bipartisan consensus that over the long term, China will remain the US' biggest strategic concern. America's core Asia strategy — its Indo-Pacific policy — is meant to counter Beijing. This means that when it comes to Washington's geopolitical priorities, Islamabad risks being left on the outside, looking in — there is limited space for it in US strategic calculations. Not surprisingly, while most South Asian states are described in the US' strategy documents as being part of the Indo-Pacific policy, Pakistan is not.[10]

Similarly, Washington's deepening partnership with New Delhi imposes limits on US–Pakistan relations. Just as there is a strong bipartisan consensus in Washington around the imperative of countering China, there is also one around the idea that India is America's best strategic bet in South Asia. Though not an alliance, the US–India security partnership is rapidly gaining steam through US arms sales and the inking of foundational defence deals. One of the key current goals of US–India security relations is to implement those foundational accords that entail the two militaries working more closely together and the transfer of high-end US military technologies to the Indian Armed Forces. The US government's messaging on India is often soaring. Prior to becoming president, Biden had called the US–India partnership the defining relationship of the 21st century, and prominent Democrats in both the executive and legislative branches have repeated that phrase during his presidency.[11] This reflects just how much forward movement the relationship has enjoyed over the last few decades. Indeed, US officials privately admit that the partnership's progress has been so rapid that it is difficult to keep up with it.[12] All this underscores both the strategic importance that Washington ascribes to the partnership with India and the limits of deeper US cooperation with Pakistan, which views with concern America's deepening security partnership with its Indian rival.

Third, mistrust is likely a factor, especially on the US side. Many senior officials in the Biden administration, including the president himself, served in the Barack Obama administration during one of the worst periods ever for US–Pakistan relations in 2011. That year included the US troops' surge in Afghanistan when Pakistan's sponsorship of the Taliban was particularly problematic; the discovery of Osama Bin Laden in Pakistan and the US' unilateral raid to apprehend him; a spat over a Central Intelligence Agency operative's killing of two Pakistanis on a busy street in Lahore; and a serious crisis, resulting in Pakistan's closure of NATO's supply routes on its soil after NATO aircraft killed 24 Pakistani border troops. This history, and the baggage that comes with it, means that some Biden administration officials' memories of the relationship likely are not rosy, which could cloud their perceptions about the partnership with Pakistan today. It may well help explain, at least in part, why Biden has declined to speak directly with the two Pakistani prime ministers who have been in office during his term — an omission that has upset some senior officials in Islamabad.[13]

Parameters of Future Partnership

What, then, might the relationship look like in the coming months and years?

Security versus Non-security Cooperation

Above all, it will be a less ambitious relationship than it was when US forces were in Afghanistan. Expectations will need to be kept in check. US officials today speak of seeking "small wins" for the relationship,[14] and of centring attention around issues like climate change, humanitarian relief and pandemic assistance (which happen to be foreign policy priorities for the Biden administration overall), along with trade and investment. However, this type of non-security partnership, while seemingly emphasising softer, lower-hanging-fruit type areas of collaboration, will not come easy. Severe economic stress in Pakistan, worries about Pakistani government corruption and concerns about Pakistan's investment environment complicate greater non-security cooperation. At the same time, various forms of social and development sector assistance, ranging from the building of schools to supporting cultural preservation projects, will continue apace. These efforts, led by the US State Department and the US Agency for International Development (USAID), have long been an unheralded success story for US–Pakistan relations.[15]

Security will likely not be a strong component of future cooperation even though security-related tensions have eased. Indeed, Pakistan-sponsored terrorism is less of a concern for Washington, given that US forces have left Afghanistan. Additionally, in 2023, Islamabad, in order to be removed from a watch list associated with the global terrorist financing watchdog known as the Financial Action Task Force, took steps (including new prosecutions of Lashkar-e-Taiba leader Hafiz Saeed) against India-focused terror groups that have long concerned Washington. Moreover, both Washington and Islamabad worry about the Islamic State–Khorasan Province (ISKP, an ISIS-K affiliate) threat in Afghanistan.

However, this is unlikely to spur deeper security cooperation. Here, the India factor looms large. Washington seeks good relations with both New Delhi and Islamabad, but it clearly privileges its ties to New Delhi. It will not want to take its relationship to a place where New Delhi would get worried, and stepped-up US–Pakistan security relations would be that place. Other factors militating against deeper US–Pakistan security cooperation are mistrust, the fact that all US security aid to Pakistan has been frozen since 2018, and differing threat perceptions of Afghanistan-based terror groups. Both Washington and Islamabad view ISIS-K and Tehreek-e-Taliban Pakistan (TTP) [or Pakistani Taliban] as threats, but America worries more about the former and Pakistan more about the latter. The TTP, which carried out a horrible campaign of violence in Pakistan from 2007 to 2014, has resurged in recent months, but unlike during its earlier campaign, it is not threatening attacks against the US or American interests in Pakistan and the broader South Asia. The group's current leader has explicitly said its fight is only in Pakistan.[16]

If there is to be new security cooperation, it will likely revolve around intelligence sharing, so that both countries can better monitor the location and movement of ISIS-K and TTP fighters. There is also the possibility of Pakistan letting the US use its airspace for future counterterrorism operations in Afghanistan.[17] Another possible space for collaboration is Afghanistan–Pakistan border security, which was the focus of a US–Pakistan counterterrorism dialogue in March 2023. However, with US security aid frozen, the scope for collaboration here is limited, though Washington may view stepped-up intelligence sharing as a tactic to help strengthen Islamabad's capacity to manage its border and the risk of cross-border terrorism.

The main legacy component of US–Pakistan security cooperation — military education and training programmes — will likely continue. Ironically, despite serious security tensions over the years, officer-to-officer relations within the two militaries remain strong and that is likely attributable to the programmes that have enabled officers to spend time in training academies in the other country. In recent years, the focus has been on Pakistani officers spending time in the US; this is the purpose of the International Military Education and Training, which is run by the US government. Due to security concerns, there are noknown programmes today that place US officers in Pakistani military facilities.[18]

The China Factor

The China factor will limit US–Pakistan partnership, but US–China competition is too fierce for the US to simply cede Pakistan to the China camp. Indeed, American officials hope to build up enough cooperation with Pakistan to ensure that Islamabad is not entirely dependent on China. This is a strategy that Washington is pursuing with other countries in South Asia and Southeast Asia as well. However, it will be especially challenging with Pakistan, given that Islamabad is already so heavily reliant on China — more so than are most countries in Asia.

Indeed, this presents a policy conundrum for Washington. The tactic that would work best to reduce Pakistani reliance on China is unlikely to be deployed while the tactic that would work the least to reduce that reliance is likely to be deployed instead. Here, some elaboration is in order.

To have the best chance of reducing Pakistani reliance on China, the US would look to the space where Washington has the most comparative advantage over Beijing. This would be in the realm of military technology. Chinese military equipment may have improved in quality in recent years, but many forms of US military technology continue to be superior to that of China. And yet, Washington is unlikely to restore security assistance to Pakistan for the reasons noted above.

Instead, Washington is likely to focus on infrastructure assistance. The Biden administration is using the International Development Finance Corporation (DFC), a new US government agency meant to sponsor infrastructure projects in the Indo-Pacific region, as a tool to push back against China's Belt and Road Initiative (BRI) investments. With South Asia now emerging as a new battleground for US–China competition, it is just a matter of time before the region becomes a target for DFC investments. DFC funds have already been earmarked for several clean energy infrastructure projects in India.[19] Though Pakistan is not formally considered a part of the Indo-Pacific policy, it will not be excluded from potential DFC projects. When Dilawar Syed, Special Representative for Commercial and Business Affairs at the US State Department, spent his week in Pakistan in July 2022, a top DFC official accompanied him.[20]

American authorities have described Chinese infrastructure investment projects as predatory, entrapping (due to debt) and generally undesirable, and argue that American investments — in line with the Indo-Pacific policy's free, open and rules-based principles — can be more transparent and equitable. US officials have made this argument about investments in a Pakistan context as well.[21] Washington likely senses an opportunity in Pakistan, given the reduced pace of activities associated with the China–Pakistan Economic Corridor, the Pakistan component of the BRI, due to Chinese and Pakistani economic slowdowns and Chinese concerns about increasing terrorism threats in Pakistan.

However, even if fuelled by a dynamic new tool like DFC, Washington would struggle to be impactful — from a great power competition perspective — with new infrastructure projects in Pakistan. This is because of its own concerns about the investment and broader economic climate there, as well as due to the fact that China is so much more present in Pakistan when it comes to large infrastructure projects. In effect, it would take a monumental and unrealistic amount of effort for Washington to catch up. Additionally, Beijing has the capacity to quickly mobilise and deploy large amounts of capital, technology and labour abroad — a capacity not enjoyed by Washington. Beijing is further advantaged by its warm relations with many political and military leaders in Pakistan, and by the Pakistani public's pro-China sentiment.

The Promise and Peril of Climate Change Cooperation

In sum, there is some scope for expanding US–Pakistan relations, especially in the non-security realm, and one can expect to see collaborations, mainly in the form of assistance from the US State Department and USAID, focused on addressing Pakistan's economic and development challenges. Education, energy and women's empowerment are areas ripe for collaboration. Trade and investment will be priorities as well, though Pakistan's severe economic stress will pose challenges.

Climate change arguably has the highest ceiling for bilateral cooperation over the longer term. It is a top priority for both governments; Pakistan is one of Asia's most climate-vulnerable states; there is fresh momentum for such cooperation after the 2022 floods; climate change effects can imperil stability, a top US interest in Pakistan; and the effects of climate change will inevitably intensify in the coming years. Additionally, the agreement at the 2022 United Nations Climate Change Conference to establish a new loss and damage fund to assist climate-vulnerable countries suggests that international climate assistance may be emerging as a global norm. US–Pakistan climate cooperation can take a variety of forms, such as the provision of American assistance to make Pakistan more climate-resilient (from financing stronger building materials to funding repairs of dilapidated water infrastructure) as well as DFC projects that fund clean energy infrastructure. Washington can also help scale up Pakistan's fledging renewables sector by providing badly needed technologies such as batteries to enable more solar power storage.[22]

However, even a high-potential space like climate change cooperation is fraught with obstacles. Pakistan's economic crisis — one of its worst in decades — and crippling political paralysis will raise concerns about the Pakistani state's willingness and capacity to take on new assistance and use it for its desired purpose. Washington and other key donors will also want to see indications that Islamabad is committed to taking ownership of its climate challenges and to changing the policies — unregulated deforestation and construction along rivers, subsidies for water-wasting forms of irrigation, a lack of attention to wastewater and other forms of pollution — that have contributed to Pakistan's climate vulnerability. Such changes are unlikely to occur anytime soon, given what Pakistan has on its immediate and even medium-term plate.

The Onus on Pakistan

Ultimately, if there is to be sustained forward movement in the relationship in the coming months and years, the onus will be on Islamabad to make a case to a distracted and sceptical Washington that enhanced partnership is essential. And that will not be an easy case to make.

Islamabad's default argument, one advanced for years, is that Pakistan is a strategically significant state because of its size, location, large population and geopolitical relationships, as well as due to its nuclear weapons and militant actors. Islamabad has argued, in effect, that it is too big to fail, that Washington needs to have a close relationship with such a pivotal and volatile state and that if it does not, bad things could happen for Pakistan and, by extension, for the US. However, while this argument has gained traction in Washington over the years, is not enough to change the current US approach to its relationship with Pakistan.

Pakistan's Three Hard-sell Pitches

There are three other pitches that Pakistan can make to the US, which, if successful, can create new pathways for partnership.

First, it can demonstrate that it can generate agency for itself even against an unfavourable geopolitical backdrop, given its alliance with China and America's growing partnership with India. In previous years, Pakistan secured agency by serving as a mediator, most notably in the early 1970s, when it helped the Richard Nixon administration normalise relations between Washington and Beijing. More recently, Islamabad was an intermediary in Afghanistan, leveraging its close ties with the Taliban (which otherwise galled Washington) to help bring the group to the table for negotiations with the Donald Trump administration.

Today, however, mediation may no longer be the source of agency for Pakistan that it was in the past. The US' relations with China are deeply fraught, but Washington does engage directly with Beijing and has no need for Pakistani intervention. Similarly, Washington has open channels with the Taliban that it can use to pursue its limited interests in Afghanistan. Tensions between the Taliban and Islamabad since the Taliban takeover will further discourage Washington from considering Pakistan as a mediator. At any rate, the Biden administration has appointed Qatar to represent its interests in Afghanistan — an indication of the limited utility it envisions for Pakistan in its post-withdrawal Afghanistan policy.[23]

One agency-generating alternative for Pakistan is to better avail opportunities for multilateral cooperation with Washington. Despite its struggles at home and image problems abroad, Islamabad does have convening power, from hosting training exercises for militaries representing dozens of countries to holding events for the arts that draw participants from around the world.[24] Pakistan has also held leadership roles in groupings as diverse as the G77 nations and the Organization of Islamic Cooperation. By drawing on its convening power and ample multilateral engagement, it can host discussions on issues of importance to both Pakistani and US interests, especially those that relate to shared, transnational threats. One possibility would be for Islamabad to host a summit on climate change that brings together vulnerable developing states, as well as the main polluting states, such as the US.

A second pitch Pakistan can make is that it can offer unique commercial benefits to Washington that set it apart from its South Asian neighbours. Admittedly, this is a hard sell. Pakistanis often point to their growing middle class and large numbers of urban, technology-savvy, English-speaking youth as tantalising market opportunities for foreign investors. However, in reality, these same benefits are present in Bangladesh and especially India on a greater scale, and with fewer concerns about economic stress and security risks. This means Pakistan will need a new narrative. If it can craft one, that would provide a big boost to future US–Pakistan relations.

A third pitch — the easiest lift of the three — is to encourage Washington to ramp up bilateral engagement outside government-to-government channels. In 2011, a very tense year for US–Pakistan relations, US Special Representative for Afghanistan and Pakistan, Marc Grossman, estimated that 90 percent of US–Pakistan relations were being pursued through official channels.[25] And yet, there is a rich legacy of robust and largely tension-free engagement outside official channels — commercial diplomacy (fuelled in part by the US–Pakistan Business Council), education exchanges (Pakistan has the largest Fulbright programme of any country) and diaspora engagement (the Pakistani–American community has at one point been one of the fastest-growing Asian diasporas in the US).[26] Additionally, there is a longstanding tradition of US–Pakistan Track Two dialogues.[27] If these dialogues are intensified — and especially if they feature newer and younger voices — they can help develop new, innovative ideas for cooperation and partnership.

Prospects for a bigger and better US–Pakistan relationship may be limited, but that does not mean there cannot be scope for more quiet and informal types of cooperation, away from the official channels that have often been sources of volatility and tension.

Endnotes

1. See, for example, Fahd Humayun, "Pakistan and the US have made up, but will it last?", *Foreign Policy*, 16 September 2022, https://foreignpolicy.com/2022/09/16/Pakistan-US-diplomacy-floods-climate/; and Ameena Tanvir, "What is the future of Pakistan–US relations after Imran Khan's ouster?", *South Asian Voices*, 19 May 2022, https://southasianvoices.org/what-is-the-future-of-pakistan-u-s-relations-after-imran-khans-ouster/.
2. Madiha Afzal, "The Biden administration's two-track Pakistan policy misses the mark", Order from Chaos blog, Brookings Institution, 2 March 2023, https://www.brookings.edu/blog/order-from-chaos/2023/03/02/the-biden-administrations-two-track-pakistan-policy-misses-the-mark/; https://www.brookings.edu/blog/order-from-chaos/2023/03/02/the-biden-administrations-two-track-pakistan-policy-misses-the-mark/.
3. One of the most comprehensive accounts of how the complexities in US–Pakistan partnership have played out over the years is Dennis Kux, *The United States and Pakistan, 1947–2000: Disenchanted Allies* (Baltimore, MD: Johns Hopkins University Press, 2001). Two useful more recent studies are Husain Haqqani, *Magnificent Delusions: Pakistan, the United States, and an Epic History of Misunderstanding* (New York: Public Affairs, 2013); and Daniel S. Markey, *No Exit from Pakistan: America's Tortured Relationship with Islamabad* (Cambridge, UK: Cambridge University Press, 2013).
4. "The United States and Pakistan launch year-long campaign commemorating 75 years of US–Pakistan relations", US Embassy, Islamabad, Pakistan, 22 March 2022, https://pk.usembassy.gov/the-united-states-and-pakistan-launch-year-long-campaign-commemorating-75-years-of-u-s-pakistan-relations/.
5. See, for example, "Secretary Antony J. Blinken with Pakistani Foreign Minister Bilawal Bhutto Zardari to commemorate the 75th anniversary of US–Pakistan relations", US State Department, 26 September 2022, https://www.state.gov/-secretary-antony-j-blinken-with-pakistani-foreign-minister-bilawal-bhutto-zardari-to-commemorate-the-75th-anniversary-of-u-s-pakistan-relations/.

6. "US Ambassador Donald Blome visits AJK to strengthen US–Pakistan trade and people-to-people ties", US Embassy, Islamabad, Pakistan, 5 October 2022, https://pk.usembassy.gov/u-s-ambassador-donald-blome-visits-ajk-to-strengthen-u-s-pakistan-trade-and-people-to-people-ties/.
7. For a detailed account of the US–Pakistan tensions provoked by the war in Afghanistan, see Steve Coll, *Directorate S: The CIA and America's Secret Wars in Afghanistan and Pakistan* (New York: Penguin Press, 2018); and Mark Mazzetti, *The Way of the Knife: The CIA, a Secret Army, and a War at the Ends of the Earth* (New York: Penguin Books, 2014).
8. US International COVID-19 vaccine donations tracker, Kaiser Family Foundation (based on US State Department data), https://www.kff.org/coronavirus-covid-19/issue-brief/u-s-international-covid-19-vaccine-donations-tracker/.
9. "Afghanistan has broken shackles of slavery: PM Imran Khan", *Geo News*, 16 August 2021, https://www.geo.tv/latest/365546-afghanistan-has-broken-shackles-of-slavery-pm-imran-khan.
10. This has been the case during both the Trump and Biden administrations. See "Indo-Pacific Strategy Report: Preparedness, Partnerships, and Promoting a Networked Region", Department of Defense, 1 June 2019, https://media.defense.gov/2019/Jul/01/2002152311/-1/-1/1/Department-Of-Defense-Indo-Pacific-Strategy-Report-2019.PDF; "A free and open Indo Pacific: Advancing a shared vision", Department of State, 4 November 2019, https://www.state.gov/wp-content/uploads/2019/11/Free-and-Open-Indo-Pacific-4Nov2019.pdf; and "Indo-Pacific strategy of the United States", The White House, February 2022, https://www.whitehouse.gov/wp-content/uploads/2022/02/U.S.-Indo-Pacific-Strategy.pdf.
11. See "India–US relationship 'defining partnership' for this century: Former Ambassador Richard Verma", *The Hindu*, 18 February 2023, https://www.thehindu.com/news/international/india-us-relationship-defining-partnership-for-this-century-former-ambassador-richard-verma/article66524141.ece; and "India-US relationship can define 21st century, says Congressman Ro Khanna", *Outlook India*, 3 January 2023, https://www.outlookindia.com/international/india-us-relationship-can-define-21st-century-says-congressman-ro-khanna-news-250392.
12. This comment was heard during a private discussion with the author.
13. Katrina Manson, "Pakistan's security adviser complains Joe Biden has not called Imran Khan", *Financial Times*, 3 August 2021, https://www.ft.com/content/f3d50eb9-5b2f-4472-ad7e-1a216e8e9ae1.

14. That term was heard in private discussions the author had with US officials.
15. However, even these seemingly innocuous aid programmes have contributed to bilateral tensions. See "Aiding without abetting: Making US Civilian assistance to Pakistan work for both sides", Wilson Center Working Group on Pakistan, Wilson Center, 2011, https://www.wilsoncenter.org/publication/aiding-without-abetting-making-civilian-assistance-work-for-both-sides.
16. Arif Rafiq, "The Pakistani Taliban's radical rebranding; Is there more than meets the eye?", Middle East Institute, 24 February 2022, https://www.mei.edu/publications/pakistani-talibans-radical-rebranding-there-more-meets-eye.
17. After the US exit from Afghanistan, media reports emerged about Washington exploring the possibility of gaining access to military bases in Pakistan to support potential US counterterrorism activities in Afghanistan. Such basing arrangements, which were in place during the Cold War and in the initial years after the 9/11 attacks, are unlikely to be reinstituted, given how politically risky they would be in an era when anti-Americanism in Pakistan has surged since Khan accused the Biden administration of sponsoring his ouster. Interestingly, David Hale, the previous US Ambassador to Pakistan, said in 2021 that he did not think the Biden administration's officials had ever sought basing arrangements to start with. See "Beyond Afghanistan: US perspectives on the future of US–Pakistan Relations", Wilson Center, 19 July 2021, https://www.wilsoncenter.org/event/beyond-afghanistan-us-perspectives-future-US–Pakistan-relations.
18. David O. Smith, a retired US military officer who was based at the Pakistan Army Command and Staff College in Quetta in 1982, has published a revealing account of the experiences of American military personnel at Pakistani Army education and training facilities. See David O. Smith, *The Quetta Experience: A Study of Attitudes and Values within the Pakistan Army* (Washington DC: Wilson Center, 2018), https://www.wilsoncenter.org/publication/the-quetta-experience-attitudes-and-values-within-pakistans-army.
19. "DFC Delivers on US climate finance with more than 2.3B committed for climate-linked projects in FY 2022", Media Release, US International Development Finance Corporation, 9 November 2022, https://www.dfc.gov/media/press-releases/dfc-delivers-us-climate-finance-more-23-billion-committed-climate-linked.
20. Amin Ahmed and Baqir Sajjad Syed, "Visitors from Washington look to Rejuvenate ties after Lull", *Dawn*, 4 July 2022, https://www.dawn.com/news/1698096.

21. This argument was first made publicly by Alice Wells, the top South Asia official at the US State Department, in 2019. See "A Conversation with Ambassador Alice Wells on the China–Pakistan Economic Corridor", Wilson Center, Washington DC, 19 November 2019, https://2017-2021.state.gov/a-conversation-with-ambassador-alice-wells-on-the-china-pakistan-economic-corridor/index.html.
22. See Michael Kugelman, "Long-term international climate assistance to Pakistan is a Hard Sell, but necessary. Here's why", *Just Security*, 9 September 2022, https://www.justsecurity.org/83004/long-term-international-climate-assistance-to-pakistan-is-a-hard-sell-but-necessary-heres-why/.
23. Lara Jakes, "Qatar to represent US interests in Afghanistan, Blinken Says", *The New York Times*, 12 November 2021, https://www.nytimes.com/2021/11/12/us/politics/us-qatar-afghanistan.html.
24. "Pakistan Navy to host 50 nations in maritime exercises from February 10", *Reuters*, 8 February 2023, https://www.usnews.com/news/world/articles/2023-02-08/pakistan-navy-says-it-will-host-50-nations-in-maritime-exercises. And for many years, the Karachi and Lahore Literature Festivals have featured authors, poets, and scholars from around the world.
25. Husain Haqqani, *op. cit.*, p. 320.
26. Faiza Mirza, "Pakistanis are second fastest growing group in US, says report", *Dawn*, 9 July 2012, https://www.dawn.com/news/732915/pakistanis-are-second-fastest-growing-race-in-us-says-report.
27. Michael Kugelman and Raoof Hasan, "What a year of track II discussions says about the future of US–Pakistan relations", *War on the Rocks*, 30 November 2017, https://warontherocks.com/2017/11/year-track-ii-discussions-says-future-u-s-pakistan-relations/.

Chapter 6

Nepal and Bhutan: The United States Returns to the Himalayas

Nishchal N. Pandey

Background

Nepal established diplomatic relations with the United States (US) in 1947 even before it did so with its own two immediate neighbours — India and China. The Rana regime in power in Kathmandu at the time probably felt that this was needed as a symbolic assertion of independence vis-à-vis Nepal's giant neighbours that were both undergoing political turbulence. Over the past seven and a half decades, Kathmandu and Washington have progressively enhanced their friendship, resulting in wide-ranging cooperation. The year 2022 marked the 76th year of diplomatic relations. During this period, while Nepal has transformed from the autocratic Rana regime to a party-less Panchayat system and then from a monarchy to a federal republic, both countries have been engaged in various bilateral cooperation and development partnerships, including cooperation in health, education, poverty alleviation and development of physical infrastructure, as well as in Nepal's democratic transformation.

The closeness of the bilateral ties has not been hindered by the significant distance between the two countries. On 28 April 1960, King

Mahendra became the first head of state from South Asia to address the joint session of the US Congress. In December 1983, King Birendra paid a state visit to the US at the invitation of President Ronald Reagan. While speaking at the state dinner during the visit, Reagan remarked, "Nepal is a neighbour of the US at the other side of the world".[1] From the US side, there has yet to be a presidential visit to Nepal although Vice-President Spiro T. Agnew paid a visit to Kathmandu in 1970. In the wake of the 9/11 terrorist attacks in the US and Nepal's own Maoist insurgency, which the US had referred to as terrorism, US Secretary of State Colin Powel visited Nepal in 2002 during his five-nation tour of South Asia.

Post-2006, Nepal went through much political instability not only with the twice-conducted constituent assembly elections but also with repeated changes in the government. During this period, Nepal did not see any high-level visits from the US — mid-level American officials made only routine trips. In 2015, following the deadly earthquake that struck Nepal, the US was steadfast in its assistance in relief, rescue and reconstruction efforts.

This chapter will examine the issues concerning Nepal–US ties at the present moment, the prognosis for the future, the possibility of causing irritation in New Delhi and Beijing of increased American engagement with Nepal and the options for Kathmandu if the US and China come to a direct confrontation in Nepal, turning it into a "boxing ring".[2]

US–Nepal Development Cooperation

While the US was only second to the UK in terms of countries with which Nepal established diplomatic ties, it was among the first countries to provide development assistance to the Himalayan state. The relationship between the US and Nepal started with an assistance agreement in 1951. Over the last 70-plus years, the support and contribution from the US Agency for International Development (USAID) has helped Nepal achieve some of its remarkable development successes, notably in the areas of family planning, malaria eradication, agriculture and forestry. Since the end of the Maoist insurgency in 2006, American cooperation has centred on the institutionalisation of peace and democracy. The nature of the US' cooperation with Nepal has evolved over the last seven and a half decades. "From the early days of malaria eradication in Terai to roads, bridges and building basic infrastructure, USAID has been supporting livelihood improvement, market integration with the rural community, disaster resilience and capacity building programs".[3] Another success story has been the Ambassador's Fund for Cultural Preservation, which has restored not only the Hanuman Dhoka Palace but also the historic octagonal Krishna Temple at Patan Durbar Square. Then-US Ambassador to Nepal, Randy Berry, said, "The temple has been fully restored. Now, not only is it beautiful, but its improved structural framework is more resilient to future earthquakes".[4]

Moreover, officers of the Nepal Army, Armed Police Force and Nepal Police receive international exposure through training and exchange programmes conducted by the Asia-Pacific Center for Security Studies in Hawaii and the Near East South Asia Center for Strategic Studies in Washington, which helps the Nepali side familiarise itself with new issues and concerns emerging in the global arena. Educational tours such as the International Visitors Leadership Programme have helped dozens of prominent Nepalese academics, media representatives, businesspersons and government officials get acquainted with the functioning of American institutions.

On 5 May 2022, a new Development Objective Agreement was signed between the two governments. The five-year aid agreement outlines the broad development areas of cooperation between Nepal and the US. The grant, worth US$659 million over five years, will help Nepal achieve its objective of becoming a middle-income nation. It needs to be noted here that Nepal is scheduled to graduate from a least developed country to a developing country in 2026. However, with the outbreak of the COVID-19 pandemic, the outbreak of the Russia–Ukraine war, the rise in oil prices and increasing inflation, coupled with the decline in tourists, the challenges on the economic front for Nepal are daunting. In addition, Nepal is extremely vulnerable to natural calamities like glacial lake outbursts, earthquakes and flooding. It is hoped that American assistance at this crucial juncture will advance Nepal's sustainable development efforts through enterprise-driven economic growth and increased resilience for communities most at risk of natural disasters and climate change.

Increasing High-Level US Delegation Visits to Nepal

After a lull for about a decade since 2006, the US has again started to engage Nepal. However, this time, it was more at an operational level. Admiral Harry B. Harris, Commander of the US Indo-Pacific Command, participated in the opening of the US-sponsored multi-national United Nations (UN) peacekeeping exercise at the Birendra Peace Operations Training Centre (BPOTC) at Panchkhal, a three-hour drive from Kathmandu. Nepal is one of the top troops contributing nation in UN peacekeeping and hopes that the BPOTC emerges as an institution of excellence for training regional and international peacekeepers. Harris' successor, Admiral Philip S. Davidson, visited Nepal in January 2019 and interacted not only with the political party leaders and senior army officers but also with think-tank heads and academics. He provided a briefing on the concept of the Indo-Pacific and the need for closer cooperation with the Nepal Army.[5]

In an effort to seek support and endorsement for the US Millennium Challenge Corporation (MCC) Nepal Compact, as well as in the wake of the ratification by the Nepalese parliament in February 2022, there were a flurry of high-level visits from the US to Nepal.

In February 2020, the MCC's Deputy Vice President for Europe, Asia, Pacific and Latin America, Jonathan Brooks, travelled to Nepal. This was followed by a visit by the Chair of the US House Foreign Affairs Committee Subcommittee on Asia, the Pacific and Nonproliferation, Representative, Ami Bera, to Kathmandu in the same month. Fatema Z. Sumar, Vice President of Compact Operations at the MCC, and Donald Lu, US Assistant Secretary for South and Central Asian Affairs, along with US Deputy Assistant Secretary for South and Central Asian Affairs, Kelly Keiderling, were in Kathmandu in September and November 2021, respectively.

On 28 September 2022, US Acting Assistant Secretary for Global Public Affairs, Elizabeth Kennedy Trudeau, visited Kathmandu. Trudeau looks after public diplomacy, manages media, initiates Track Two diplomacy and works on shaping public opinion in favour of the US government. During her two-day visit, Trudeau met with minority group activists, media contacts and embassy exchange programme alumni for roundtable discussions on disinformation and the media's role in a democracy.

Trudeau's visit took place two weeks after Li Zhanshu, head of the Standing Committee of the Chinese National People's Congress, returned home from his Nepal trip. The Chinese have been trying to reunite the various factions of the erstwhile communist party whereas the US and India are not comfortable with the reality that the Communist Party of Nepal (Unified Marxist–Leninist) [CPN (UML)] leader, K. P. Sharma Oli, becomes the *de facto* head again if the Nepal Communist Party (NCP) is to reunite, as the CPN (UML) would become the largest communist bloc in the country.

The MCC Nepal Compact: Protests and Ratification

Aiming to improve Nepal's energy connectivity and reduce transmission costs through the construction of about 300 kilometres of electricity transmission lines and support for the maintenance of 300 kilometres of roads within five years of the project's period, the MCC Nepal Compact (worth US$500 million) was signed on 14 September 2017 by Nepal's Finance Minister Gyanendra Bahadur Karki and Acting Chief Executive Officer of the MCC, Jonathan Nash. The project had been under discussion between Nepal's finance ministry officials and the US government for some years prior to 2017. However, Nepal's foreign and defence ministries were not in the loop during the initial discussions and negotiations. The project was also not well presented to the wider Nepali public. The Left parties in Nepal began voicing their concerns about this project being under the Indo-Pacific strategy of the US military to counter China's Belt and Road Initiative.[6]

Street Protests against the MCC Nepal Compact

The suspicion and narrative of the MCC Nepal Compact being anti-China garnered so much support in Nepal that it became a contentious issue, leading to a series of street protests throughout the country, with many questioning the American intention behind supporting Nepal and the necessity of parliamentary ratification for the project.

On 10 February 2022, eight fringe parties, particularly those with a communist ideology, staged a demonstration outside the House of Representatives in Kathmandu against the possible endorsement of the MCC Nepal Compact. The aggressive protesters who tried to breach the 'no protest zone' outside the parliament were baton-charged by security forces in an attempt to bring the situation under control. Some protesters also pelted stones and bricks at the security forces, and several people on both sides suffered injuries. Parties such as the Netra Bikram Chand-led NCP, Mohan Bikram Singh-led NCP Masal, Mohan Baidya-led NCP Revolutionary Maoist, Rishi Kattel-led NCP, Biswobhakta Dulal aka "Aahuti"-led Baigyanik Samajbadi Communist Party and Chandra Prakash Gajurel-led Deshbhakt Janaganatantrik Morcha, and supporters of the fringe communist parties staged the demonstration. To add fuel to the fire, the right-wing Rastriya Prajatantra Party also held its own protest against the MCC Nepal Compact.

A general strike was also called by the protesters, along with the call to shut down schools, disrupting transportation in the country. The police in Kathmandu detained dozens of protesters who tried to block traffic and attempted to set vehicles on fire. Clearly, the US had never been in such a huge controversy in Nepal ever before as it did during the MCC Nepal Compact episode.

On 18 February 2022, tensions ran high in Kathmandu in front of the parliament building as demonstrators protesting against the MCC Nepal Compact were from the student wings of the ruling parties themselves. The CPN (Maoist Centre) and CPN (UML) — the two coalition partners in Prime Minister Sher Bahadur Deuba's government — protested against the MCC Nepal Compact as the parliament convened its meeting to discuss the project.[7] Hundreds of protesters carried banners and placards demanding that the government not ratify the MCC Nepal Compact.

It was in the midst of this tense atmosphere that Lu conveyed the message to Deuba and CPN (Maoist Centre) Chair, Pushpa Kamal Dahal, that if the MCC Nepal Compact failed parliamentary ratification, Washington would be forced to reconsider its Nepal policy. The harsh tone of his message then prompted Beijing to slam Washington for giving Nepal a "gift with an ultimatum" and even warn the US against using "coercive diplomacy" in Nepal.[8]

During a media briefing in Beijing, Chinese foreign ministry spokesperson, Wang Wenbin, said, "We oppose coercive diplomacy and actions that pursue selfish agenda at the expense of Nepal's sovereignty and interests".[9] China, while appreciating the world's development cooperation with Nepal, said such cooperation should be based on "full respect for the will of the Nepalese people". It should come with "no political strings attached". Beijing also stated that "China welcomes the international community to cooperate with Nepal, contribute to Nepal's economic development and livelihood improvement, but this should be done based on Nepalese people's willingness without political conditions".[10]

Finally, on 27 February 2002, after five years of procrastination and the Americans being subjected to public humiliation, the Nepalese parliament finally ratified the MCC Nepal Compact. However, there was also an "interpretative declaration" of the parliament incorporated into the agreement, which later legal experts would opine as legally "not binding".[11] Deliberations began after three partners in the government — CPN (Maoist Centre), CPN (UML) and the Janata Samajbadi Party — finally agreed to vote in favour of the MCC Nepal Compact with an interpretative declaration.

Nepal's Ministry of Foreign Affairs (MoFA) then provided a pointed but restrained statement to the comments and counter comments made by the US and China on the agreement. It clarified that any decision to accept development assistance by Nepal is based on its national interests and priorities. "The sovereign parliament of Nepal alone decides what development assistance is needed in the best interest of Nepal and Nepali people. We sincerely hope for the continued goodwill of our friends", MoFA's spokesperson, Sewa Lamsal, said in the statement issued in response to media queries on the views that appeared in various media on the MCC's assistance to Nepal.[12] The foreign affairs ministry further stated that Nepal has always been pursuing an independent, balanced and non-aligned foreign policy: "In pursuant to this policy, as a sovereign country, Nepal has accepted and utilised development assistance as per her national requirement and priority", the spokesperson said.[13] The MoFA statement came as there were growing concerns in Nepal that the country was already dragged into the geopolitical rivalry between China and the US.

Following the ratification of the MCC Nepal Compact, Nepal–US ties witnessed an upward trajectory. However, Nepal soon went to general elections in November 2022, which threw up a badly hung parliament. Political instability was apparent as the prime minister's position shifted from Deuba to Pushpa Kamal Dahal (also known as Prachanda). Initially, the Maoist cadres were in the streets protesting against the MCC Nepal Compact, but now, as a ruling party, the onus is on Prachanda to ensure that the project implementation is conducted smoothly.

Prior to the elections, Lu paid his second visit to Nepal on 28 July 2022. The US official's visit took place when another American programme — the State Partnership Program (SPP) — became a highly debated issue in Nepal. It was widely viewed that Lu's visit was arranged to convince the Nepali partners of the benign nature of the programme with no threat to Nepal's prickly neighbours. The SPP is an exchange programme between the national guard of a US state and a partnering country. Nepal was inducted to the SPP in 2019, according to the US embassy in Kathmandu, following two requests in 2015 and 2017. However, speaking at the International Relations Committee of the House of Representatives, Foreign Minister Narayan Khadka and Chief of the Army Staff General Prabhu Ram Sharma reiterated that Nepal has never been a part of the SPP, and no agreement or memorandum of understanding was signed to that effect although the US has been asking Nepal to join the programme since 2015.[14]

After the SPP became a politically debatable subject, the US embassy in Nepal responded that it is Nepal's sovereign decision to participate in the SPP, and that any country can simply submit a letter to cancel its participation. On 21 June 2022, after a nationwide controversy over the SPP, the Nepalese government decided to withdraw from the project. The SPP dispute occurred just weeks before Deuba's planned trip to the US in mid-July 2022 — this would have marked the first formal visit by a sitting Nepalese prime minister in two decades. However, the visit was later cancelled due to the SPP controversy.

Both the MCC and the SPP sagas highlight the lack of coordination among the various Nepalese agencies, ministries and departments. In such a scenario, the US pushes Nepal to "run without learning to walk". Nepalese institutions — primarily MoFA and the Ministry of

Defence — are weak and information is not shared between them on a regular basis. The National Security Council regularly sends messages and reports to the Prime Minister's Office, but one is not certain who reads or acts on them. This has led to costly misjudgements and avoidable misunderstandings with donor nations, especially on matters relating to national security. The MCC Nepal Compact and the SPP are cases in point.

At times, news is made public first by foreign entities before the relevant Nepalese institutions act on them. This generates unnecessary debate within the country. In many cases, in addition to opposition protests, the political parties in power also do not stop their student wings from going against the government, thereby resulting in a bizarre situation. Given that the geopolitical landscape has become a predominant factor in the conduct of foreign policy, there is a need for Nepalese institutions to be extra cautious and show cohesion and unity in the conduct of the country's affairs.

American Interest in the Tibetan Refugees Issue

One of the issues extremely sensitive to China and in which Nepal easily gets entangled is the presence of Tibetan refugees in Nepal. Since the beginning of this century, the inflow of Tibetans from Tibet into Nepal has been dwindling. Also, those currently in the country have their children or even grandchildren born in the country.

In February 2005, the Deuba government closed the office of the Representative of the Dalai Lama in Kathmandu. The office used to function like an unofficial embassy. In 2008, in the run-up to the Beijing Olympics, the Tibetan refugees staged daily protests in front of the consular section of the Chinese embassy. Each year, during the birthday of the Dalai Lama and Tibet's liberation day, the Nepal Police would be on high alert to stop any untoward incident in front of the Chinese embassy. Despite stringent measures in place, a Tibetan monk self-immolated himself on 6 August 2013 in the Boudhanath area of Kathmandu. The US' interest on this issue has always been there, evident by the fact that the Khampa rebellion in the late 1960s was clandestinely supported by the US' Central Intelligence Agency.[15] About 25,000

Tibetans continue to reside in Nepal and some of them even own hotels and carpet factories. China has been hyper-sensitive to the possibility of a repeat of the Khampa rebellion via a politically unstable and weak Nepal. To add to this, American officials have nowadays been pressurising Nepal into issuing identity cards to Tibetan refugees creating further anxiety for Nepal's security apparatus. It needs to be underscored that Nepal does not officially accord refugee status to the Tibetans.

On 20 May 2022, US Under Secretary for Civilian Security, Democracy and Human Rights, Urza Zeya, arrived in Nepal on a three-day visit. She is also the US Special Coordinator for Tibetan issues. She travelled to Nepal from India where she met the exiled Tibetan spiritual leader, the Dalai Lama, in Dharamshala. A day after her arrival in Kathmandu, Zeya visited the Tibetan refugee camp in Jawalakhel, Lalitpur. Later that day, she also went to Kathmandu's Boudha, home to many Tibetan refugees. She was escorted to the refugee camp by Nepal Police.

Zeya's visit to the camp immediately drew criticism from political figures and former diplomats who claimed that the visit went against Nepal's 'One-China' policy. They believed that the US' involvement in the affairs of the Tibetan refugees residing in Nepal could deteriorate Kathmandu's relations with Beijing. The main opposition party, the CPN (UML), objected to Zeya's visit to the camp with Chairman Oli expressing his discontent. "This government does not care about the national interest. The government has violated Nepal's established norms by letting US official visit [the] Tibetan refugee camp in Nepal. This government has become weak", he said. "Who allowed the US official to visit the Tibetan refugee camp? Is this the neutrality and national independent foreign policy envisioned by the constitution?" Lu questioned.[16]

Zhao Lijian, a spokesperson for China's Ministry of Foreign Affairs, said during a media conference that the US "should stop meddling in China's internal affairs under the pretext of Tibet-related issues, and offer no support to the anti-China separatist activities of the Dalai clique".[17] A few days after Zeya's visit, at the 14th meeting of the Nepal–China Bilateral Consultative Mechanism, Chinese officials allegedly voiced their concerns about her engagements with the Tibetan refugees in Kathmandu. Then, in July 2022, Liu Jianchao, Chairman of the Chinese Communist Party's (CCP) international liaison department, paid a visit to Kathmandu.

During his talks with the heads of Nepal's communist parties, he urged them to reaffirm their support for the 'One-China' policy. It must be underscored here that almost all communist parties of Nepal have party-to-party ties with the CCP.

Another Congressional delegation, led by Senator Kirsten Gillibrand (New York), which included Senators Sheldon Whitehouse (Rhode Island), Cory Booker (New Jersey) and Mark Kelly (Arizona), and Representative Mondaire Jones, visited Nepal on 22 April 2022 where they met with Nepal's political leaders. Deuba thanked the US Congress for its support to Nepal, notably during the earthquake in 2015 and the recent COVID-19 pandemic. Both sides emphasised the value of parliamentary exchanges in fostering the multifaceted partnership between Nepal and the US. The delegation reaffirmed its commitment to collaborating closely with Nepal on issues of mutual concern. The discussions also focused on agriculture and food security, as well as Nepal's contributions to UN peacekeeping operations.

Despite the promulgation of a federal, secular, republican constitution in 2015, Nepal has been grappling with the twin challenges of political instability and low economic growth. The recently held general elections (November 2022) could not provide a clear mandate. At first, the Chairman of CPN (Maoist Centre), Prachanda, teamed up with the second largest party, CPN (UML), but differences with the latter's leader, Oli, soon surfaced on the issue of the election of the president. This prompted Prachanda to move closer to the largest party, the Nepali Congress, leading to the en masse resignation of the CPN (UML) ministers in February 2023.

While it is a regular practice for Nepalese politicians to vent their ire on 'foreign conspiracy' the moment they lose power, what is significant is that the US, which was never controversial in Nepalese politics, suddenly and rapidly gained prominence inside the rumour mills of Kathmandu. "As Nepal becomes a playground for international geopolitics, its politics of musical chairs has become murkier".[18] According to outgoing foreign minister, Bimala Rai Paudyal, "uninvited foreign guests" were to blame for the "political instability" that led to the CPN (UML) exiting the government. Her party spokesman has indicated that she was "probably" referring to the high-level visits from the US and India before the seismic political changes in Kathmandu.[19]

Despite the concerns and anxiety, the US has, no doubt, contributed significantly to Nepal's overall development. The US is the first choice for Nepalese students wanting to pursue higher education overseas[20] — Nepal is among the top 25 student-sending countries to the US.[21] Many Nepalese also have the opportunity to live in the US through the "Diversity Visa" lottery scheme. Since 1962, nearly 4,000 US Peace Corps volunteers have served in Nepal, teaching in rural schools and helping in farms.[22] Some of them have gone on to become senators and influential officials in the US government and they hold Nepal close to their hearts.

The swift implementation of the MCC Nepal Compact will resolve the Himalayan kingdom's infrastructure bottlenecks and address long-term maintenance needs. In the process, it will, hopefully, negate the false propaganda spread to the Nepali public. However, it will largely depend on the speed with which the projects are implemented. Land acquisition, tree felling and access roads to the construction area are still some challenges. In April 2023, the Millennium Challenge Account-Nepal (MCA-Nepal)[23] launched a global tender to build a transmission line which will reach Maheshpur in India via Lapsifedi in Kathmandu, and Ratmate substation in Nuwakot, Makwanpur, Dhading, Tanahun, Palpa, Chitwan and Nawalparasi. This project will be constructed to carry a high voltage of 400 kilovolts of electricity.

Under this project, there is also a plan to maintain and improve 77 kilometres of roads. An ultra-modern road will be paved on the 77-kilometre stretch from Dhankhola to Shivakhola in Dang. MCA-Nepal said that the design of the substation and transmission line of the project has already been prepared. Since the timeframe for the full implementation of the MCC Nepal Compact is only five years and one year has already elapsed, there is a need for the swift implementation of the building of the transmission lines and road construction or else the criticism aired by the various political party leaders during the ratification will be validated in that the "US actually wishes to clutch Nepal under its security grip under the guise of the MCC".[24]

The US and Bhutan: Engagement with Formal Ties

The US and Bhutan do not have formal diplomatic relations as it is an established norm of Bhutanese foreign policy not to have diplomatic relations with the permanent five members of the UN Security Council (UNSC). Although Bhutan joined the UN way back in 1971, the US still deals with Bhutan through its embassy in New Delhi. In fact, only three countries in the world (Iran, North Korea and Bhutan) do not have diplomatic ties with the US.[25]

As a result of its introduction of Bhutanese refugee resettlement, the US currently hosts the second largest cluster of Bhutanese citizens outside of Bhutan.[26] The Lhotsampas are now spread in all 50 states of the US. The Bhutanese diaspora has emerged as an important factor in shaping Bhutan–US relations. Many young Lhotsampas are active on social media and other platforms. They are disseminating information about Bhutan to the wider American public like never before. It is certain that a new generation of Bhutanese entering the US will function as a strong leverage for the US to forge stronger ties with the Himalayan kingdom in the future.

On 11 January 2015, US Secretary of State, John Kerry, met with Bhutanese Prime Minister Tshering Tobgay at the Vibrant Gujarat Summit in India. Bhutan has carefully navigated itself between India and China and also forged partnerships with Japan, the European Union (EU), Canada and other countries without jeopardising its special relations with India. However, as relations warm up between the US and India, it is possible that Bhutan too opens up to non-UNSC member countries, especially in the EU.

John J. Sullivan, US Deputy Secretary of State, paid a visit to Bhutan in 2019 and discussed a range of issues, including the importance of protecting and enhancing a "rules-based order in the Indo-Pacific". The US donated 6,00,000 COVAX vaccines to Bhutan during the COVID-19 pandemic, which greatly helped the country. In fact, Bhutan reported only 21 COVID-related deaths.[27] The US also annually hosts Bhutanese under the Hubert Humphrey, Fulbright and International Visitors programmes but military-to-military ties with the Royal Bhutanese Army are minimal unlike between the US and the Nepalese Army.

Conclusion

While Bhutan does not have formal ties with the US, Nepal–US relations have come a long way in the past 75 years. The US has consistently supported Nepal on several fronts, ranging from malaria eradication in the terai and providing help during the earthquake to the MCC Nepal Compact and assistance during the outbreak of the COVID-19 pandemic.

Nepal and Bhutan both voted in favour of the UN resolution that "Russia immediately, completely and unconditionally withdraws all its military forces from the territory of Ukraine within its internationally recognised borders", but both India and China abstained from the voting.[28] Nepal and Bhutan's radically diverged stance from that of India and China's positions in the Russia–Ukraine conflict ipso facto sides with the stance of the US and the rest of the EU.

Caught between two large regional powers — India and China — in a fraught geopolitical environment, it remains to be seen how Nepal and Bhutan manage their relations with the US for their benefit without ruffling the feathers of the two Asia giants next door.

Endnotes

1. "Toasts of the President and King Birendra Bir Bikram Shah Dev of Nepal at the state dinner", The American Presidency Project, 9 December 1983, https://www.presidency.ucsb.edu/documents/toasts-the-president-and-king-birendra-bir-bikram-shah-dev-nepal-the-state-dinner.
2. "Nepal and its neighbours", *The Economist*, 12–18 March 2022.
3. Keshab Poudel, "Nepal-US relations at 75", *Spotlight*, 30 April 2022, https://www.spotlightnepal.com/2022/04/30/nepal-us-relations-75/.
4. "The US supports the preservation of cultural heritage sites in Patan Durbar Square", *The Annapurna Express*, 1 June 2022, https://theannapurnaexpress.com/news/the-us-supports-the-preservation-of-cultural-heritage-sites-in-patan-durbar-square-6258.
5. The author was invited to one of the interactions with Admiral Davidson.
6. "NCP leaders suspicious about MCC grant, demand clarification", *myRepublica*, 17 December 2019, https://myrepublica.nagariknetwork.com/news/ncp-leaders-suspicious-about-mcc-grant-demand-clarification/.
7. Hemanta Shrestha, "Coalition partners' student wings protest against MCC", *The Kathmandu Post*, 18 February 2022, https://kathmandupost.com/visual-stories/2022/02/18/coalition-partners-student-wings-protest-against-mcc.
8. Anil Giri, "China nudges Nepal on One-China policy", *The Kathmandu Post*, 26 May 2022, https://kathmandupost.com/national/2022/05/26/china-nudges-nepal-on-one-china-policy.

9. "We oppose coercive diplomacy and actions that pursue selfish agenda at the expense of Nepal's sovereignty and interests", *People's Review*, 18 February 2022, https://www.peoplesreview.com.np/2022/02/18/we-oppose-coercive-diplomacy-and-actions-that-pursue-selfish-agenda-at-the-expense-of-nepals-sovereignty-and-interests/.
10. "China opposes 'coercive diplomacy' of US in pushing MCC compact in Nepal", *Global Times*, 18 February 2022, https://www.globaltimes.cn/page/202202/1252597.shtml.
11. Durga Prasad Bhurtel, "Interpretative declaration: Makes no change in compact", *The Himalayan Times*, 4 March 2022, https://thehimalayantimes.com/opinion/interpretative-declaration-makes-no-change-in-compact.
12. "Decision to accept development assistance is based on national interests, priority: Nepal", *myRepublica*, 20 February 2022, https://myrepublica.nagariknetwork.com/news/decision-to-accept-development-assistance-taken-by-nepal-on-the-basis-of-national-interests-priority-mofa/.
13. *Ibid.*
14. Anil Giri and Tika Pradhan, "Government decides to stay away from SPP", *The Kathmandu Post*, 21 June 2022, https://kathmandupost.com/national/2022/06/21/government-decides-to-stay-away-from-spp.
15. Prem Singh Basnyat, "A forgotten history", *myRepublica*, 22 June 2019, https://myrepublica.nagariknetwork.com/news/a-forgotten-history/.
16. "Oli questions government: Who allowed US Under Secretary Zeya to visit Tibetan refugee camp?", *The Annapurna Express*, 26 May 2022, https://theannapurnaexpress.com/news/oli-questions-government-who-allowed-us-under-secretary-zeya-to-visit-tibetan-refugee-camp-6139.
17. "Foreign Ministry Spokesperson Zhao Lijian's Regular Press Conference on May 19, 2022", Ministry of Foreign Affairs of the People's Republic of China, 19 May 2022, https://www.fmprc.gov.cn/mfa_eng/xwfw_665399/s2510_665401/202205/t20220519_10689491.html.
18. Bharat Bhushan, "Game of thrones in Nepal: The great game in the Himalayas", *Business Standard*, 6 March 2023, https://www.business-standard.com/article/opinion/game-of-thrones-in-nepal-the-great-game-in-the-himalayas-123030600082_1.html.
19. *Ibid.*
20. "The United States remains the first choice for international students", US Embassy in Nepal, 17 November 2020, https://np.usembassy.gov/the-united-states-remains-the-first-choice-for-international-students/.
21. "International Scholarships for Nepalese Students in USA", AECC Global, https://www.aeccglobal.com.np/scholarships/usa.

22. "208th Group of peace corps volunteers arrive in Nepal", US Embassy in Nepal, 14 June 2023, https://np.usembassy.gov/208th-group-of-peace-corps-volunteers-arrive-in-nepal/.
23. The MCC administers the MCA. When a country is awarded the MCC, it sets up its own local MCA.
24. Dev Gurung, "Nepal Aaja", *YouTube*, https://www.youtube.com/watch?v=0vwKnMy8_hs.
25. David Mark, "On the outs with America–North Korea, Iran and... Bhutan?", *Splice Today*, 30 December 2014, https://www.splicetoday.com/politics-and-media/on-the-outs-with-america-north-korea-iran-and-bhutan.
26. Note: Bhutan does not, however, consider them as bona fide citizens of Bhutan.
27. "Bhutan: The latest coronavirus counts, charts and maps", *Reuters*, 15 July 2022, https://www.reuters.com/graphics/world-coronavirus-tracker-and-maps/countries-and-territories/bhutan/.
28. Anil Giri, "UN vote on Ukraine shows geopolitical shift in South Asia, observers say", *The Kathmandu Post*, 4 March 2022, https://kathmandupost.com/politics/2022/03/04/un-vote-on-ukraine-shows-geopolitical-shift-in-south-asia-observers-say.

© 2024 World Scientific Publishing Company Pte. Ltd.
https://doi.org/10.1142/9789811276439_0007

Chapter 7

United States–Bangladesh Relations since Joe Biden's Assumption of Office

Farooq Sobhan

On 7 January 2023, Bangladesh's newly appointed Ambassador to the United States (US), Muhammad Imran, presented his credentials to US President Joe Biden. In his written remarks presented to the Ambassador, Biden stated, "As 2022 marks the 50th anniversary of US–Bangladesh relations, I would like to acknowledge our enduring partnership with Bangladesh."[1] Biden further mentioned in his letter to the Ambassador that his administration "looks forward to working with you to deepen our relations as we address the opportunities and challenges ahead" and that "…our nations will continue to work on democratic governance, climate change, refugees, and maritime security. We are invested in your success and support the ability of all Bangladeshis to freely participate in and contribute to their country's development."[2]

Since January 2021, the US and Bangladesh have had a complex relationship that has been marked by both cooperation and differences. On the one hand, during the past two years, bilateral relations have witnessed high-level visits, increased trade and military cooperation. It can, therefore, be argued that the two countries have further strengthened their diplomatic and economic ties. On the other hand, under the Biden administration, in contrast to that of Donald Trump, during bilateral meetings, issues such as holding free and fair elections, upholding human rights, freedom of the press and labour matters, as well as a host of other issues have been the focus of attention. In sum, the Biden administration has made democracy, human rights and the Indo-Pacific strategy among the main pillars of its foreign policy agenda.[3]

Areas of Bilateral Cooperation

Economic Cooperation

Since 2021, the US and Bangladesh have worked together to increase trade and investment and expand overall economic cooperation.

The US–Bangladesh Trade and Investment Cooperation Forum Agreement (TICFA) was signed on 25 November 2013 and provides a platform for the two countries to collaborate on economic and trade matters and discuss any obstacles.[4] Since the signing of TICFA, there has been an increase in American assistance to support sustainable agriculture and increased food security, modernise small-scale farming and strengthen the trade and investment partnership between the two countries. Bilateral cooperation has also expanded in other areas such as energy, infrastructure development, education, healthcare, transportation and logistics, among others.[5]

The Biden administration has also emphasised the importance of creating a level playing field for American workers and businesses, and the US is working closely with Bangladesh to ensure that trade and investment between the two countries benefit both nations.[6] Bangladesh's exports to the US during 2021–2022 were nearly US$10.5 billion, while its imports were close to US$3 billion.[7]

In December 2022, the two countries convened the sixth meeting of the TICFA Council, which discussed a range of issues impacting their bilateral trade relationship. Bangladesh's delegation was led by its Commerce Secretary, Tapan Kanti, while the US side was led by Assistant US Trade Representative for South and Central Asia, Christopher Wilson.[8] The key issues addressed at the meeting included production sharing of US cotton-based ready-made garments (RMG), trade and investment climate, intellectual property rights, technical cooperation for quality certification infrastructure, labour issues and International Development Finance Corporation (DFC) funding. For Bangladesh, a major area of focus was obtaining preferential market access for Bangladesh's RMG exports to the US.[9]

Another interesting facet of US–Bangladesh relations includes the issue of inward remittances — a major contributor to Bangladesh's economy — accounting for approximately seven percent of its gross domestic product. According to the Bangladesh Bank, between October and December 2022, Bangladesh received a total of US$4.82 billion in remittances. The largest portion of this figure was from the US, amounting to US$966.89 million or 20.06 percent of the total amount. For the second year in a row, the largest flow of remittances originated from the US[10] rather than Saudi Arabia, which has historically occupied the top position for inward remittances for the past few decades.

Security and Defence Cooperation

The US and Bangladesh have a long-standing history of security cooperation in various fields. Bangladesh is located at a strategic crossroads in South Asia and has faced a range of security challenges, including terrorism, natural disasters and extremist violence. In recent years, the two nations have made significant efforts to enhance their security cooperation with a focus on countering terrorism, promoting regional stability, ensuring maritime security and sharing intelligence,[11] as well as undertaking counterterrorism training[12] and joint exercises.

In March 2022, the US and Bangladesh conducted a 25-day joint exercise in Dhaka — Exercise Tiger Lightning-3 — which included participants from the US Pacific Army Command and the Bangladesh Army.[13] Additionally, the US has provided support to Bangladesh in the form of training and equipment to improve the capabilities of the Bangladesh Navy and Air Force.

In December 2022, the navies from both countries undertook a four-week exercise in Bangladesh, the Second Joint Combined Exchange Training exercise involving the US Naval Special Warfare and the Bangladesh Navy Special Warfare Diving and Salvage.[14] Further american assistance has included the provision of patrol boats, training for border guards and the establishment of a border security cooperation programme.[15] These efforts have helped to improve Bangladesh's ability to control its borders and prevent the smuggling of weapons, drugs and people.

With regard to bilateral security cooperation, for the US, a top-most priority includes collaborating with its South Asian partners, such as Bangladesh, on promoting regional stability in the Indo-Pacific region. The Biden administration's new Indo-Pacific strategy has drawn renewed interest from American policymakers, while Dhaka has reached out to Washington as part of a "third-way balancing" effort to use its ties with the US as an alternative to India or China.[16]

The US has expressed its support for Bangladesh's efforts to maintain its sovereignty and territorial integrity in the face of regional challenges, including the Rohingya refugee crisis and the ongoing tensions between India and China.[17]

The US has been providing humanitarian assistance to the Rohingya refugees in Bangladesh and has, at every opportunity, promised to continue to provide support for the Rohingyas in Bangladesh. This commitment was reiterated by US Assistant Secretary of State for the Bureau of Population, Refugees and Migration, Julieta Valls Noyes, during her visit to Bangladesh in December 2022.[18] In March 2023, the US government announced that it was providing US$24 million in additional humanitarian assistance for the nearly one million Rohingya refugees in Bangladesh. Since the latest Rohingya crisis began in August 2017, the US has provided over US$2 billion in humanitarian support for the Rohingyas.[19]

Maritime security has been another area of cooperation between the two nations. The US has been providing training and assistance to Bangladesh to enhance its maritime capabilities[20] and the two nations have been conducting joint exercises to improve coordination and interoperability.[21] In 2021, the US Coast Guard conducted a maritime law enforcement training programme with the Bangladesh Coast Guard, which was aimed at enhancing Bangladesh's ability to combat illegal fishing and smuggling.[22]

Furthermore, the US and Bangladesh have been working to strengthen their defence ties. In June 2021, the two nations signed a memorandum of understanding (MoU) to enhance defence cooperation and promote military-to-military engagement. The MoU outlines areas of cooperation such as joint exercises, military education and training, and defence research and development.[23]

During the past two years of the Biden administration, US–Bangladesh security cooperation has continued to remain robust and has seen significant progress, with a focus on countering terrorism, promoting regional stability, ensuring maritime security and strengthening defence ties.

Energy Cooperation

An important area of cooperation has been renewable energy. The US has been providing technical assistance and funding to help Bangladesh develop its renewable energy sector. In June 2021, the US Agency for International Development (USAID) announced a US$17 million project to support the development of 1,200 megawatts of renewable energy in Bangladesh. This project is expected to help reduce greenhouse gas emissions and improve energy security in the country.[24]

Climate Change Cooperation

Since Biden took office in January 2021, climate change cooperation between the US and Bangladesh has taken on renewed significance. The Biden administration has made combating climate change a top priority and has sought to re-engage with the international community on this issue. One of the first actions taken by the Biden administration was to rejoin the Paris Agreement, an international treaty aimed at combating climate change.[25] Bangladesh has been a strong supporter of the Paris Agreement and has been working to implement its provisions. In fact, Bangladesh, a country particularly vulnerable to the impact of climate change, has been a key partner in these efforts.[26]

As evidence of its emphasis on climate change and with Bangladesh being one of the most affected countries in the world, John Kerry, US Special Presidential Envoy for Climate, visited Bangladesh from 9 to 11

April 2021 to discuss the country's vulnerability to the impact of climate change and explore opportunities for collaboration on climate action. During his visit, Kerry met with Bangladeshi officials, civil society representatives and private sector leaders to discuss issues related to climate adaptation and mitigation, clean energy and sustainable development. He also visited a coastal community affected by climate change to observe the impact of sea-level rise and highlight the urgent need for action. Kerry's visit was part of the Biden administration's efforts to elevate climate change to a top priority in its foreign policy agenda and to collaborate with other countries to address this global challenge.[27]

The Health Sector

The US is one of the largest development partners of Bangladesh, providing assistance in areas such as health, education and economic growth. These are critical areas that Bangladesh continues to address in its journey towards shedding its status as a least developed country in 2026.[28]

Following the outbreak of the COVID-19 pandemic, the US was quick to provide urgent support to Bangladesh. This included providing US$2.5 million through USAID to Bangladesh's efforts to combat the pandemic. The priority areas of support included "strengthening infection prevention and control measures in health facilities, improving specimen transport and referral systems, and increasing risk awareness communication and outreach".[29]

Peter D. Haas, US Ambassador to Bangladesh, announced that by November 2022, his government had provided 100 million vaccine doses to Bangladesh, making it the largest COVID-19 vaccine donor to Bangladesh. He added that since the start of the pandemic, American support had trained more than 50,000 healthcare providers and other workers on safely administering vaccines across all of Bangladesh's 64 districts, as well as donated freezer vans, freezer units and vaccine carriers to help move 71 million doses of vaccines to remote areas.[30] Haas added that the US had provided Bangladesh with COVID-19-related development and humanitarian assistance amounting to US$140 million.[31]

High-level Bilateral Engagements

Bangladesh's Foreign Minister meets US Secretary of State

On 4 April 2022, at the invitation of US Secretary of State Antony J. Blinken to mark 50 years of diplomatic ties between the US and Bangladesh, Bangladesh's Foreign Minister A. K. Abdul Momen visited Washington for a series of high-level meetings.[32]

The meeting between Abdul Momen and Blinken focused on strengthening the bilateral relationship between Bangladesh and the US and deepening cooperation on a range of issues, including economic development, security and human rights. Blinken expressed appreciation for Bangladesh's generosity in hosting the Rohingya refugees and reiterated the US' commitment to supporting Bangladesh in addressing the Rohingya crisis and ensuring their safe and voluntary return to Myanmar.[33]

Abdul Momen, in turn, emphasised the importance of economic and trade cooperation between the two countries and highlighted the fact that the US is Bangladesh's largest trade and investment partner.[34] As American investment is largely in the energy sector, the minister suggested that there could also be investments in areas such as pharmaceuticals and information technology.[35]

8th US–Bangladesh Partnership Dialogue

On 20 March 2022, the 8th US–Bangladesh Partnership Dialogue was held in Dhaka after a two-year hiatus due to the COVID-19 pandemic. The dialogue serves as an umbrella platform for "elevating the robust ties" between Dhaka and Washington, and for discussing and engaging in diplomatic efforts.[36]

Ambassador Victoria Nuland, the third highest ranking official at the US State Department, called the dialogue an "appetizer for the feast", while the Bangladesh delegation, led by Foreign Secretary Masud Bin Momen, dubbed the meeting as "the beginning of a rejuvenated robust engagement with our US friends".[37] The dialogue included a "renewed, multi-faceted and deepening" emphasis on trade, investment, labour, human rights, governance and global threats such as climate change, terrorism and maritime security, as well as regional issues such as the Indo-Pacific strategy and the Rohingya crisis.[38] Both delegations also discussed the Russia–Ukraine war, during which the US asked Bangladesh for its support in ending the conflict. Bangladesh, in turn, stressed its "deep concerns" about the US' sanctions imposed on the Rapid Action Battalion (RAB) and requested that the sanctions be lifted without delay. It also requested the reinstatement of the Generalised System of Preferences (GSP) facilities, which was withdrawn following the Rana Plaza tragedy in 2013.[39]

One of the key outcomes of the dialogue was the signing of the US–Bangladesh Framework for Economic Partnership, which aims to deepen economic ties between the two countries by promoting trade and investment, enhancing economic governance and expanding cooperation in areas such as energy, infrastructure and digital connectivity. The framework also aims to promote people-to-people ties and cultural exchanges between the two countries. Furthermore, the two sides discussed security cooperation, including counterterrorism and maritime security, and explored ways to enhance collaboration in these areas. They also discussed ways to strengthen democratic institutions and promote human rights and good governance in both countries.[40]

8th Bangladesh–US Bilateral Security Dialogue

The partnership dialogue in Dhaka was followed by the 8th Bangladesh–US Bilateral Security Dialogue in Washington on 4 April 2022. The dialogue is essentially a forum for consultations between the two countries on security issues of mutual interest.[41] Masud and US Under Secretary of State for Arms Control and International Security, Ambassador Bonnie Jenkins, led the talks and discussed a wide range of issues relating to defence and security cooperation between the two countries. Other items on the agenda included discussions on United Nations (UN) peacekeeping and Bangladesh–US security cooperation, including cooperation in military training, maritime security, proposed defence agreements, defence purchase and capacity development. Several regional issues were also discussed, including the Rohingya crisis, the Indo-Pacific, counterterrorism and civilian security cooperation.[42]

On the Indo-Pacific strategy, a productive discussion took place, with Bangladesh expressing its support for inclusive socio-economic development in the Indo-Pacific region. In addition, a central component of the dialogue involved persuading Bangladesh to sign twin foundational defence agreements that were first discussed in 2019 — the General Security of Military Information Agreement and the Cross-Servicing Agreement.[43] The US also expressed its willingness to assist Bangladesh in the modernisation and institutional development of its armed forces.[44]

The two sides also discussed regional security issues, including the situation in Afghanistan and the Rohingya refugee crisis, and explored ways to deepen collaboration on these issues. The US side reiterated its support for Bangladesh's efforts to address the Rohingya refugee crisis and ensure the safe and voluntary return of the refugees to Myanmar.[45]

Visit of USAID Deputy Administrator to Bangladesh

In May 2022, USAID's Deputy Administrator Isobel Colemen paid a four-day visit to Bangladesh to evaluate the need for humanitarian assistance to approximately one million Rohingya refugees. Coleman appreciated Bangladesh's role in hosting such a large number of refugees for a protracted period of time. She emphasised that the US government will remain by the side of the Rohingyas. During her visit, Coleman announced the launch of a US$20.5 million environmental conservation project to protect biodiversity in the country and develop climate resilience.[46]

9th Bangladesh–US Defence Dialogue

The 9th defence dialogue between Bangladesh and the US was held in Hawaii on 17 and 18 May 2022. According to Bangladesh Armed Forces' publicity wing, the Inter-Services Public Relations, the purpose of the dialogue was to facilitate a broad discussion on bilateral defence and military cooperation as a complement to the strategic dialogue. It added that the US will continue to support the Bangladesh Armed Forces in defence development and training and that "the dialogue will enhance defence and military cooperation in the areas of global and regional security, technology, defence equipment, disaster management, peacekeeping operations, training, visits, joint exercises and deployments workshops, among others." The statement further mentioned that the two countries' armed forces have been working together in UN peacekeeping missions and the war on terror, and that the exchange of military visits of senior officials between the two countries was another feature of military cooperation.[47]

US–Bangladesh High-level Economic Consultation

The next high-level engagement between the two governments took place on 2 June 2022 when US Under Secretary of State for Economic Growth, Energy and the Environment, Jose W. Fernandez, and Adviser for Private Industry and Investment to the Prime Minister of Bangladesh, Salman F. Rahman, met for the Second US–Bangladesh High-Level Economic Consultation in Washington. Against the backdrop of 50 years of diplomatic relations between the two nations, the meeting served to cover a wide range of important issues, including strengthening business engagement, climate change, health, trade and labour issues.[48]

In keeping with Bangladesh's efforts to obtain improved market access for its apparel exports to the US market, the Bangladesh side raised the issue of preferential market access. The US side paid special attention to labour rights, and while it appreciated Bangladesh's progress in improving labour standards, it stressed the need for additional steps to respect internationally recognised labour rights,[49] such as those enshrined in Bangladesh's International Labour Organization (ILO) road map. The Bangladesh side agreed to fully implement the four key components of the ILO road map. Dhaka also pledged to expand workers' rights to freedom of association and collective bargaining in the export processing zones and eventually throughout its economy. Both parties concluded that the successful implementation and enforcement of international labour regulations can help both countries emerge from the pandemic more robustly, share economic gains and unlock greater economic opportunities with other trade partners by developing a more congenial business atmosphere.[50]

The US provided an overview of the Indo-Pacific Economic Framework for Prosperity (IPEF), and, in response, Bangladesh welcomed more information about the supply chain resilience and decarbonisation components of the IPEF. Bangladesh also expressed interest in receiving American technical support to use its ocean resources sustainably and further develop its blue economy with a view to protecting the environment and achieving economic growth.[51]

US Deputy Secretary of State speaks to Bangladesh's State Minister for Foreign Affairs

Just days before the US' Christmas holidays in December 2022, US Deputy Secretary of State Wendy Sherman made a phone call to Bangladesh's State Minister for Foreign Affairs, Shahriar Alam. According to a press release issued by the US embassy in Dhaka, the discussion covered the subject of "strengthening US–Bangladesh relations, the importance of holding free and fair elections, and the safety and security of US embassy personnel."[52]

Visit of US Senior Director for South Asia, National Security Council, to Bangladesh

Early in January 2023, the first of three back-to-back visits by senior US officials to Dhaka took place. Rear Admiral Eileen Laubacher, Senior Director for South Asia at the National Security Council, paid a four-day visit to Bangladesh where she held official meetings with Masud and visited the Rohingya refugee camp in Cox's Bazaar. The focus of the discussions was principally on security and defence issues, the repatriation of the Rohingyas in Bangladesh to Myanmar, defence cooperation, the Indo-Pacific strategy, maritime security and strengthening capacities of the law enforcement agencies, among other issues.[53]

Visit of US Assistant Secretary for Central and South Asia to Bangladesh

The visit of US Assistant Secretary for Central and South Asia, Donald Lu, to Bangladesh may only have been for a day, but the significance of his visit did not go unnoticed. Lu is the senior most official from the US State Department in charge of South Asia, and his second visit to Dhaka in less than a year carried a major message. Apart from echoing the comment, "I am here to strengthen the friendship between the two countries; while the present world is struggling for peace and justice",[54] Lu made clear the US government's position on various critical bilateral issues.

Addressing reporters, Lu highlighted the need for Bangladesh to improve labour rights, which would then allow it to draw funds from the US government's DFC. The Bangladesh foreign minister responded that the government has plans to reform the labour sector and was committed to improving labour rights. The minister also expressed the hope that such steps would allow Bangladesh to regain the GSP facility that the US had suspended in 2013.[55]

On the sanctions against the RAB, Lu praised the progress made by the law enforcement agency on the human rights front. Regarding the Indo-Pacific strategy, Lu added that the US "desires to put more resources and attention to the Indo-Pacific, including right here to Bangladesh". Lu also emphasised the importance of Dhaka holding free and fair elections due in 2024. Both the Bangladesh foreign minister and foreign secretary agreed that US–Bangladesh relations were excellent and would be further strengthened in the coming years.[56]

Visit of US State Department Counselor to Bangladesh

On 14 and 15 February 2023, Derek Chollet, Counselor at the US State Department and Foreign Policy Advisor to the US Secretary of State, visited Bangladesh. He met with senior government officials, civil society members and representatives from the humanitarian organisations, and called on Bangladesh's Prime Minister Sheikh Hasina.[57]

During his visit, Chollet discussed continued US support to Bangladesh on the Rohingya issue, the importance of free and fair elections and the protection of human rights, cooperation to mitigate climate change and a free and open Indo-Pacific region.[58]

Prior to travelling to Dhaka, Chollet said in an online interview with a Bangladeshi talk show programme that Bangladesh has had "a remarkable journey — 51 years. We are interested in deepening the ties".[59] Chollet also remarked that the US sees "huge potential" in its relationship with Bangladesh and there is a lot of "room to grow".[60] He also discussed ways for a sustainable solution to the Rohingya crisis with the Bangladeshi authorities, as well as ways of enhancing bilateral relations between the two countries.[61]

Challenges

While the above-mentioned points make apparent that the US and Bangladesh have a long-standing relationship covering a wide range of subjects, there remain multiple challenges and points of differences between the two countries.

The thorniest issue during the past two years has undoubtedly been the US' sanctions against the RAB. On 10 December 2021, under the Global Magnitsky Human Rights Accountability Act, the US Department of State announced sanctions on the elite law enforcement agency in Bangladesh, its Director General and four other senior serving and former officers, along with their immediate family members, for their involvement in gross violations of human rights. The sanctions mean that these individuals are barred from entering the US, and any assets they have within US jurisdiction are frozen.[62]

The Bangladesh government has strongly objected to the sanctions, calling them "unilateral and unjustified". In response, Haas emphasised that the sanctions were not targeted at the Bangladesh government but rather at individuals responsible for human rights abuses.

For several years, a major concern of the US has been the issue of labour rights in Bangladesh, particularly the lack of the right of workers in Bangladesh's garment industry to form or join trade unions. The government has been criticised for not doing enough to protect workers' rights to unionise.[63]

Another major issue for the US is the human rights situation in Bangladesh. The US State Department's 2021 Human Rights Report highlighted concerns over extrajudicial killings, disappearances and arbitrary detention by Bangladeshi security forces.[64] Additionally, the Bangladesh government's crackdown on freedom of expression and the press has drawn criticism from human rights organisations and the US government.[65]

Biden's administration has made promoting and strengthening democracy a top priority in its foreign policy. It has stated that democracies are more stable, prosperous and secure, and that supporting democracy and human rights is not just a moral imperative but also in America's national interest.[66] The administration has taken several steps towards this goal, including launching a global Summit for Democracy, increasing funding for democracy and human rights programmes and imposing sanctions on individuals and entities that undermine democracy and human rights. In the case of Bangladesh, the US government has flagged the issue of Bangladesh's weakening democracy and emphasised the importance of defending and strengthening democratic institutions, including a free press, an independent judiciary and fair elections.[67]

In a virtual discussion on 'Bangladesh–US Relations: Prognosis for the Future' in December 2021, US Ambassador to Bangladesh, Earl Miller, emphasised the need for economic development to go together with democratic development, with respect for democracy and human rights being mutually reinforcing. He stated that the US supported free, fair, credible, participatory and peaceful elections that reflect the will of the Bangladeshi people, and a plural and democratic electoral process with protection for the voters and participants set out in Bangladesh's constitution. Miller also stressed the importance of freedom of the press and expression, and the need for voices of dissent and disagreement to be heard and respected. He was of the view that frequent and lively debate was crucial for the flourishing of strong democracies.[68]

During Chollet's recent visit to Dhaka, he did not refrain from underscoring the importance his administration is giving to the issue of democracy. In a roundtable discussion with representatives from Bangladesh's media fraternity, he remarked, "If there's an erosion of democracy, it's going to be a limit on our ability to cooperate with each other. We see great potential in this relationship. But the reality is that the United States' strongest partnerships are with strong democracies."[69] Chollet added that as Bangladesh had failed to come up with a plan of action for democracy, it was excluded from the US' Summit of Democracy on 29 and 30 March 2023 for the second time. Bangladesh was not invited to attend the first summit held virtually in December 2021.[70]

Another serious concern highlighted by the Biden government includes the laws governing Bangladesh's digital space. During his speech in Dhaka in February 2023, Haas raised his government's concerns about the Bangladesh government's regulations for digital, social media and over-the-top platforms, as well as the draft Data Protection Act (DPA). He said if the DPA was passed with strict data localisation requirements, it may force some American companies to leave the Bangladesh market. He added that online platform regulations may also dissuade companies from investing in Bangladesh if they face criminal liability for user content. Haas echoed that this could have an extremely negative impact on Bangladesh, putting over 2,000 startups out of business and making their services inaccessible. He further stated that the draft regulations' broad definitions for criminal online content worry civil society organisations and journalists because they could restrict fundamental human rights and freedoms.[71]

In addition, the US government has raised concerns about the Bangladesh government's Digital Security Act (DSA), which was passed in 2018. The act includes provisions that give authorities broad powers to arrest and prosecute individuals for online speech deemed to be "propaganda", "hurting religious sentiment" or "defaming" the state or its founding father. The US government has criticised the act for its potential impact on freedom of expression and human rights. At an event marking World Press Freedom Day, Haas said his government had made its concerns about the DSA apparent to both government officials and in its annual Human Rights Report.[72]

Conclusion

Relations between Bangladesh and the US have continued to evolve positively since Biden took office. Both countries have established strong diplomatic and economic ties and Biden's administration has demonstrated a commitment to strengthening the relationship in the areas of development, security, climate change, trade and investment. With continued cooperation and collaboration, Bangladesh and the US can work together to promote stability, prosperity and security in the region.

The visit of Lu to Dhaka in January 2023 was particularly significant for several reasons. First, he praised the Bangladesh government on the RAB making "tremendous progress"[73] on improving its record on human rights issues. However, it was made clear by both Lu and Chollet that the sanctions against the RAB would remain as Dhaka must first undertake major reforms.

Bangladesh is also taking seriously the threat of sanctions by the US against Russia. In early January 2023, Bangladesh did not allow a sanctioned Russian ship, carrying equipment for its Rooppur nuclear power plant that Russia and India are helping to build, to dock at one of its ports.[74] For Bangladesh, this was a difficult decision and one that has upset Russia. However, Bangladesh has decided to toe the line and not risk upsetting the US, lest it face retaliatory action.

During her visit to Dhaka in December 2022, US Deputy Assistant Secretary in the Bureau of South and Central Asian Affairs, Afreen Akhter, referred to Bangladesh as an important strategic partner. The US also condemned the genocide of the Rohingya refugees in Myanmar — a stance that helped Dhaka highlight the atrocities and the resultant refugee burden on Bangladesh.

In the coming months, Bangladesh will have to tackle two major challenges in its relations with the US. The first will be the ability of Bangladesh to maintain friendly and cordial relations with both the US and China at a time when the relations between these two countries have deteriorated sharply. Will Bangladesh be obliged or pressured into siding with one of these two countries in preference to the other?

The second challenge relates to the forthcoming parliamentary elections.[75] On 15 March 2023, *New Age*, a Dhaka-based daily newspaper, published an article by Haas under the heading 'Road to Bangladesh's Future'. The article coincided with Haas completing One year of his tenure as America's Ambassador in Bangladesh. He writes, "One important waypoint is the upcoming parliamentary elections. The United States does not have a favourite in these elections, but we want to see a free and fair elections conducted in accordance with international standards."[76]

On 13 March 2023, Hasina addressed a press conference in Dhaka. According to press reports, she said vested quarters at home and abroad were trying to frame Bangladesh's next parliamentary elections as a questionable one, but she made it crystal clear that she will not succumb to any kind of pressure. She said, "I believe in the people's power and the blessings of the Almighty. My father's blessing is also with me. We don't care about any pressure."[77]

In conclusion, it can be argued that US–Bangladesh relations have been on an upward trajectory. This is despite American sanctions against the RAB and its officers for human rights violations and disappearances, and despite Bangladesh not having been invited to either of the two democracy summits in December 2021 and March 2023. It is evident from the number of bilateral dialogues and visits of senior officials from both countries to each other's capitals that both countries are intent on strengthening their economic, political, defence and security relations. For the US, there is sufficient merit in strengthening its ties with the small but strategic South Asian country.

Endnotes

1. "US invested in Bangladesh's success: Biden", *The Daily Star*, 8 January 2023, https://www.thedailystar.net/news/world/news/us-invested-bangladeshs-success-biden-3215401.
2. *Ibid.*
3. "US foreign policy under Biden", *World Politics Review*, 21 November 2022, https://www.worldpoliticsreview.com/biden-us-foreign-policy.
4. "US-Bangladesh Trade and Investment Cooperation Forum Agreement (TICFA) Meeting", US Embassy in Bangladesh, 22 November 2015, https://bd.usembassy.gov/u-s-bangladesh-trade-investment-cooperation-forum-agreement-ticfa-meeting/.
5. "US relations with Bangladesh — Bilateral relations fact sheet", Bureau of South and Central Asian Affairs, US Department of State, 19 July 2022, https://www.state.gov/u-s-relations-with-bangladesh/.
6. "Remarks by Ambassador Haas at US–Bangladesh business forum", US Embassy in Bangladesh, 10 May 2022, https://bd.usembassy.gov/remarks-by-ambassador-haas-at-u-s-bangladesh-business-forum/.

7. BSS, "PM invites US to make larger investments in Bangladesh", *The Daily Star*, 23 September 2022, www.thedailystar.net/news/bangladesh/news/pm-invites-us-make-larger-investments-bangladesh-3126301.
8. "United States and Bangladesh Convene 6th meeting of the US–Bangladesh trade and investment cooperation forum agreement council", US Trade Representative, 6 December 2022, ustr.gov/about-us/policy-offices/press-office/press-releases/2022/december/united-states-and-bangladesh-convene-6th-meeting-US-Bangladesh-trade-and-investment-cooperation.
9. "Bangladesh stresses preferential RMG market access to USA", *Bangladesh Sangbad Sangstha*, 7 December 2022, https://www.bssnews.net/news-flash/98474.
10. Mehedi Hasan, "Remittance inflow to Bangladesh accounted for 6.6% of GDP in 2020", *Dhaka Tribune*, 18 May 2021, https://archive.dhakatribune.com/business/2021/05/18/remittance-inflow-to-bangladesh-accounted-for-6-6-of-gdp-in-2020.
11. "US donates metal shark and defender patrol boats to the Bangladesh Navy and Bangladesh coast guard", United States Embassy in Bangladesh, 9 September 2021, https://bd.usembassy.gov/u-s-donates-metal-shark-and-defender-patrol-boats-to-the-bangladesh-navy-and-bangladesh-coast-guard/.
12. "Bangladesh Army completes joint training with India–US", *Bangladesh Live News*, 17 June 2022, https://www.bangladeshlivenews.com/en/bangladesh/details/bangladesh-army-completes-joint-training-with-india-us.
13. "Joint exercise of Bangladesh, US armies concludes in Rajendrapur", *The Business Standard*, 31 March 2022, https://www.tbsnews.net/bangladesh/joint-exercise-Bangladesh-US-armies-concludes-rajendrapur-394814.
14. "Bangladesh, US Navy conduct joint military exercises", Bangladesh Institute of Maritime Research and Development, 15 November 2022, https://bimradbd.org/news-details/maritime-news/bangladesh-us-navy-conduct-joint-military-exercises.
15. "US support for Bangladesh's border security," United States Embassy in Bangladesh, 2023, https://bd.usembassy.gov/our-relationship/policy-history/border-security-cooperation-program/.
16. Anu Anwar, Geoffrey Macdonald, Daniel Markey, and Jumaina Siddiqui, "Bangladesh's balancing act amid the US Indo-Pacific strategy", United States Institute of Peace, 1 April 2022, https://www.usip.org/publications/2022/04/bangladeshs-balancing-act-amid-us-indo-pacific-strategy.

17. "Joint statement on the virtual strategic dialogue between the United States of America and Bangladesh", US Department of State, 6 November 2020, www.state.gov/joint-statement-on-the-virtual-strategic-dialogue-between-the-united-states-of-america-and-bangladesh.
18. "US pledges to continue its support to Rohingyas, host communities", *Dhaka Tribune*, 22 December 2021, https://www.dhakatribune.com/bangladesh/2022/12/08/us-pledges-to-continue-its-support-to-rohingyas-host-communities.
19. "US announces $26m new humanitarian aid for Rohingyas", *The Business Standard*, 9 March 2023, https://www.tbsnews.net/rohingya-crisis/us-announces-26m-new-humanitarian-aid-rohingyas-596502.
20. "US–Bangladesh security cooperation," US Embassy in Bangladesh, accessed February 18, 2023, https://bd.usembassy.gov/our-relationship/security-cooperation/.
21. "Navy, coast guard and Bangladesh hold annual CARAT exercise", US Navy, 28 July 2021, https://www.navy.mil/Press-Office/Press-Releases/display-pressreleases/Article/2737048/navy-coast-guard-and-bangladesh-hold-annual-carat-exercise/.
22. "US coast guard conducts maritime law enforcement training program with Bangladesh coast guard", US Coast Guard, 21 May 2021, https://content.govdelivery.com/accounts/USDHSCG/bulletins/2d17f2d.
23. "US–Bangladesh defense cooperation: A historic MOU", US Embassy in Bangladesh, 28 June 2021, https://bd.usembassy.gov/u-s-bangladesh-defense-cooperation-a-historic-mou.
24. "USAID launches a new clean energy project: Bangladesh advancing development and growth through energy (badge)", US Agency for International Development, 21 June 2021, https://bd.usembassy.gov/usaid-launches-a-new-clean-engergy-project-bangladesh-advancing-development-and-growth-through-energy-badge/.
25. "Executive order on tackling the climate crisis at home and abroad", The White House, 27 January 2021, https://www.whitehouse.gov/briefing-room/presidential-actions/2021/01/27/executive-order-on-tackling-the-climate-crisis-at-home-and-abroad/.
26. "John Kerry's Bangladesh visit highlights climate cooperation". US Embassy in Bangladesh, 12 April 2021, https://bd.usembassy.gov/john-kerrys-bangladesh-visit-highlights-climate-cooperation/.
27. *Ibid.*

132   F. Sobhan

28. "Bangladesh finally gets nod to graduate from LDC", *The Daily Star*, 25 November 2021, www.thedailystar.net/business/news/bangladesh-finally-gets-nod-graduate-ldc-2902456.
29. UNB, "Coronavirus: US mobilises $2,500,000 to support Bangladesh", *The Daily Star*, 22 March 2020, https://www.thedailystar.net/coronavirus-live-update-us-mobilises-2500000-support-bangladesh-1879828.
30. "US COVID-19 vaccine donations to Bangladesh surpass 100 million mark", US Embassy in Bangladesh, 9 November 2022, https://bd.usembassy.gov/28797.
31. *Ibid.*
32. "Momen meets Blinken in Washington on 50 years of US–Bangladesh ties", *The Daily Star*, 5 April 2022, https://www.thedailystar.net/news/bangladesh/diplomacy/news/bangladesh-demand-withdrawal-sanctions-momen-blinken-meet-us-state-dept-2998241.
33. *Ibid.*
34. *Ibid.*
35. *Ibid.*
36. "Bangladesh–US partnership dialogue eyes 'closer understanding' on key issues", *The Business Standard*, 20 March 2022, https://www.tbsnews.net/bangladesh/Bangladesh-US-partnership-dialogue-eyes-closer-understanding-key-issues-387898.
37. "US–Bangladesh relationship: What's in the feast?", *The Daily Star*, 24 March 2022, https://www.thedailystar.net/news/bangladesh/diplomacy/news/US-Bangladesh-relationship-whats-the-feast-2989131.
38. "Experts call for enhanced Bangladesh–US liaison to lift sanctions on RAB", *The Business Standard*, 22 February 2022, https://www.tbsnews.net/bangladesh/experts-call-enhanced-Bangladesh-US-liaison-lift-sanctions-rab-376798.
39. "Treasury sanctions perpetrators of serious human rights abuse on international human rights day", US Department of Treasury, 10 December 2021, https://home.treasury.gov/news/press-releases/jy0526.
40. "US–Bangladesh sign framework for economic partnership", *Dhaka Tribune*, 21 June 2021, https://www.dhakatribune.com/business/2021/06/21/US-Bangladesh-sign-framework-for-economic-partnership.
41. "Bangladesh, US hold virtual bilateral security dialogue," *Dhaka Tribune*, 22 July 2021, https://www.dhakatribune.com/bangladesh/foreign-affairs/2021/07/22/Bangladesh-US-hold-virtual-bilateral-security-dialogue.

42. "US keen to enhance security cooperation with Bangladesh", *The Daily Ittefaq*, 7 April 2022, https://en.ittefaq.com.bd/1352/US-keen-to-enhance-security-cooperation-with.
43. "US wants 2 defence deals with Bangladesh", *The Daily Star*, 18 October 2019, https://www.thedailystar.net/frontpage/us-wants-2-defence-deals-bangladesh-1815466.
44. "US keen to enhance security cooperation with Bangladesh", *Dhaka Tribune*, 5 April 2022, https://www.dhakatribune.com/bangladesh/2022/04/07/us-keen-to-enhance-security-cooperation-with-bangladesh.
45. *Ibid*.
46. "Deputy Administrator Isobel Coleman travels to Bangladesh", US Agency for International Development, 13 May 2022, https://www.usaid.gov/news-information/press-releases/may-13-2022-deputy-administrator-isobel-coleman-travels-bangladesh.
47. "Bangladesh–US defence dialogue held", Inter Services Public Relations Directorate, Bangladesh, 25 May 2022, https://www.ispr.gov.bd/en/9th-Bangladesh-US-bilateral-defence-dialogue-held.
48. "US–Bangladesh high-level economic consultation", US State Department, 2 June 2022, https://www.state.gov/u-s-bangladesh-high-level-economic-consultation/.
49. "Bangladesh seeks preferential market access to the US", *Prothom Alo*, 4 June 2022, http://prothomalo.com/business/local/bangladesh-seeks-preferential-market-access-to-the-us.
50. "U.S.–Bangladesh high-level economic consultation", US State Department, 2 June 2022, https://www.state.gov/u-s-bangladesh-high-level-economic-consultation/.
51. *Ibid*.
52. "Deputy Secretary of State Sherman's call with state minister for foreign affairs of Bangladesh Shahriar Alam", US State Department, 22 December 2022, https://bd.usembassy.gov/29082/.
53. "Meeting with US official: Strengthening defence cooperation stressed", *Prothom Alo*, 10 January 2023, https://en.prothomalo.com/bangladesh/66pjbt4gjc.
54. "I have come to Dhaka to strengthen friendship: Donald Lu", *Bangladesh Live News*, 16 January 2023, https://www.bangladeshlivenews.com/en/bangladesh/details/i-have-come-to-dhaka-to-strengthen-friendship-donald-lu/.

55. "Donald Lu in Dhaka: US underscores labour reform for enhanced funding", *The Financial Express*, 15 January 2023, https://beta.thefinancialexpress.com.bd/national/donald-lu-in-dhaka-us-underscores-labour-reform-for-enhanced-funding.
56. *Ibid.*
57. "State Department's Counselor Derek Chollet & Interagency Delegation Visit Bangladesh to demonstrate continued support for US–BD partnership", US Embassy, Dhaka, 15 February 2023, https://bd.usembassy.gov/29302/.
58. *Ibid.*
59. "US sees huge potential to grow its relations with Bangladesh: Counsellor Chollet", *The Business Standard*, 10 February 2023, https://www.tbsnews.net/economy/us-sees-huge-potential-grow-its-relations-bangladesh-counsellor-chollet-583114.
60. "US wants deeper ties with Bangladesh, says Counselor Chollet", *The Financial Express*, 10 February 2023, https://thefinancialexpress.com.bd/national/us-wants-deeper-ties-with-bangladesh-says-counselor-chollet-1676034736.
61. "State Department's Counselor Derek Chollet & interagency delegation visit Bangladesh to demonstrate continued support for US–BD partnership", US Embassy in Bangladesh, 15 February 2023, https://bd.usembassy.gov/29302/.
62. "US stands firm on sanctions on rights abusers in Bangladesh", *Asia Times*, 22 April 2022, https://asiatimes.com/2022/04/us-stands-firm-on-sanctions-on-rights-abusers-in-bangladesh/.
63. "Bangladesh: Protect garment workers' rights", Human Rights Watch, 6 February 2014, https://www.hrw.org/news/2014/02/06/bangladesh-protect-garment-workers-rights.
64. 2021 Country reports on human rights practices: Bangladesh, US Department of State, 13 April 2022, https://www.state.gov/reports/2021-country-reports-on-human-rights-practices/bangladesh.
65. "Bangladesh: End crackdown on freedom of expression online", Amnesty International, 25 July 2021, https://www.amnesty.org/en/latest/press-release/2021/07/bangladesh-end-crackdown-on-freedom-of-expression-online/.
66. Remarks by President Biden on "America's place in the world", The White House, 4 February 2021, https://www.whitehouse.gov/briefing-room/speeches-remarks/2021/02/04/remarks-by-president-biden-on-americas-place-in-the-world.

67. "Bangladesh–United States relations", US Department of State, 22 July 2022, https://www.state.gov/u-s-relations-with-bangladesh/.
68. "Stronger democratic institutions, governing structures to fuel Bangladesh's future success: US envoy", *Daily Sun*, 9 December 2021, https://www.daily-sun.com/post/592796/Stronger-democratic-institutions-governing-structures-to-fuel-Bangladeshs-future-success:-US-envoy.
69. "Eroding democracy could limit US cooperation with Bangladesh: US official", *The Business Standard*, 15 February 2023, https://www.tbsnews.net/bangladesh/eroding-democracy-could-limit-us-cooperation-Bangladesh-US-counselor-chollet-585694.
70. *Ibid.*
71. Remarks by Ambassador Haas at Panel Discussion for "Online freedom and business investment in Bangladesh", US Embassy in Bangladesh, 5 February 2023, https://bd.usembassy.gov/29243/.
72. "US concerned about Bangladesh's digital security act", *Dhaka Tribune*, 24 May 2022, https://www.dhakatribune.com/foreign-affairs/2022/05/24/us-concerned-about-bangladeshs-digital-security-act/.
73. "US wants fair polls in Bangladesh: Lu", *New Age*, 15 January 2023, https://www.newagebd.net/article/191739/rab-made-tremendous-progress-in-respecting-rights-donald-lu.
74. "Russian ship returning without offloading Rooppur equipment", *The Daily Star*, 19 January 2023, https://www.thedailystar.net/news/bangladesh/news/russian-ship-returning-without-offloading-rooppur-equipment-3225141.
75. "Bangladesh PM announces general elections in January 2024", *VOA*, 9 December 2022, https://www.voanews.com/a/bangladesh-pm-announces-general-elections-in-january-2024-/6869119.html/.
76. Peter D. Haas, "Road to Bangladesh's future", *New Age*, 15 March 2023, https://www.newagebd.net/article/196827/road-to-bangladeshs-future.
77. "PM: No pressure can make me bend", *Dhaka Tribune*, 13 March 2023, https://www.dhakatribune.com/bangladesh/2023/03/13/pm-says-will-never-bow-down-to-foreign-pressure-reiterates-holding-fair-polls/.

Chapter 8

The United States and Sri Lanka: Winning Back Colombo

Asanga Abeyagoonasekera

"How do you fix a broken country?" was the CNN headline in July 2022 reporting the Sri Lankan crisis.[1] With the political economy in crisis, the island nation needs immediate stability. Among the possible saviours, the United States (US) will be a pivotal partner in Sri Lanka's efforts to achieve stability. In this regard, the foreign policy focus of American President Joe Biden's administration will be critical for the present-day unstable environment in Sri Lanka.

Never in Sri Lanka's political history, since independence in 1948, has a serving executive president been ousted by a people's uprising. President Gotabaya Rajapaksa, appointed by a popular mandate in late 2019, was removed from office on 9 July 2022 when protesters stormed the presidential residence and took control, demanding his resignation. The downfall came with an unprecedented economic crisis, with soaring food prices and severe shortages of essential supplies triggering mass protests. Behind the economic turmoil was political instability where senior ministers stepped down from the regime several months before due to Gotabaya's autocratic rule. However, post the uprising, immediate measures were taken to stabilise the country with assistance from India, the US, China, Japan, the European Union (EU) and the International Monetary Fund (IMF). The IMF's financial assistance of US$2.9 billion and debt restructuring with creditors were seen as the only prudent measures to come out of the debt-ridden crisis. Sri Lanka's foreign debt stood at US$51 billion and it had suspended repayment of nearly US$7 billion due in 2022.[2]

Apart from domestic economic and political challenges, the island nation had to manoeuvre multiple external challenges, such as the COVID-19 pandemic and the war in Ukraine, which impacted oil prices and crippled the tourism industry. The impact of the great power rivalry between the US and China and between India and China was also clearly visible. Sri Lanka's foreign policy was tilted towards China during the Gotabaya regime and was not limited to just Chinese infrastructure projects — a unique political model was in the making, supported by the Chinese Communist Party (CCP). The US and its allies, including Sri Lanka's close neighbour, India, were concerned about the strong Chinese position in Sri Lanka's foreign policy.

Against the backdrop of the Sri Lankan crisis, this chapter assesses the US' position and how Washington should re-engage with Sri Lanka in the face of growing Chinese interest. This chapter attempts to unpack Biden's foreign policy in Sri Lanka during the crisis and the US' bilateral economic relationship with Sri Lanka as well as discusses issues of democracy, human rights and American military assistance.

US Bilateral Assistance

The US, as a bilateral development partner, has been playing a pivotal role in Sri Lanka. From assistance during the Asian tsunami in 2004 and developing coastal fisheries harbours to humanitarian aid through the US Agency for International Development (USAID) and combating the COVID-19 outbreak, where US$5 million of assistance and medical equipment was donated to Sri Lanka, the US has been committed to helping Sri Lanka during its times of distress.

In Colombo's present crisis, the US has increased its commitment. Janet L. Yellen, US Secretary of the Treasury, over a telephone conversation with Sri Lankan President Ranil Wickremesinghe, expressed Washington's "support for Sri Lanka's steps towards an IMF-supported programme to advance economic reform and achieve a strong and durable recovery".[3] The long delay from Sri Lanka's official and private creditors, especially

China, on debt restructuring resulted in the island nation not being able to conclude the financial assistance package with the IMF for US$2.9 billion. This 17th IMF assistance package will be an initial step in stabilising the Sri Lankan economy, helping to regain confidence among other lenders and for credit agencies to look at Sri Lanka positively. Moving towards a more structured process with progressive reforms, Sri Lanka will gain credibility in the international arena. This will be the first time Sri Lanka will reach out to the IMF as a bankrupt nation with depleted foreign reserves — this is perhaps the only difference from the previous 16 times.

Wickremasinghe's progressive approach and commitment towards the IMF will directly strengthen US–Sri Lanka bilateral relations and further work towards achieving US foreign policy objectives, which include bringing Sri Lanka closer to the US Indo-Pacific strategy. The US has welcomed the quick progress made by the Wickremasinghe government and its commitment to improving transparency and redemocratising the country following the autocratic rule of the Rajapaksas. However, ultra-nationalist political factions in Sri Lanka have criticised Wickremasinghe for his quick progressive recalibration towards the IMF reforms and alignment with American policies — they see it as a threat to Sri Lanka's sovereignty. According to Asoka Bandarage, "there are already signs that these policies would be detrimental to the well-being of ordinary Sri Lankans and the sovereignty of the country".[4] This is a poor assessment, and it is misleading and harmful to the US–Sri Lanka position and the progressive reforms taking place in the country. The leftist and ultra-nationalist political factions will weaponise the "neo-liberal reforms" in the coming election.

Since 1977, the US has consistently appreciated the pro-market-led economic reforms in Sri Lanka, then introduced by President J. R. Jayawardena, who was a close family relation of the current president. The economic liberalisation and strong relationship with the US established then were fundamental ingredients for the continuation of the relationship. In the past, there were only two state visits by Sri Lankan leaders to the US — the first by Jayawardena and the other by Wickremasinghe as prime minister. During Jayawardena's presidency, the US viewed with sensitivity India's intervention in Sri Lanka, especially during the ethnic conflict.

However, the present-day position of the US has changed due to the strong relationship with India.

Bilateral Trade Between Sri Lanka and the US

The Sri Lankan economy has faced two external shocks in the past few years — the COVID-19 pandemic, which crippled its tourism industry, and the Russian-Ukraine war, which impacted oil and commodity prices (see Figure 8.1). Despite the external shocks, Sri Lanka's export revenue from the US has been considerable. According to the Sri Lanka Export Development Board, in 2020, during the pandemic environment, the US was the largest among the top five export destinations for Sri Lanka.[5] For over a decade, the US has been the leading export destination for Sri Lanka. In 2021, the export value from Sri Lanka to the US was US$3.1 billion, an increase of 22.3 percent over 2020.[6]

The US and Sri Lanka marked 75 years of bilateral relations in 2023. While celebrating 75 years of Sri Lanka's independence and US–Sri Lanka relations, Biden delivered a message through US Under Secretary for Political Affairs, Victoria Nuland, to the Sri Lankan president on

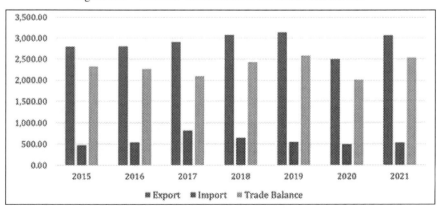

Figure 8.1: Bilateral Trade between Sri Lanka and the US.

Source: Sri Lanka Customs, "Trade Relations between Sri Lanka and the US", Embassy of Sri Lanka in the United States, 10 June 2023, https://slembassyusa.org/new/trade/trade-relations-between-sri-lanka-and-the-u-s.html.

1 February 2023. The message emphasised the strong bilateral relations that "have tackled formidable global challenges, including the combating of climate change, addressing the scourge of human trafficking and maintaining a secure, free and open Indo-Pacific", further elaborating the importance of deepening bilateral trade and economic ties with a shared commitment to democracy, freedom, opportunity and equality.[7]

At the crucial moment when Sri Lanka was facing its worst economic crisis in 2022, with extended fuel and cooking gas queues and depleted foreign reserves to fund the essential imports, Colombo requested for immediate international assistance with an intense liquidity and insolvency crisis, further defaulting on its borrowings. India was one of the first nations to assist Sri Lanka through a credit line for fuel and essentials for the public.

Julie Chung, US Ambassador in Sri Lanka, said, "As Sri Lankans endure some of the greatest economic challenges in their history, our efforts to support economic growth and strengthen democratic institutions have never been more critical".[8] The US announced a US$120 million new financing package for Sri Lanka's small and medium-sized businesses. A US$27 million contribution to Sri Lanka's dairy industry, US$5.75 million to those who had been the hardest hit by the economic crisis and US$6 million in new grants to provide livelihood and technical assistance on financial reform were offered as an immediate relief to stabilise the situation. This assistance from the US was announced during the visit by Robert Kaproth, US Deputy Assistant Secretary of Treasury for Asia, and Ambassador Kelly Keiderling, Deputy Assistant Secretary of State for South and Central Asia, to the island.[9]

Biden's Foreign Policy Focus on Sri Lanka

In essence, the Biden administration stepped up its bilateral efforts with Sri Lanka with an eye on its foreign policy imperative. To quote Donald Lu, US Assistant Secretary for Central and South Asia, "Our relationship with India is one of the key partnerships that will determine the security of Asia, the United States and the world."[10] There has been a significant shift and focus on India and the Indian Ocean as part of the Biden administration's Indo-Pacific commitment. The US 2022 National Security Strategy (NSS) placed significant emphasis on the Indo-Pacific, referring to the phrase 32 times in the 48-page strategy document. The NSS explained that "no region will be of more significance to the world and to everyday Americans than the Indo-Pacific".[11] The immediate American attention to the Indo-Pacific region will naturally reflect attention towards the geo-strategically located Sri Lanka in the Indian Ocean. Growing Chinese influence through infrastructure projects, which could transform into 'forward military bases' in the Indian Ocean, such as Hambantota Port — built and leased by China — has drawn considerable attention from the Pentagon.[12] Sri Lanka, located 32 kilometres away from India and close to the sea lines of communication (SLOCs) of the east–west trade, as well as a key energy supply route, is of immediate interest to the US foreign policy calculus. According to the 2022 US Report on 'Military and Security Developments Involving the People's Republic of China', approximately 76 percent of oil import and 23 percent of gas import transit through the South China Sea, and the Strait of Malacca is a priority for China in the next 15 years.[13] In this context, Sri Lanka's geographical location at the SLOCS is of Beijing's strategic interest. The US has identified China's strategic manoeuvres from infrastructure diplomacy and political and military assistance to the Indian Ocean littorals, including Sri Lanka, as a threat to Washington's foreign policy and security interests.

Biden's foreign policy focus and interest in Sri Lanka have been visible in three areas, namely, promoting democracy, human rights with reconciliation and the threat to American policies of growing Chinese influence in Sri Lanka. In this regard, the US has a particular focus towards the Indian Ocean's maritime security, where US assistance to upgrade the Sri Lankan coast guard was a priority. Unlike his predecessor, Donald Trump, Biden has taken a stricter posture on human rights and democratic backsliding; on China's aggression, it has been more of a bipartisan consensus.

Nuland's visit to Sri Lanka in February 2023 to mark the 75th anniversary of US–Sri Lanka relations symbolised "continued US support for Sri Lanka's efforts to stabilise the economy, protect human rights and promote reconciliation".[14] Nuland explained the US position on redemocratising the nation as a priority; she referred to the postponement of the local election in March 2023, claiming that they are not "giving people across the country a voice in their future". The local election will be a trendsetter for the next parliamentary and presidential election in which the government has understood the significant risk of losing the polls due to the prevailing economic crisis — one that has made the regime unpopular. The economic hardship, with mounting food prices and human rights concerns, where the protestors were detained under the Prevention of Terrorism Act (PTA), will be decisive factors in the election. The postponement of the election will send the wrong signals to the US and the international community, and reflect the government's political insecurity to test public opinion.

This was Nuland's second visit to Sri Lanka in less than a year, pledging American support and assurance to stabilise the economic crisis. There were multiple efforts by the US to stabilise the economy and assist the new political model — an executive president (Wickremasinghe) appointed by the members of parliament until the remainder of his term, a parliament majority backed by Rajapaksa's political party, Sri Lanka Podujana Peramuna, and a prime minister, Dinesh Gunawardena, who is a firm Rajapaksa political associate. The hybridity of the regime — a president with a liberal centre-right political ideology and a prime minister, and his ruling majority, with a centre-left political ideology and an ultra-nationalist posture — is a political mismatch. A similar bipartisan model was exercised during the 2015–2019 regime and faced many political challenges in its efforts to sustain power.

The current economic crisis and the new political model provide a better opportunity for the US and its allies than the previous autocratic regime to work with the island state. The disruption and the people's uprising provided two clear advantages to the US. The first was to influence the recalibration of Sri Lanka's foreign policy, which was tilted towards China by the Rajapaksa presidency. The second was economic assistance to Sri Lanka, allowing the US, India and Japan to establish a stronger position in Sri Lanka than before.

The US on Sri Lanka's Maritime Security

Sri Lanka's geostrategic location and maritime domain are of great interest to the US. Sri Lanka possesses a territorial sea of 21,500 square kilometres and an exclusive economic zone of up to 200 nautical miles (370 kilometres) from the coastal line — an extent of 517,000 square kilometres. Sri Lanka's position at the east–west trade routes makes the island nation an important destination for trade and maritime security in the Indian Ocean. There has been a maritime security and safety interest, and the US has agreed to "pursue joint initiatives to enhance security".[15] With the implementation of the Indo-Pacific strategy, the Biden administration identifies Sri Lanka as an important partner in the Indian Ocean. Strengthening bilateral military cooperation is a priority for the US in Sri Lanka to achieve its Indo-Pacific maritime domain objectives. The recent 20-member high-level delegation, along with Jedidiah Royal, US Principal Deputy Assistant Secretary of Defence for Indo-Pacific Security Affairs, clearly indicated that the US is doubling its priority in US–Sri Lanka defence cooperation.[16]

There is a clear interest for the US to develop Sri Lanka's capacity in the maritime domain. Sri Lanka's Ambassador to the US, Mahinda Samarasinghe, explained this interest at the 75th anniversary of US–Sri Lanka relations:

> "We are conscious of our positioning and our relevance to the United States' Indo-Pacific strategy. We look to engage with the four-nation Quadrilateral Security Dialogues [Quad] as an interested nation. We look to enhance our maritime surveillance capacities and would value continued United States support in combatting drug and human trafficking in the region."[17]

This position reflects the Wickremasinghe administration's pro-US stance.

The US Navy donated a US Coast Guard high endurance cutter which has helped to increase Sri Lanka's ability to patrol its territorial waters. The strengthening of the coast guard will assist in fighting illegal, unreported and unregulated fishing and illegal goods shipment, as well as provide search and rescue operation capabilities. There have been several US Navy port calls and a close partnership with the Sri Lanka Navy to establish a Sri Lankan Marine Corps. The US has also extended a hand to the "Sri Lanka Navy and Air Force to build cooperation on humanitarian assistance and disaster relief".[18] By cooperating with the US and India, Sri Lanka has a strong opportunity to strengthen its maritime security and contribute towards a rules-based order in the Indo-Pacific.

Redemocratising and Fighting Corruption

Biden's administration came to power amidst significant domestic challenges to American democracy, including the attack on 6 January 2021 on the US capital and several other illiberal manoeuvres by the former administration. To address the democratic backsliding, the Biden administration doubled its commitment to revisit and resurrect the principles and values of US democracy projects buried by Trump. China's rise with an alternative political model that developing nations with democratic footing were ready to emulate was seen as a threat to the US and its allies. Sri Lanka was on this trajectory when Gotabaya decided to exercise a "Chinese development model" as the way forward for Sri Lanka.[19] This China posture was explained during a telephone conversation with Chinese President Xi Jinping where Gotabaya was ready to adopt the CCP's strategies and stated, "Sri Lanka hopes to learn from the CCP's governance experience, and especially looks forward to strengthening exchanges and cooperation on poverty alleviation and rural vitalisation strategies."[20]

China comfortably exerted its influence on Sri Lanka during the Gotabaya rule. This guaranteed continuous support, including in the United Nations (UN) Human Rights Council (UNHRC), where Sri Lanka reciprocated by supporting China's human rights concerns in Xinjiang.[21] At the same time, Gotabaya began to move towards autocratic rule through structural changes to the constitution, multiple interferences by the executive branch in the judiciary, such as pardoning a political convict, and interference in the bureaucracy which threatened the overall democratic model of the country.[22] Witnessing the dangerous trajectory of the country, the Biden administration decided not to invite Sri Lanka to the first Summit of Democracy in December 2021.[23] The heavily militarised model, exercised with multiple military appointments to civilian administration positions, came to the attention of Washington, which viewed Sri Lanka's transition from democratic to autocratic rule with the military at the forefront, similar to that in Myanmar and Pakistan, as a clear danger to American interest.[24]

The overall democratic backsliding of Sri Lanka was a concern not only to the US but also to many other liberal democratic nations in the West, where Sri Lanka has its most significant trade volume of exports, such as the EU. The autocratic posture of Gotabaya, with several family members holding vital ministerial positions, including that of the prime minister and ministers for finance, defence, youth, telecommunications and sports, was also a concern for other senior ministers, revealing the internal dysfunctionality after a senior minister, Susil Premajayantha, was removed from office.[25] USAID democracy projects were functioning amidst the challenging political environment. The US was extremely concerned about the country losing its democratic values and China taking advantage of the militarised political environment to install an alternative governance mechanism.

While the Sri Lankan people's uprising in 2022 to ouster the Gotabaya family rule was focused mainly on the country's economic woes, it was also a reaction against the rampant corruption of the regime and its ruling elites. The IMF was right about Colombo fighting corruption as a central pillar to achieving structural reforms in the country. It identified widespread corruption throughout government institutions, which were politicised by the Gotabaya regime. The present Wickremasinghe regime's acceptance of USAID's 'Democratic, Prosperous Sri Lanka with the Ability to Survive Amidst Disasters' project will pave the way for the introduction of the 'dekleptification guide'.[26] The 'dekleptification guide' is a valuable resource for USAID working in countries trapped in severe corruption, particularly those whose courageous citizens open windows of opportunity for reforms. Sri Lankan reforms taking place at the state level, along with the IMF, will allow USAID to set the agenda for broader social participation in anti-corruption measures and implement strategies in Sri Lanka. It is also an opportunity for the US, India and Western democracies to assist Sri Lanka in recalibrating its prior democratic norms and values. It also provides the space for these countries to regain the lost traction due to heavy Chinese influence in Sri Lanka's foreign policy.

Human Rights and Reconciliation

Washington has had a delicate relationship with Colombo due to human rights concerns of the past in Sri Lanka. The US refrained from fully assisting Sri Lanka, strategically distancing itself due to Tamilian grievances. In the 1980s, the US was concerned about helping Jayawardena as it did not want to be perceived to be assisting regimes that suppress the minorities. With Wickremasinghe in power, a similar minority-centred human rights approach by the US is likely to continue in Sri Lanka. To address this, Wickremesinghe has pledged to revisit the 1987 devolution of power known as the 13th Amendment.[27]

British Liberal Democrat leader Ed Davey clearly explained to the United Kingdom (UK) parliament the needs of Colombo, saying Sri Lanka requires two packages — political and economic.[28] The political package was to reinstall the democratic processes and address the minority concerns by addressing human rights issues which are of concern in the UK where many members of the Sri Lankan Tamil diaspora reside and who demand their rights. The same is visible in the US, Canada, France and many other countries. The protests outside of Sri Lanka against the Gotabaya regime included the Tamils highlighting their own grievances, along with the dysfunctionality of the government. The Sri Lankan diaspora held the autocratic family rule and rampant corruption by Gotabaya's family members accountable for the crisis. The diaspora also lobbied strongly for the implementation of measures to address human rights concerns and to prosecute the Rajapaksa family. The letter by Tamil American United in the US to the US House of Representatives was a clear example of the Sri Lankan diaspora putting pressure on the Western governments.[29] The Sri Lankan diaspora in the US are influential stakeholders who are able to exert pressure on the US government to address democratic backsliding and human rights concerns in Sri Lanka. On its part, the US tends to take a pro-diaspora posture as the regimes in power have made pledges in the UNHRC to introduce political solutions through the devolution of power, but they have has never really made a genuine attempt to deliver in this regard.[30]

In December 2022, the US State Department sanctioned Prabath Bulathwatte, former head of a clandestine Sri Lankan Army platoon known as the Tripoli Platoon.[31] The Tripoli Platoon was reportedly Gotabaya's hit squad when he was defence secretary. Journalists were said to be tortured in the Tripoli Platoon's unmarked white vans and often never seen again. The degrading treatment and punishment of Sri Lankan journalist Keith Noyahr in May 2008 and the assassination of Lasantha Wickramatunga, Editor of *Sunday Leader*, were examples in this respect. The Center for Justice and Accountability notes as follows, "While Gotabaya was Secretary of Defence from 2005 to 2015, dozens of journalists were killed, tortured, abducted or disappeared."[32]

The families of the victims in these disappearance cases requesting justice have been a serious concern for the international community, especially for the Biden administration, which issued sanctions. The various regimes following the war have made multiple commitments in the UNHRC to address such disappearances and grievances of the Tamil community impacted by the civil war that ended in 2009. They also further promised transitional justice mechanisms to introduce a genuine reconciliation process to the nation. However, 14 years have passed since the end of the civil war. There has not been a clear reconciliation process due to the ultranationalist posture of the ruling coalition governments which have regarded the international commitments and recommendations as Western interference in a sovereign regime. The Sri Lankan government co-sponsored its resolution in the UNHRC and renegaded on its commitment. The lack of firm commitment has widened the trust deficit between the government and the Tamil community. The Biden administration has strongly signalled to Colombo to move into a genuine reconciliation process to address the minority concerns. The same signal was seen from New Delhi when S. Jaishankar, India's External Affairs Minister, visited Sri Lanka in January 2023 where he pointed towards fully implementing the 13th Amendment — the devolution of power — which was the initial political solution introduced to address the minority concerns. According to Jaishankar, "the full implementation of the 13th Amendment and early conduct of the provincial election are critical", and the "durable efforts towards reconciliation are in the interests of all sections in Sri Lanka". India has expressed this position multiple times in the past to the governments in Sri Lanka. However, Sri Lanka has failed to implement the amendment.[33]

During an interactive dialogue at the 51st Session of the UNHRC with the office of the UN High Commissioner for Human Rights in Sri Lanka,

India's Permanent Representative to the UN, Mani Pandey, highlighted the "full implementation of the 13th Amendment of the Constitution, delegation of powers to [the] Provincial Councils and holding of Provincial Council election at the earliest"[34] while Chinese Permanent Representative to the UN, Ambassador Chen Xu, expressed the view that China "opposes any country taking advantage of the current difficult situation in Sri Lanka to seek self-interest, and urges relevant parties to respect the human rights development path that Sri Lanka has independently chosen according to its national conditions, and abandon the practice of using human rights to exert political pressure and interfere in other's internal affairs."[35] The direct reference was to India and the Western nations, including the US, which have pushed for political reform through the devolution of power to address minority concerns. This polarisation between the Western states and China is reflected in domestic politics and street protests by ultra-nationalists, such as the burning of the 13th Amendment by Buddhist priests, highlighting the danger to the country's sovereignty.[36]

Another challenge facing the Sri Lankan regime is the PTA and its use against many civilians, including the protestors at the recent uprising who broke into the president's residence and his office. Nuland highlighted that the PTA reforms should bring results and adhere to international standards.[37] On the PTA and the new Anti-Terrorism Act (ATA), the US has indicated its displeasure and abuse of human rights, along with the EU, due to the arbitrary detention of many innocent civilians.[38] According to Meenakshi Ganguly, South Asia Director at Human Rights Watch: "The proposed counterterrorism law (ATA) would permit the Sri Lankan government to continue to use draconian measures to silence peaceful critics and target minorities."[39]

The US on China in Sri Lanka

The Pentagon National Defence Strategy, released in 2022,[40] takes a much stronger position against China, stating that the US will strengthen its partnership with India to enhance its ability to deter China's aggression in the Indo-Pacific region. The US' posture in South Asia will impact the nations in India's immediate periphery such as Sri Lanka, which has close collaboration with China.

According to the US National Security Strategy (NSS), released in October 2022, the Biden administration's interest in South Asia focuses on three domains: climate change, the pandemic and Beijing's coercive behaviour. The administration's focus on the Quad and AUKUS (a trilateral security pact comprising Australia, the UK and the US) on "weaving our allies and partners closer together — including by encouraging tighter linkages between like-minded Indo-Pacific and European countries"[41] — is a clear strategy of dealing with the geopolitical rivalry between the US and China and between India and China in the Indo-Pacific region.

The Biden administration's threefold NSS focus on China — to invest in competitiveness, align with allies and compete responsibly with Beijing — is a clear indication to nations like Sri Lanka with a significant Chinese influence. Chinese influence in Sri Lanka grew with Chinese infrastructure diplomacy conducted through the Belt and Road Initiative. Large-scale projects, CCP funding, human rights support for the regime in Colombo and military assistance were visible Chinese influences in Sri Lanka. Chinese geoeconomic interests, such as in Hambantota Port, gradually transformed into geopolitical ambitions with civil–military operations. The call by Yang Wang 5 — known as the Chinese spy ship[42] — in Hambantota Port took place despite multiple futile warnings from New Delhi to the Sri Lankan government. This was a clear example of China's considerable influence on the island state. Upon its arrival, Sri Lankan politicians attended the ceremony to welcome the Chinese vessel.[43] The strong Chinese political agency and capturability of the political elites in Sri Lanka have been considerable. The Chinese hybrid civil–military manoeuvres such as the 'spy-balloon' in the US or the 'spy-ship' in Sri Lanka, which led to enormous attention in Washington and New Delhi, are parallels. While Washington has doubled its containment strategy against Chinese belligerent behaviour, Sri Lanka will be subject to considerable attention in the strategic circle in Washington. India's focus on China in its immediate southern periphery, where wind power projects in the north of Sri Lanka were replaced by India,[44] and Chinese engagement in the fisheries sector of Sri Lanka[45] will lead to considerable attention from New Delhi's security circle.

The Biden administration's NSS and Indo-Pacific strategies aim to contain China's aggressive behaviour in the different geographical theatres. The 2014 Chinese submarine visit to Sri Lanka, followed by infrastructure lease acquisitions in Hambantota Port for 99 years in 2017 and obtaining the Colombo port city special economic zone were opaque and non-transparent agreements without proper consultation and due diligence and they attracted considerable US attention. The protestors also questioned not only the US but also the long-term strategic intent of the Chinese during the 2022 uprising. Corruption is another factor that has been a concern in Chinese projects raised by Sri Lankan policymakers and the public. When some projects were suspended, the government did not have the strength to continue with the investigations due to China's financial entanglement and considerable political influence. It was Wickremasinghe, the present president who was the prime minister back then, who suspended the Chinese projects and, months after, resumed the same projects.

Lu highlighted the association of China to the present economic crisis at the Sub-committee on Asia, the Pacific, Central Asia and Non-proliferation when he pointed out that "the economic collapse in Sri Lanka owes its origins in parts to the predatory loans by China".[46] Beyond the Chinese projects being a cause for the economic collapse in Sri Lanka, the unsustainable loans with high-interest rates, such as 6.5 percent for some loans in Hambantota Port, also added to the crisis. The expected financial returns were minimal to almost nothing, such as in the case of the Mattala Rajapaksa International Airport, known as the world's emptiest airport.[47] A more important concern for the economic crisis was the financial mismanagement and ill policy prescription adopted by Gotabaya's autocratic regime, which was reluctant to get international assistance. Sri Lanka's ill-advised ultra-nationalist inward policy prescription was evident when the government decided to wait and do nothing until its foreign reserves were depleted to near zero; this is perhaps the only country in the recent past that did not seek international assistance, such as from the IMF, at a crucial juncture just before the crisis erupted. The regime transformed its narrative and projected the IMF and Western intervention as a danger to sovereignty. The same narrative was used to push out many important projects, such as a US grant of US$480 million from the Millennium Challenge Corporation,[48] the Japanese Light Rail Transit (LRT) project and the tripartite India, Japan and Sri Lanka's East Container Terminal (ECT).

However, the past seemingly irrational position on the US, Japan and India has changed with Wickremasinghe's presidency. In June 2022, the

Sri Lankan cabinet approved a grant of US$57 million for a project by USAID, with a project period of 2026. The USAID programme will focus on capacity building for a 'Democratic, Prosperous Sri Lanka with the Ability to Survive Amidst Disasters'.[49] The programme will look at democratic governance, growth based on a secure market and strengthening the resources required to sustain pressure and stress. The new administration also positively revisited Japan's LRT project when Japan's Ambassador to Sri Lanka, Hideaki Mizukoshi, mentioned to Wickremasinghe's Senior Adviser, Ruwan Wijewardena, that "as soon as the Sri Lankan government has reached an agreement with the IMF, the project can be implemented again".[50] During the official visit to Japan in May 2023, Wickremesinghe expressed his regret to the Japanese government for the suspension of the LRT project by his predecessor and pledged to recommence the project.[51] India was also assured the continuation of the port project in Sri Lanka with a shift from the ECT to the West Container Terminal at the same port with an investment of US$700 million from India's Adani group. Sri Lankan Foreign Minister, Mohamed Uvais Mohamed Ali Sabry, explained that the port deal with Adani is like a "government-to-government kind of deal" — a clear indication that the Wickremasinghe government is ready to strengthen bilateral relations with India.[52]

The positive posture towards the US, Japan and India by the Wickremasinghe government indicates a drastic shift from Gotabaya's earlier hard-line position. The change from Gotabaya's anti-US position to Wickremasinghe's pro-US stance could be assessed from the positive trajectory developed in a short time by Wickremasinghe due to his political maturity. The West had possibly established trust with Wickremasinghe's commitments when he was five times prime minister. However, the present duality of the regime and how long the new model can be sustained is also a concern to the West, since Wickremasinghe is aligned with Gotabaya's political faction.

The acceptance of American assistance in strengthening democracy and good governance is an initial step to recalibrating the lost US confidence and rebalance China's strong influence in the island nation. The US holds the policy view that countries like Sri Lanka require assistance to minimise China's growing impact due to Colombo's incapacity to manage Chinese pressure. Wickremasinghe understands the delicate balance he would need to achieve with the US, India and China to navigate the economic challenges at a critical juncture where assistance is required from all quarters.

The risky China tilt that the Gotabaya regime presented threatened Colombo's balanced foreign policy and crippled the economy. Balancing the Chinese is an opportunity for Wickremasinghe to prove his ability in foreign policy management and in re-engaging the US and the West — an important indicator that he is able to lead the nation better than his predecessor.

However, the Gotabaya shadow, with his party having a majority in the parliament, will have earlier ultra-nationalist sentiments in the government's political ideology, which the president must navigate cautiously. Balancing foreign policy and domestic politics will stabilise Sri Lanka until the next election. However, the US will need to work with all political leaders during the interim period. There is a high possibility of a victor of the opposition, Samagi Jana Balawegaya and National People's Power, a leftist party, at the local election — this will be a trendsetter for the next presidential and parliamentary election.

Conclusion

The people's uprising in 2022 created an open space for the US to push its foreign policy agenda in Sri Lanka. The vacuum occurred with the ousting of an autocratic family rule, with the US making an immediate appeal for reforms to redemocratise the nation. Biden's policy to win back Sri Lanka was executed through multiple strategies. The core of Biden's policy is on rebuilding democracy, an initiative propelled from the early days of the US administration by initiatives, such as the Summit of Democracy. Rebuilding democracy was integrated into the Biden foreign policy agenda to firmly ally with like-minded democratic partners and target autocratic and repressive regimes. In Sri Lanka, the US' foreign policy to build and strengthen democracy was executed through USAID. The new Sri Lankan leader, a close ally of the US, has agreed to introduce various reforms resetting the previous autocratic sentiments, especially China's influence on the island. The US will work on a human rights and reconciliation agenda and push for political reforms to introduce devolution of power for the minority community. New Delhi has already communicated to Colombo its intention of prioritising the devolution of power — the

13th Amendment. Wickremasinghe's position to fully implement the 13th Amendment was expressed.

On the geopolitical front, while US–China tension has intensified throughout the term of the Biden administration, the US bi-partisan consensus has been to identify China as a direct threat to its national security. Considerable attention to China's aggressive behaviour in different geographies, including Sri Lanka, is considered a threat to American foreign and national security policies. The US administration accepts Wickremasinghe's progressive reforms. However, Washington will need to work with all political leaders during the interim period until the next election. In the coming months, the US will double its efforts in Sri Lanka to sustain a more pro-US position, assisting with economic stability, democracy, human rights, fighting corruption and enhancing security.

Endnotes

1. Heather Chen, "Sri Lanka crisis: How do you fix a broken country?", *CNN*, 16 July 2022, https://www.cnn.com/2022/07/15/asia/sri-lanka-crisis-economy-fix-gotabaya-rajapaksa-saturday-intl-hnk/index.html.
2. PTI, "US Delegation Meets Sri Lankan President Rajapaksa: Discusses Economic Crisis", *Outlook India*, 27 June 2022, https://www.outlookindia.com/international/us-delegation-meets-sri-lankan-president-rajapaksa-discusses-economic-crisis-news-205005.
3. "Readout: Secretary of the Treasury Janet L. Yellen's Call with Sri Lankan President Ranil Wickremesinghe", U.S. Department of the Treasury, 6 March 2023, https://home.treasury.gov/news/press-releases/jy1322.
4. Asoka Bandarage, "IMF Led Privatization, Land and Resource Grab in Sri Lanka", *Critical Asian Studies*, 20 December 2022, https://criticalasianstudies.org/commentary/2022/12/20/commentary-asoka-bandarage-imf-led-privatization-land-and-resource-grab-in-sri-lanka.
5. "2020 Marks A Successful Year For Sri Lanka Exports", Sri Lanka Economic Development Board, 20 January 2021, https://www.srilankabusiness.com/news/2020-marks-a-successful-year-for-sri-lanka-exports.html.
6. "Market And Country Brief: United States of America 2022", Sri Lanka Economic Development Board, 2022, https://www.srilankabusiness.com/pdfs/market-profiles/2022/usa-2022.pdf.

7. "US President extends warm wishes to Sri Lanka on its 75th Anniversary of Independence", Presidential Secretariat, 3 February 2023, https://www.presidentsoffice.gov.lk/index.php/2023/02/03/us-president-extends-warm-wishes-to-sri-lanka-on-its-75th-anniversary-of-independence/.
8. Bharatha Mallawarachi, "Senior US officials visit Sri Lanka to help resolve crisis", *AP News*, 27 Jun 2022, https://apnews.com/article/politics-asia-economy-sri-lanka-fbf25f19499c9912708adaa58a1f9dea.
9. *Ibid.*
10. Donald Lu, "Testimony on U.S.-India Relations SFRC Subcommittee on the Near East, South Asia, Central Asia, and Counterterrorism", U.S. Foreign Senate, 2 March 2022, https://www.foreign.senate.gov/imo/media/doc/030222_Lu_Testimony.pdf.
11. "National Security Strategy 2022", *The White House*, 2023, https://www.whitehouse.gov/wp-content/uploads/2022/10/Biden-Harris-Administrations-National-Security-Strategy-10.2022.pdf.
12. "Military and Security Developments Involving the People's Republic of China, 2021", Annual Report to the Congress, Office of Secretary of Defence, United States, 2021, https://media.defense.gov/2021/Nov/03/2002885874/-1/-1/0/2021-CMPR-FINAL.PDF.
13. *Ibid.*
14. "US Under Secretary of State Victoria Nuland in Sri Lanka", *News First*, 1 February 2023, https://www.newsfirst.lk/2023/02/01/us-under-secretary-of-state-victoria-nuland-in-sri-lanka/.
15. "U.S. Relations With Sri Lanka — Bilateral Relations Fact Sheet", Bureau of South and Central Asian Affairs, The State Department, United States, 21 June 2022, https://www.state.gov/u-s-relations-with-sri-lanka/.
16. Uditha Devapriya, "In Sri Lanka, Opposition Parties Allege a Secret CIA Visit", *The Diplomat,* 9 March 2023, https://thediplomat.com/2023/03/in-sri-lanka-opposition-parties-allege-a-secret-cia-visit/.
17. "Ambassador Mahinda Samarasinghe addressed the members of the Cosmos Club and invitees" Embassy of Sri Lanka in the United States, https://www.youtube.com/watch?v=QW4RCy8XF10.
18. "U.S. Relations With Sri Lanka — Bilateral Relations Fact Sheet", *op. cit.*
19. Mira Srinivasan, "Expect China-style development for Sri Lanka: Gotabaya", *The Hindu*, 9 October 2020, https://www.thehindu.com/news/international/expect-china-style-development-for-sri-lanka-gotabaya/article32816165.ece.
20. "Xi Jinping Speaks with Sri Lankan President Gotabaya Rajapaksa on the Phone", Ministry of Foreign of the People's Republic of China, 29 March

2021, https://www.fmprc.gov.cn/mfa_eng/gjhdq_665435/2675_665437/2782_663558/2784_663562/202103/t20210330_9168772.html.
21. Asanga Abeyagoonasekera, *Teardrop Diplomacy: China's Sri Lanka Foray* (New Delhi: Bloomsbury 2023), https://www.bloomsbury.com/in/teardrop-diplomacy-9789356401174/.
22. Anbarasan Ethirajan, "Duminda Silva: Anger as Sri Lanka frees politician sentenced for murder", *BBC*, 26 June 2021, https://www.bbc.com/news/world-asia-57608573.
23. Easwaran Rutnam, "Democracy summit: US snubs Sri Lanka", *Daily Mirror*, 25 November 2021, https://www.dailymirror.lk/front_page/Democracy-summit-US-snubs-Sri-Lanka/238-225483.
24. Sachini Perera, "When the Pandemic is a Portal to Militarization", *Groundviews*, 30 May 2020, https://groundviews.org/2020/05/30/when-the-pandemic-is-a-portal-to-militarization/.
25. "Fired Sri Lanka minister says removal a blessing, symbolic of economic mismanagement", *Economy Next*, 4 January 2022, https://economynext.com/fired-sri-lanka-minister-says-removal-a-blessing-symbolic-of-economic-mismanagement-89311/.
26. "Dekleptification Guide: Seizing Windows of Opportunity to Dismantle Kleptocracy", U.S. Agency for International Development, September 2022, https://www.usaid.gov/sites/default/files/2023-02/USAID-Dekleptification-Guide.pdf.
27. Rathindra Kuruvita, "Sri Lankan President Pledges Full Implementation of 13th Amendment", *The Diplomat*, 6 February 2023, https://thediplomat.com/2023/02/sri-lankan-president-pledges-full-implementation-of-13th-amendment/.
28. "British MP calls for international arrest warrant against Gotabaya Rajapaksa", *FirstPost*, 14 July 2022, https://www.firstpost.com/world/british-mp-calls-for-international-arrest-warrant-against-gotabaya-rajapaksa-10908881.html.
29. "Self-determination and justice for the Tamil people in Sri Lanka", Tamil Americans United, 22 January 2023, https://twitter.com/Tamils_Action/status/1618436324499030016?s=20.
30. "Sri Lanka agrees to co-sponsor UNHRC resolution: US", *Business Standard*, 16 March 2017, https://www.business-standard.com/article/pti-stories/sri-lanka-agrees-to-co-sponsor-unhrc-resolution-us-117031600751_1.html.
31. "Combating Global Corruption and Human Rights Abuses", US Department of State, 9 December 2022, https://www.state.gov/combating-global-corruption-and-human-rights-abuses/.

32. "Report on Attacks against Journalists in Sri Lanka", Center for Justice and Accountability, 9 February 2021, https://cja.org/what-we-do/litigation/wickrematunge-v-rajapaksa/advocacy/.
33. Meera Srinivasan, "India did not wait, did what was right to help Sri Lanka: Jaishankar", *The Hindu*, 20 January 2023, https://www.thehindu.com/news/national/india-did-not-wait-for-others-did-what-was-right-for-sri-lankas-recovery-eam-jaishankar/article66412365.ece.
34. "India urges devolution, China alleges politicization", *The Morning*, 7 June 2023, https://www.themorning.lk/articles/218203.
35. *Ibid.*
36. P. K. Balachandran, "Sri Lankan Tamils seek pruning of Governor's powers", *NewsIn Asia*, 14 February 2023, https://newsin.asia/sri-lankan-tamils-seek-pruning-of-governors-powers/.
37. Zulfick Farzan, "US wants Sri Lanka to go ahead with elections", *NewsFirst*, 1 February 2023, https://www.newsfirst.lk/2023/02/01/us-wants-sri-lanka-to-go-ahead-with-elections/.
38. "2021 Country Reports on Human Rights Practices: Sri Lanka", US Department of State, 2021, https://www.state.gov/reports/2021-country-reports-on-human-rights-practices/sri-lanka/.
39. "Sri Lanka: Reject New Counter-Terrorism Bill", Human Rights Watch, 7 April 2023, https://www.hrw.org/news/2023/04/07/sri-lanka-reject-new-counterterrorism-bill.
40. "2022 National Defence Strategy of the United States of America", U.S. Departmentr of Defense, 27 October 2022, https://media.defense.gov/2022/Oct/27/2003103845/-1/-1/1/2022-National-Defense-Strategy-Npr-Mdr.Pdf.
41. "National Security Strategy 2022", *The White House*, 2023, *op. cit.*
42. Yvette Tan, "Chinese 'spy ship' Yuan Wang 5 docks in Sri Lanka despite Indian concern", *BBC*, 16 August 2022, https://www.bbc.com/news/world-asia-62558767.
43. Meera Srinivasan and Ananth Krishnan, "Chinese vessel reaches Sri Lanka's Hambanthota port", *The Hindu*, 16 August 2022, https://www.thehindu.com/news/international/chinese-vessel-reaches-sri-lankas-hambantota-port/article65774283.ece.
44. Meera Srinivasan, "Indian power projects replace Chinese ventures in Sri Lanka", *The Hindu*, 29 March 2022, https://www.thehindu.com/news/international/indian-power-project-replaces-chinese-venture-in-sri-lankas-northern-islands/article65269733.ece.

45. Asanga Abeyagoonasekera, "The baneful existance of Chinese cucumber farms in Sri Lanka", Monographic Series, Washington DC: The Millennium Project, South Asia Foresight Network, 2023, https://southasiaforesight.org/safn-monographic-series-volume-1-2023-2/.
46. "Strengthening U.S. Engagement in Central Asia", U.S. House Foreign Affairs Committee Democrats, 2022, https://www.youtube.com/watch?v=CKOml8h1vm4.
47. Wade Shepard, "The story behind worlds emptiest international airport", *Forbes*, 28 May 2016, https://www.forbes.com/sites/wadeshepard/2016/05/28/the-story-behind-the-worlds-emptiest-international-airport-sri-lankas-mattala-rajapaksa/?sh=317bf80c7cea.
48. "Do not recommend Sri Lanka signing MCC in its current state: review committee chair", *EconomyNext*, 3 July 2020, https://economynext.com/do-not-recommend-sri-lanka-signing-mcc-in-its-current-state-review-committee-chair-71661/.
49. P. K. Balachandran, "Economic Crisis Forces Sri Lanka to Shed Fears and Move Closer to US, Middle East", *The Diplomat*, 6 July 2022, https://thediplomat.com/2022/07/economic-crisis-forces-sri-lanka-to-shed-fears-and-move-closer-to-us-middle-east/.
50. "Japan willing to reconsider restarting halted projects including LRT project, President's senior adviser says", *ColomboPage*, 10 December 2022, http://www.colombopage.com/archive_22B/Dec10_1670695087CH.php.
51. "President apologizes to the Japanese Government over the termination of the Colombo Light Rail Transit (LRT) project", *Sunday Island Online*, 26 May 2023, https://island.lk/president-apologizes-to-the-japanese-government-over-the-termination-of-the-colombo-light-rail-transit-lrt-project/.
52. Suhashini Haidar, "Adani project is like a government-to-government deal, says Sri Lankan FM: Sri Lankan Foreign Minister Ali Sabry", *The Hindu*, 5 March 2023, https://www.thehindu.com/news/international/adani-investment-has-come-in-we-are-not-panicking-about-projects-sri-lankan-foreign-minister-ali-sabry/article66583333.ece.

Chapter 9

The United States and the Maldives: Setting Strategic Ties

Amit Ranjan

As a small archipelago located at a strategic point in the Indian Ocean, the Maldives has become an important country for the United States (US) in the latter's pursuit of its strategic objectives in the Indo-Pacific region. Highlighting the significance of Malé, the US' country report on the Maldives states, "With the growing importance of the Maldives in the broader Indo-Pacific strategy, it is a priority to open a mission in the country. Having a physical presence in the country will provide a more effective platform for furthering our interests in Maldives, allow us [the US] to better execute our strategic objectives, and facilitate the deepening of people-to-people ties".[1] Then, the 2019 Indo-Pacific strategy report underlined:

> Following the recent democratic transition in the Maldives [in 2018], the United States has begun to explore avenues to expand security cooperation, with particular emphasis on providing capacity-building opportunities to the Maldives National Defence Forces and Maldivian Coast Guard. Key areas of focus include maritime domain awareness [MDA] — to enable [the] Maldivian forces...to monitor and patrol its sovereign maritime area and contribute to regional efforts to protect sea lines of communication; HA/DR [High Availability/Disaster Recovery readiness; and counter-terrorism capability.[2]

In recent years, at least, Washington has primarily taken the lead in strengthening bilateral ties with Malé. The Maldives has reacted positively and welcomed the US' initiatives. Before the US, during President Abdulla Yameen's term (2013–2018) in the Maldives, China was an important partner of the island country. Much before the US and China made their forays into the Maldives, India was Malé's main economic aid and "net security" provider. India felt marginalised during Yameen's presidency. However, after Yameen lost the 2018 presidential elections, India regained its lost position in the Maldives. Since 2018, the Maldivian government, under Ibrahim Mohamed Solih, has been pursuing an "India First" policy, while the opposition parties are focused on an "India Out" campaign.

This chapter examines the reasons for powerful states and small nations interacting with each other. In examining the US' engagements with the Maldives, mostly theories from the realist school are used as they largely underline Washington's foreign policy.[3] This chapter then analyses US–Maldives bilateral ties and how these impact New Delhi and Beijing in different ways. This chapter primarily argues that the US' policy towards the Maldives is aimed at checking the increase in Chinese assertiveness in the Indo-Pacific region. Second, this chapter contends that India welcomes American strategic presence in the Maldives, mainly because it believes Washington can help New Delhi overcome the "Chinese challenge" in the Indo-Pacific region, South Asia and along its border. Unlike India, Beijing has countered charges made by Washington against it and has taken measures to renew ties with Malé.

The US' Engagement with the Maldives: Theoretical Underpinnings

Theoretically, major powers ally with other countries to balance their adversary(ies). The balance of power is core to the classical realism and neorealist theory. The balance can be internal by increasing economic capability, developing strategies and increasing military power. External balancing occurs when the state forms alliances to counter status quoists or revisionist states.[4] Modifying the balance of power, Stephen M. Walt argues that states pursue policies to balance threats. Alliance formation is determined by the threat perceived by the member states.[5] During the Cold War years (1948–1991), both the US and the erstwhile Soviet Union established close ties with strategically located small countries to gain the upper hand against the other. The small states accepted the invitation to join one or the other blocks because of political, economic and ideological reasons. As anticipated by Kenneth N. Waltz, realism retains its significance as nothing much has changed in the system in the post-Cold War days.[6] A few years after the end of the Cold War, the US discovered a new rival — China. Now, to fulfil its objectives, the US is allying with like-minded countries to balance and counter Beijing.

In the post-Cold War era, Washington's Indo-Pacific strategy has slowly changed from engaging with China to checking its assertion in the region and globally.[7] Such policy changes result from increasing rivalry in the face of clashes of political and economic interests between the US and China. During Donald Trump's presidency (2017–2021), China and the US entered into a trade war over tariffs and other trade economic measures adopted by Washington. The Chinese saw it as an act of engaging in protectionist policies and took retaliatory measures. In the face of the trade war, the US enhanced its strategic measures to check and counter China's presence in various parts of the world, including the Indo-Pacific region.

The US' objective in the Indo-Pacific region under President Joe Biden's administration is largely a continuation of policies pursued by the Trump administration. The 2019 Indo-Pacific strategy stated:

> As China continues its economic and military ascendance, it seeks Indo-Pacific regional hegemony in the near-term and ultimately global pre-eminence in the long-term…These actions endanger the free flow of trade, threaten the sovereignty of other nations and undermine regional stability. Such activities are inconsistent with the principles of a free and open Indo-Pacific.[8]

The strategy report also mentioned Russia's efforts to use economic, diplomatic and military means to achieve influence in the Indo-Pacific region. Likewise, the Indo-Pacific strategy, published in February 2022, mentioned the following:

> Under President Biden, the United States is determined to strengthen our long-term position in and commitment to the Indo-Pacific…This intensifying American focus is due in part to the fact that the Indo-Pacific

faces mounting challenges, particularly from the PRC [People's Republic of China]…The PRC's coercion and aggression spans the globe, but it is most acute in the Indo-Pacific…Our collective efforts over the next decade will determine whether the PRC succeeds in transforming the rules and norms that have benefitted the Indo-Pacific and the world…Our objective is not to change the PRC but to shape the strategic environment in which it operates, building a balance of influence in the world that is maximally favourable to the United States, our allies and partners, and the interests and values we share.[9]

Unlike powerful states, for James N. Rosenau, small states are more vulnerable to the vagaries of the international system.[10] To deal with their vulnerabilities, realists feel that small states usually follow two strategies — balancing the threat by allying with a powerful state or collecting medium or small-sized states or bandwagoning with a powerful state that threatens the small state.[11] Balancing is in contrast to bandwagoning.[12] Balancing is a costly activity in which most states would not like to engage, but they do to survive and protect their values. Unlike balancing, bandwagoning rarely involves any cost and is done with the expectation of possible gains. States bandwagon to make profits at the expense of their autonomy and to explore opportunities to engage with bigger powers.[13]

There are two main forms of bandwagoning. The first — jackal bandwagoning — is for profit. In this form, revisionist states bandwagon to share in the spoils of victory. The second is piling-on bandwagoning, which occurs after a war when the states typically bandwagon with the victor to claim an unearned share of the spoils.[14] Some small countries also believe in hedging, a mix of confrontational and cooperative elements.[15] Hedging is essentially a combination of balancing and bandwagoning.[16] Alyson J. K. Bailes, Bradley A. Thayer and Baldur Thorhallsson observed that many small states prefer to ally with big powers seeking "shelter" for external and domestic reasons.[17] In matters of foreign policy, small states have limited options.[18] Despite their limitations, small states have significance in power politics for various reasons, such as strategic location, ideology and resources, among others. Therefore, as Robert O. Keohane underscored, like bigger states, small states are important constituents of the international system; hence, they must also be studied carefully.[19]

There is no universally agreed definition of a small country or small state. In the past, attempts to define small states have included geographical size, population size and a country's degree of influence in international affairs.[20] Considering factors such as geographical size and features, population size and gross domestic product (GDP), the Maldives fits the definition of a small state.[21] The Maldives is an archipelago of 1,192 coral islands (or about 1,200 islands), of which only one-sixth are inhabited by the country's 569,871 people (in 2023).[22] The Maldives's GDP is likely to reach US$5.75 billion in 2023.[23]

As a small country, the Maldives has no power ambition. The island state has entered into close ties with regional powers, mainly for economic and political reasons and to find solutions to the environmental crisis causing an existential threat to the country. There is also no big conventional security-related threat to the Maldives. India takes care of whatever little threat, mainly internal, faced by the Maldives. For example, in 1988, an attempt was made to oust President M. Maumoon Abdul Gayoom from power with the help of mercenaries. The Indian military carried out Operation Cactus to clear Malé of the mercenaries. Then, in 2013, former president, Mohamed Nasheed, after being thrown out of power in 2012 and with the court ordering his arrest, took refuge in the Indian High Commission in Malé. He left the High Commission after a deal was made between the Maldivian government and him.[24] India has also helped the Maldives to deal with natural disasters. For example, in December 2004, after a tsunami struck the Maldives, India was the first country to come forward with relief materials and aid to Malé. India provided an initial budgetary support of US$1.18 million to meet the country's tsunami-related challenges.[25] Then, in 2014, at the request of the Maldivian government, India swiftly supplied drinking water to Malé, which faced a water crisis due to the breakdown of the Reverse Osmosis water plant. Within 12 hours, the Indian Air Force deployed three C-17 and three IL-76 aircrafts that airlifted packaged water from New Delhi to Arakkonam and then to Malé. Under Operation Neer (Water) between 5 and 7 September 2014, the Indian Air Force supplied 374 tonnes of drinking water to Malé. In addition, two Indian ships — INS Deepak and INS Shukanya — supplied around 2,000 tonnes of water to meet the water-related demands of residents in Malé.[26] Besides India, China has also extended help to the Maldives to meet challenges posed by natural disasters. In the last few years, India has provided economic assistance and competed with China in helping the Maldives.

Hence, Malé does not really need the US for economic assistance and security against threats. The US–Maldives relationship is mainly driven by Washington's desire to counter China in the Indo-Pacific region. The next section examines recent developments in the US–Maldives relationship.

The US–Maldives Relations in Recent Years

One of the most talked about events between the US and the Maldives in recent years is the signing of the framework for defence and security relationship on 10 September 2020. A media release by the US Department of Defense stated, "The framework sets forth both countries' intent to deepen engagement and cooperation in support of maintaining peace and security in the Indian Ocean".[27] The two countries also agreed to work towards scheduling the first defence and security dialogue between them.[28] They also reiterated their respective countries' commitment to a free and open Indo-Pacific region that promotes the security and prosperity of all nations in the region.[29]

Earlier, to deepen their strategic relations, in 2013, the US and the Maldives agreed on a draft of the Status of Forces Agreement (SOFA). Some of the provisions of that draft were leaked out.[30] Journalist Azra Naseem saw the contents, which were published on the Maldivian current affairs blog, *Dhivehi Sitee*. It included the following:[31]

(a) The US would have unfettered access to, and use of, not just the military facility (or facilities) to be established but also over all Maldivian aerial ports and seaports for whatever purpose it wants.
(b) The designated areas agreed between the Maldives and the US would be sealed off for "exclusive use by the US forces".
(c) The US would have the authority to secure "the vicinity" around the island(s) in whatever way the US deems is necessary for [the] safety [of] Americans.

(d) The US personnel based in [the] Maldives would have all diplomatic privileges, exemptions and immunities equivalent to that offered by the Vienna Convention.
(e) US vehicles and vessels would be free to move within all Maldivian territory and territorial seas as they wish. US aircrafts and vessels could not be boarded and inspected.
(f) All Maldivian ports and the designated facilities and areas can be used for anything from transit and training to humanitarian activities and "such other purposes" as the Maldives and the US agree.
(g) The US would be free to construct, alter and improve various structures and hire contractors. With few exceptions, [the] contractors will enjoy all privileges and exemptions given to US military personnel.
(h) The US will initially have the designated area(s) for 10 years and will continue automatically unless the SOFA is terminated by one party with one year's notice.
(i) Disputes have to be settled exclusively through negotiation between the two parties.

Many in the Maldives saw the SOFA as an attempt by the Mohamed Waheed Hassan government (2012–2013) to allow the US to set up a military base in the country. This was refuted by Defence Minister Colonel (Retired) Mohamed Nazim, who continued his position in the next government under Yameen. In an interview with *Sunonline* in April 2013, Nazim said that the SOFA "does not involve establishing a base".[32] However, as opposition mounted against the SOFA, the newly elected government of Yameen did not further pursue the agreement proposed by the US.[33] A minister at the President's Office, Mohamed Shareef, stated, "We have told them [the US] that we can't do it because both India and Sri Lanka are also not happy with it".[34]

The second important development in the relationship between the US and the Maldives was a visit by US Secretary of State, Michael R. Pompeo, to the Maldives in October 2020. The US and the Maldives established diplomatic relations in 1965. In July 1992, US Secretary, James Addison Baker, while on his way to the Philippines, made a stop on the island country. Twelve years later, in July 2004, US Secretary of State Colin Powell visited the Maldives. During his meeting with Solih, Pompeo spoke about the US plans to open a resident embassy in the

Maldives for the first time since the establishment of diplomatic relations. In an exclusive interview with Aishath Shaany of *Raajje TV*, Pompeo said, "We announced today that we'll have a US embassy here, which we're very excited about. The first time in history that we'll have a permanently stationed American diplomat here to continue to build out what's been a really important security relationship, an important diplomatic relationship, and of course, a deep economic relationship between our two countries as well".[35] During his interview, Pompeo was critical of China's role in the Maldives and in the region. He said, "If you look at what China, for example, has done, it's the biggest polluter in the region. It presents the greatest threat to the people of [the] Maldives and their economy. If you want to look to the greatest risk for increasing the amount of CO_2 in the air, you need to look no further than Beijing and its surrounding environments".[36] In a press conference, Pompeo added, "Your [the Maldives's] role here in the Indo-Pacific and in the international community is increasingly important".[37]

A year after Pompeo's visit to Malé, US Assistant Secretary of State for South and Central Asia Donald Lu was in the Maldives. In an exclusive interview with *Raajje TV*, Lu said that the US–Maldives relationship has "never been better" and this is a "wonderful time to be working on so many different things together", including climate change, COVID-19 response, military cooperation and counterterrorism cooperation. Regarding the opening of the US embassy in Malé, Lu said that "his visit goes hand in hand with this".[38] In July 2022, Biden nominated Hugo Yue-Ho Yon as Ambassador Extraordinary and Plenipotentiary to the Maldives. Interestingly, Hugo's profile shows that he has worked both in Beijing and New Delhi — he was Deputy Minister Councillor for Economic Affairs at the US embassy in New Delhi and Deputy Financial Attaché at the US embassy in Beijing.[39] However, the US embassy is yet to open in Malé. The Maldives also does not have an embassy in Washington. Its permanent representative to the United Nations in New York is accredited as its Ambassador to the US. When meeting with Abdul Ghafoor Mohamed, the Maldives's Ambassador to the US, during the presentation of credentials, Biden remarked, "[The] Maldives has emerged both as a regional and global leader on climate, democracy and security".[40]

During the ceremony, Mohamed noted the progress made in the establishment of the US embassy in the Maldives in 2022.

The US increasing ties with the Maldives impact China and India. Hence, it is pertinent to understand New Delhi and Beijing's reactions to the strengthening US–Maldives ties. The next section analyses India's supportive stance on the US initiatives in the Maldives and China's adverse reaction, in view of the US–Maldives ties being part of the larger Indo-Pacific strategy to contain and check China in the region.

India, China and the US–Maldives Ties

The current political environment in South Asia has changed India's policy response to the US–Maldives defence ties. On condition of anonymity, an Indian official, privy to the developments on the SOFA in 2013, told the Indian media portal, *The Wire*, in 2020, "Yes, we [India] did discourage a SOFA in 2013 as it would have justified a similar agreement with China and an offer to us [India] as well, leaving an outcome that was less desirable than the existing state. And, in 2013, both [the US and Maldives] listened to us".[41] An Indian official told *The Hindu* that the "Indian embassy in Malé had been kept briefed about the negotiations and had been shown a copy of the two-page document signed…Neither of those objectives [agreed in the 2020 agreement] in any way impinges on India's role as a "net security provider" in the Indian Ocean and [they] are actually "complementary" to India's plans for the Indo-Pacific".[42] The same official added, "It is significant that the Maldives has taken a strategic position and signed this agreement with the US and not with China, despite the fact that it is part of [the] BRI [Belt and Road Initiative]".[43]

Unlike in 2013, India welcomed the September 2020 defence pact between the US and the Maldives because of the growing challenge from a militarily assertive China in the Indo-Pacific region, in South Asia and along its border.[44] There had been reports on the continuous transgressions by the People's Liberation Army (PLA) into Indian territory and over the India-controlled Line of Actual Control. According to Indian government data, between 2016 and 2018, there were 1,025 Chinese transgressions into Indian territory.[45] Even the Indian Army, as Indian Union Minister and former Army Chief, V. K. Singh, said, has transgressed Into Chinese territory more often than the PLA.[46] Such transgressions often create tensions along the border. In recent times, the military stand-off between India and China occurred in the Doklam trijunction. The trijunction borders China's Chumbi Valley to the north, Bhutan's Ha district to the east and the Indian state of Sikkim to the west.

On 28 August 2018, after 73 days of military stand-off at Doklam, India and China agreed on disengagement. About two years later, the military tensions between the two countries peaked in May–June 2020 when a "sizeable number" of Chinese troops entered Eastern Ladakh. On 15 June 2020, the PLA and soldiers from the Indian Army engaged in hand-to-hand fighting in which 20 Indian army personnel were killed with sharp weapons. Eight months after that clash, China acknowledged that four of its soldiers died while fighting with Indian army personnel in June 2020.[47] The two countries' armies also clashed in January 2021. Again, in September 2021, China accused India of firing shots at its border troops. At that time, India accused China of firing into the air. Then, in December 2022, despite military-level talks, Indian and Chinese troops clashed near the Twang sector of the Indian state of Arunachal Pradesh. Some soldiers were injured in that clash.[48]

In order to deal with the Chinese challenge, besides taking various measures, India has also further deepened ties with like-minded friendly countries such as the US, Japan and Australia. The Quadrilateral Security Dialogue was revitalised in 2017. The strong India–US relations can be sensed by the growing political engagement between New Delhi and Washington. Successive Indo-Pacific strategy reports have clearly mentioned the significance of India in the US' strategy in the Indo-Pacific region and Asia. Analysing India–US relations in recent years, former Indian Foreign Secretary and National Security Advisor Shivshankar Menon said during an online forum hosted by the Washington-based Carnegie Endowment for International Peace, more Indians would accept "doing things with the US, for the US, that actually US allies would do — without an alliance".[49] He also said that "the actual practice of interoperability, of taking on particular roles and of fitting into a larger common strategy — I don't see that being problematic today".[50]

The Maldives was not a very important country for China till 2011 and it did not even have an embassy in Malé prior to that. Chinese President Xi Jinping's visit to the Maldives in September 2014 remarkably changed the nature of their relations. In December 2014, Yameen signed a China-led maritime Silk Road connectivity project[51] and became a party to the BRI. In 2015, the Maldivian parliament enacted a law enabling foreigners to acquire land. Many political analysts saw the amendment in the land reform rules to primarily benefit China more than any other country that could buy land and set up a military base in the Maldives.[52] The opposition parties accused the Yameen government of planning to award parts of south-central Laamu Atoll to China to set up a military base.[53] Yameen dismissed any such accusations. In August 2017, three Chinse naval ships — Changchun, Jing Zhou and Chao Hu — harboured in Malé's commercial port.[54] Five months later, in December 2017, China and the Maldives decided to set up a Joint Ocean Observation Station, which the Maldivian opposition leaders claimed would be used for military purposes with a provision for even a submarine base. It was decided that the observatory would be set up at Makunudhoo.[55]

The Solih government, which was elected into power in 2018, discovered that the country was under severe debt, mainly due to large Chinese investments and loans taken under Yameen's term as the country's president. To help out, during Solih's visit to New Delhi in December 2018, India announced a US$1.4 billion loan to the Maldives to pay off its debt to China.[56]

Despite being out of favour during Solih's leadership, Beijing remains engaged with Malé. During the COVID-19 pandemic, China helped and provided aid materials to the Maldives.[57] After the visit by Pompeo to Malé, during which he made accusations against China, the Chinese embassy in the Maldives issued a statement that stated, "During his trip, Pompeo has tirelessly spread political rumours on China and instigated China–Maldives relationship...China's development is an opportunity, not a threat. Mutually beneficial cooperation between China and [the] Maldives is in line with the common interests of the two countries and will bring more benefits to both people".[58]

Later, in January 2022, Chinese Foreign Minister Wang Yi landed in Malé. Yi's visit was a part of his five-nation trip to Eritrea, Kenya,

Comoros, the Maldives and Sri Lanka.[59] During the visit, China and the Maldives signed five important agreements[60]:

(1) Agreement on Mutual Visa Exemption: This will allow Maldivians to travel to China on a 30-day visa-free basis once the pandemic restrictions are lifted.
(2) Agreement of Economic and Technical Cooperation on Grand Aid: This focuses on developing key areas such as social, livelihood and infrastructure projects. Under it, aid totalling US$62.63 million is to be used for projects agreed upon by both countries.
(3) A Letter of Exchange on the Feasibility Study of Management and Maintenance of China–Maldives Friendship Bridge.
(4) Supplementary Contract to the Implementation Contract for China-Aided Micro-Grid Sea-water Desalination Project in the Maldives.
(5) Agreement on Establishing a Hospital Assistance and Cooperation Programme between the Maldives's Ministry of Health and China's National Health Commission: Under this agreement, the services of a specialist Ophthalmic Centre in the Maldives have been extended for a further 2 years. The memorandum of understanding to establish this centre was signed in July 2021.

In Malé, Wang Yi said:

> China is willing to work with the Maldives to take the 50th anniversary of the establishment of diplomatic relations as an opportunity to implement the important consensus reached by the two heads of state, deepen China–Maldives traditional friendship, focus on post-pandemic recovery cooperation, work together to build the Belt and Road, and elevate the China–Maldives future-oriented comprehensive friendly partnership of cooperation to a new level for the benefit of the two countries and the two peoples.[61]

Explaining Wang Yi's visit to the Maldives, Chinese Ambassador to the Maldives, Wang Lixin, counted the following achievements[62]:

(1) It was "one important visit" as the two countries marked 50 years of their diplomatic relationship.

(2) The visit has achieved "two major goals" — reviewing and summarising the past and drawing a blueprint for the future.
(3) It has sent "three important messages". First, China has always supported the Maldives in safeguarding its sovereignty and territorial integrity through the pursuit of its independent foreign policy. Second, China, with down-to-earth actions, supports the Maldives in speeding up its socio-economic development and enhancing its capability for independent development. Third, in the 50th year, the two sides should take a broader view of their relations and open a new chapter of mutually beneficial and friendly cooperation.
(4) The visit specified "four key directions for future cooperation between the two countries", that is, first, to continue their cooperation in the fight against the pandemic; second, to continue to build the Belt and Road Initiative with high quality, accelerating cooperation on key projects and tourism, and promote the ratification and implementation of the China–Maldives Free Trade Agreement at an early date; third, to expand cooperation in emerging fields such as communication, digitisation and marine economy and back its efforts for the strategy of diversified development; and fourth, to strengthen coordination in international affairs and safeguard the international system centred on the United Nations.
(5) The two sides signed the four agreements mentioned above.

Conclusion

The US' initiatives to strengthen its bilateral ties with the Maldives, at least in recent years, is mainly to pursue its larger Indo-Pacific strategy in the region. The strategic location of the Maldives in the Indian Ocean gives the US an advantage in the Indo-Pacific region. As mentioned in various reports, the US' prime objective in the region is to check China's growing assertion and support friendly countries in dealing with Beijing. The Maldives has reacted positively to the US' initiatives because, as a small state, the Maldives needs political and economic support from a bigger power. Hence, ties with the US benefit Malé.

India and China have reacted differently to the US–Maldives ties. India has largely welcomed their relationship and sees it as a part of an effort by a friendly country to check China's growing interest in the Indo-Pacific region, South Asia and along its border. Unlike India, China has viewed the growing ties between Washington and Malé with criticism and assertions. It has also countered the US' assertions against it in the region. Despite the decline in Malé's engagement with Beijing following Solih's victory in the presidential elections in 2018, formal visits and bilateral interactions between the Maldives and China continue.

Endnotes

1. "Integrated country report: Maldives", US Department of State, March 2022, p. 6, https://www.state.gov/wp-content/uploads/2022/06/ICS_SCA_Maldives_Public.pdf.
2. "Indo-Pacific strategy report: Preparedness, partnerships, and promoting a networked region", US Department of Defense, 1 June 2019, p. 35, https://media.defense.gov/2019/Jul/01/2002152311/-1/-1/1/Department-Of-Defense-Indo-Pacific-Strategy-Report-2019.Pdf.
3. Stephen M. Walt, "The world wants you to think like a realist", *Foreign Policy*, 30 May 2018, https://foreignpolicy.com/2018/05/30/the-world-wants-you-to-think-like-a-realist/; Eric Posner, "America's return to realism", *Project Syndicate*, 3 September 2021, https://www.project-syndicate.org/commentary/america-return-to-foreign-policy-realism-by-eric-posner-2021-09; and Joshua Shifrinson and Stephen Wertheim, "Biden the realist", *Foreign Affairs*, 9 September 2021, https://www.foreignaffairs.com/articles/united-states/2021-09-09/biden-realist.
4. See Kenneth N. Waltz, *Theory of International Politics* (Massachusetts: Addison-Wesley Publishing Company, 1979), pp. 104–128.
5. Stephen M. Walt, *The Origins of Alliance* (New York: Cornell University Press, 1990).
6. See Kenneth N. Waltz, "Structural realism after the cold war", *International Security*, 2000, 25(1), 5–41.
7. "Indo-Pacific strategy report of the United States", The White House, February 2022, p. 5, https://www.whitehouse.gov/wp-content/uploads/2022/02/US-Indo-Pacific-Strategy.pdf.
8. "Indo-Pacific strategy report: Preparedness, partnerships, and promoting a networked region", US Department of Defense, 1 June 2019, p. 8, https://media.defense.gov/2019/Jul/01/2002152311/-1/-1/1/Department-Of-Defense-Indo-Pacific-Strategy-Report-2019.Pdf.

9. "Indo-Pacific Strategy Report of the United States", The White House, February 2022, p. 5, https://www.whitehouse.gov/wp-content/uploads/2022/02/US-Indo-Pacific-Strategy.pdf.
10. James N. Rosenau, "Pre-theories and theories of foreign policy", in *Classics of International Relations*, 2nd edn., John A. Vasquez and N. J. Englewood Cliffs (eds.) (New Jersey: Prentice Hall, 1966), pp. 164–175.
11. Azim Zahir, "India-China rivalry in the Indian Ocean: Emergence of a new Indo-Maldives strategic dynamic", *Journal of the Indian Ocean Region*, 2021, 17(78–95), 81.
12. Kenneth N. Waltz, *op. cit.*, p. 126.
13. Stephen M. Walt, *op. cit.*; and Kei Koga, "The concept of 'hedging' revisited: The case of Japan's foreign policy strategy in East Asia's power shift", *International Studies Review*, 2018, 20, 633–660, 637.
14. Randall L. Schweller, "Bandwagoning for profit: Bringing the revisionist state back", *International Security*, 1994, 19(1), 72–107 and 93–96.
15. John D. Ciorciari and Jurgen Haacke, "Hedging in international relations: An introduction", *International Relations of the Asia-Pacific*, September 2019, 19(3), 367–374, https://doi.org/10.1093/irap/lcz017.
16. Kei Koga, *op. cit.*, pp. 633–660.
17. Alyson J. K. Bailes, Bradley A. Thayer and Baldur Thorhallsson, "Alliance theory and alliance 'Shelter': The complexities of small state alliance behaviour", *Third World Thematics: A TWQ Journal*, 2016, 9–26.
18. Jeanne A. K. Hey, "Introducing small state foreign policy", in *Small States in World Politics: Explaining Foreign Policy Behaviour* (London: Lynne Rienner Publishers Inc., 2003), pp. 1–11; and Miriam Fendus Elman, "The foreign policies of small states: Challenging neorealism in its own backyard", *British Journal of Political Science*, April 1995, 25(2), 171–217.
19. Robert O. Keohane, "Lilliputians' Dilemmas: Small states in international politics", *International Organization*, 1969, 23(2), 291–310, 310.
20. Jeanne A. K. Hey, (2003), *op. cit.*
21. Azim Zahir, "India-China rivalry in the Indian Ocean: Emergence of a new Indo-Maldives strategic dynamic", *Journal of the Indian Ocean Region*, 2021, 17, 78–95, 81.
22. Maldives Population, *Worldometer*, https://www.worldometers.info/world-population/maldives-population/#:~:text=The%20current%20population%20of%20Maldives,the%20latest%20United%20Nations%20data.
23. "Maldives' GDP-2022 Data-2023 Forecast", *Trading Economics*, https://tradingeconomics.com/maldives/gdp#:~:text=GDP%20in%20Maldives%20is%20expected,according%20to%20our%20econometric%20models.

24. R. K. Radhakrishnan, "Nasheed leaves Indian embassy after 'deal'", *The Hindu*, 23 February 2013, https://www.thehindu.com/news/international/south-asia/nasheed-leaves-indian-embassy-after-deal/article4446333.ece.
25. "India-Maldives relations", Ministry of External Affairs, Government of India, December 2014, https://mea.gov.in/Portal/ForeignRelation/Maldives_December_2014.pdf.
26. "Operation Neer: Indian assistance to Maldives during Male water crisis", High Commission of India in the Maldives, https://hci.gov.in/male/?3840?003.
27. "The Maldives and US sign defense agreement", US Department of Defense, 11 September 2020, https://www.defense.gov/Newsroom/Releases/Release/Article/2344512/the-maldives-and-us-sign-defense-agreement/utm_campaign/digest/utm_medium/email/utm_source/nuzzel/.
28. Ibid.
29. Ibid.
30. Devirupa Mitra, "Seven years on, India now backs a defence pact between US and Maldives", *The Wire*, 13 September 2020, https://thewire.in/south-asia/seven-years-on-india-now-backs-a-defence-pact-between-the-us-and-maldives.
31. Azra Naseem, "A US military base in the Maldives?", *Dhivehi Sitee*, 24 April 2013, http://www.dhivehisitee.com/executive/us-military-base-maldives/. Also see "Agreement between the United States of America and the Republic of Maldives regarding Status of Forces and Access to and Use of Facilities in the Maldives", chrome-extension://efaidnbmnnnibpcajpcglclefindmkaj/https://www.dhivehisitee.com/images/US-Maldives-SOFA-draft.pdf.
32. "Maldives will not pursue defence agreement with US: President Yameen", *Sunonline*, 23 January 2014, https://en.sun.mv/19484.
33. Ibid.
34. Ibid.
35. "Secretary Michael R. Pompeo with Aishath Shaany of Raajje TV", *Raajje TV*, 28 October 2020, https://2017-2021.state.gov/secretary-michael-r-pompeo-with-aishath-shaany-of-raajje-tv/index.html.
36. Ibid.
37. "Pompeo says US will open embassy in Maldives for first time", *Reuters*, 28 October 2020, https://in.reuters.com/article/usa-asia-maldives/pompeo-says-us-will-open-embassy-in-maldives-for-first-time-idINL8N2HJ3LI.
38. Zunana Zalif, "Relationship between Maldives, US has 'never been better'", *Raajje TV*, 19 November 2021, https://raajje.mv/109712.

39. "President biden announces key nominees", *The White House*, 27 July 2022, https://www.whitehouse.gov/briefing-room/statements-releases/2022/07/27/president-biden-announces-key-nominees-26/.
40. "New Ambassador of Maldives, Abdul Ghafoor Mohamed, presents credentials to President Biden", *Gov. MV*, 13 December 2022, https://www.gov.mv/en/news-and-communications/new-ambassador-of-maldives-abdul-ghafoor-mohamed-presents-credentials-to-president-biden.
41. Devirupa Mitra, *op. cit.*
42. Suhasini Haidar, "India welcomes US–Maldives defence agreement", *The Hindu*, 14 September 2020, https://www.thehindu.com/news/national/india-welcomes-us-maldives-defence-agreement/article32601889.ece.
43. *Ibid.*
44. At least, there is no report of opposition in public. See Suhasini Haidar, *op. cit.*
45. "1025 Chinese transgressions reported from 2016 to 2018: Government data", *The Economic Times*, 28 November 2019, https://economictimes.indiatimes.com/news/defence/1025-chinese-transgressionsreported-from-2016-to-2018-government-data/articleshow/72262114.cms?from=mdr.
46. "India has transgressed LAC more often than China: V. K. Singh", *The Hindu*, 7 February 2021, https://www.thehindu.com/news/national/india-has-transgressed-into-lac-more-times-than-china-says-v-k-singh/article33774108.ece.
47. "China reveals four soldiers killed in June 2020 border clash with India", *Reuters*, 19 February 2021, https://www.reuters.com/article/us-china-india-border-idUSKBN2AJ04B.
48. "India-China dispute: The border row explained in 400 words", *BBC*, 14 December 2022, https://www.bbc.com/news/world-asia-53062484.
49. Cited in Matt Ho, "China-India border row: Risk of tangled ties if New Delhi looks to third parties, says expert", *South China Morning Post*, 23 September 2020, https://www.scmp.com/news/china/diplomacy/article/3102657/china-india-border-row-risk-tangled-ties-if-new-delhi-looks.
50. *Ibid.*
51. Devirupa Mitra, *op. cit.*
52. Sudha Ramachandran, "The China-Maldives connection", *The Diplomat*, 25 January 2018, https://thediplomat.com/2018/01/the-china-maldives-connection/.
53. Lia Xiaokun, "Land sale isn't for military purpose, says Maldives", *China Daily*, 25 July 2015, http://www.chinadaily.com.cn/world/2015-07-25/content_21404471.htm.

54. Shan Anees, "Three Chinese naval ships arrive in Male", *Raajje.mv*, 27 August 2017, https://raajje.mv/16679.
55. Sachin Prashar, "China's ocean observatory in Maldives sparks fresh security concerns", *The Times of India*, 26 February 2018, https://timesofindia.indiatimes.com/india/chinas-ocean-observatory-in-maldives-sparks-fresh-security-fear/articleshow/63072040.cms.
56. "Maldives dismisses reports of Indian military base in Malé in return for $1 billion aid", *The Times Now News.Com*, 30 November 2018, https://www.timesnownews.com/international/article/maldives-india-relationship-abdulla-shahid-china-ties-dismisses-reports-of-indian-military-base-in-male-in-return-for-1-billion-dollar-aid-president/323408.
57. See Amit Ranjan, "The Maldives response to COVID-19", *ISAS Brief No. 769*, 6 April 2020, Institute of South Asian Studies, National University of Singapore, https://www.isas.nus.edu.sg/papers/the-maldives-response-to-covid-19/.
58. "Statement of the Chinese Embassy in Maldives refuting China-related negative comments of US secretary of State Michael Pompeo during his visit to Maldives", Embassy of the People's Republic of China in the Republic of Maldives, 29 October 2020, http://mv.chineseembassy.org/eng/sgsd/t1827539.htm.
59. Meera Srinivasan, "Maldives, China ink key deals, agree on visa exemption", *The Hindu*, 8 January 2022, https://www.thehindu.com/news/international/maldives-china-ink-key-deals-agree-on-visa-exemption-visa-exemption/article38191082.ece.
60. "Maldives and China sign five agreements during official visit", Ministry of Foreign Affairs, Government of the Maldives, 8 January 2022, https://www.gov.mv/en/news-and-communications/maldives-and-china-sign-five-agreements-during-official-visit; and "Press Statement delivered by Foreign Minister Abdulla Shahid at the joint press conference with Chinese Foreign Minister Wang Yi", Ministry of Foreign Affairs, Government of the Maldives, 8 January 2022, https://www.gov.mv/en/news-and-communications/press-statement-delivered-by-foreign-minister-abdulla-shahid-at-the-joint-press-conference-with-chinese-foreign-minister-wang-yi.
61. "Wang Yi holds talks with Maldivian Foreign Minister Abdulla Shahid", Ministry of Foreign affairs of the People's Republic of China, 19 January 2022, https://www.fmprc.gov.cn/mfa_eng/topics_665678/kjgzbdfyyq/202201/t20220109_10480370.html.
62. "Embarking on a new journey and embracing a bright future", Embassy of the People's Republic of China in the Republic of the Maldives, 13 January 2022, http://mv.chineseembassy.org/eng/sgsd/202201/t20220113_10483554.htm.

© 2024 World Scientific Publishing Company Pte. Ltd.
https://doi.org/10.1142/9789811276439_0010

Chapter 10

Beyond Biden: India–United States Relations

S. D. Muni

Introduction

The United States's (US) foreign relations invariably carry a strong stamp of its president's personality. The personality of the US president, however, is institutionalised in the White House, which pursues its foreign policy moves in close coordination with other institutions, especially the US Department of Defense, the US State Department and the US Congress. These institutions take into account the global context of core American interests at a given point in time while formulating policy options. These institutions also factor in broader US business and social concerns. The US president can take a decision beyond the options presented to him, but he does so generally after weighing the options presented to him. Thus, the role of personality is invariably tempered by the institutional constraints of the US system.

This has been evident in several instances of the US' relations with India in the past. During the Cold War period, presidents like Dwight D. Eisenhower and John F. Kennedy wanted to be friendlier and accommodative towards India, including on issues related to Pakistan and China. However, the institutional constraints limited their options. During his visit to India in 1959, Eisenhower was prepared to consider India's unexpressed desire to resolve the Kashmir dispute by accepting the ceasefire line as the international boundary, but both the US State and Defense Departments were against it. President Ronald Reagan was open to building a robust relationship with India following Indian Prime Minister Indira Gandhi's meeting with him at Cancun, Mexico, in 1980 and her state visit to the US in 1982, but he could not do so due to domestic constraints.

The institutional constraints that led to a drift between the world's two big democracies started getting dissolved with the end of the Cold War. It took almost a decade of developments during the 1990s that underlined India's gradual rise — marked by economic opening and growth, and the declaration of nuclear status. The legacies of the drift period, however, continue to be reflected occasionally in contemporary engagements. For instance, US President Bill Clinton's first term saw an activist role of the US in the Kashmir issue, leading to the rise of the separatist organisation — the Hurriyat Conference. The Clinton presidency's approach towards India started changing, as evident in the case of Pakistan's aggression in Kargil in 1999, only following India's declaration of its status as a nuclear weapon state and the rising assertion of China against the US for Asian hegemony. Clinton's visit to India in 2000, during his second term, proved to be a landmark in changing the course of Indo-US relations. Clinton's successor, President George W. Bush, provided greater momentum to improving relations with India as the heat of Chinese assertion (recall the downing of a US spy plane by China in 2001) was being felt in Washington. Again, US President Barack Obama created a short-lived flutter in these relations when he sought cooperation and coordination with China in ensuring South Asian security during his China visit in 2009. Soon afterwards, the drift in Sino-US relations and the US announcement of a "rebalance in Asia" to contain China's assertive rise changed the course. Obama visited India twice in 2010 and 2015. In November 2009, while welcoming Indian Prime Minister Manmohan Singh to Washington, Obama projected the India–US relationship to be one of the "defining relationships of the 21st century" and his Secretary of Defense, Leon E. Pennetta, described India in 2012 as the "lynchpin" of American strategy in the Indo-Pacific region. The joint statement issued by Obama and Indian Prime Minister Narendra Modi during the latter's visit to the US in

June 2016 was captioned as 'The United States and India: Enduring Global Partners in the 21st Century'.[1] US President Donald Trump steadily built on the areas of cooperation between the two countries, and the current US President Joe Biden has carried on with the legacy of his predecessors.

Driving Forces

During the past nearly a quarter of a century, the US' approach towards India has shown a radical shift. Both at the official and public (media and policy analyst) levels, the bond of democracy is referred to generally as the driver of growing close relations between the two countries. The US, being the oldest, and India, being the largest, nay, 'mother of democracy' now, the ideological bond of democracy is no doubt a strong area of convergence. However, the role of the democracy factor in improving bilateral relations has, at best, been a debatable one. For more than 50 years, India's functioning democracy did not fit into the US' strategic priorities during the Cold War years. Pakistan, since the early 1950s, and China, during the 1970s through the 1990s, were seen as more useful allies and partners by US policymakers. The US did not see eye to eye with India on almost all Cold War-related issues. Even now, the US periodically expresses concern on democracy-related issues like human rights and religious freedom in India.[2] New Delhi has also been proclaiming its preference for democracy in foreign relations, but it has compromised on democracy issues whenever they came in conflict with its strategic interests.[3] A careful survey of the past two decades of US–India engagement suggests that this engagement has been driven by three factors other than democracy, namely, growing strategic convergence on the threat from an assertive China in the Indo-Pacific region, India's growing economic promise, and, finally, the rise of the Indo-American community within the US. These three factors, of which the strategic convergence has been the most important one, have been defining the Indo-US engagement and will possibly continue to do so irrespective of the political complexion and personality of the US president. Let us look at these factors in some detail.

Strategic Convergence on the Chinese Challenge

It has been noted earlier that Indo-US relations were characterised by a drift during the Cold War period. The shift in the US' approach towards India after the end of the Cold War was caused by two factors, namely, India's growing economic and strategic capabilities and the rise of an assertive China challenging the US' dominance in the Indo-Pacific region. Washington started realising that to face the Chinese challenge, there was an urgent need to recast the US' approach towards the region. In this change, the US' approach towards its own allies in the region such as Japan, Australia and Korea as well as the other major Asian players — India, Vietnam and the Association of Southeast Asian Nations — underwent redefinition. India was seen as a strategic anchor in the Indian Ocean that had both the capabilities and willingness to emerge as a strong counterbalance to China. Condoleezza Rice, before becoming US National Security Adviser under the Bush presidency in 2001, wrote in *Foreign Affairs*:

> What we do know is that China is a great power with unresolved vital interests…China resents the role of the Unites States in the Asia-Pacific region. This means that China is not a status-quo power but one that would like to alter Asia's balance of power in its own favor. That alone makes it a strategic-competitor and not a strategic-partner…China's success in controlling the balance of power depends in large part on America's reaction to the challenge. The United States must deepen its cooperation with Japan and South Korea and maintain its commitment to a robust military presence in the region. It should pay closer attention to India's role in regional balance…India is an element in China's calculation. And it should be in America's too.[4]

Subsequently, there were other strategic analysts and policymakers who also argued along these lines.[5] The idea of building Indian capabilities to balance rival China in the Indo-Pacific region has repeatedly been articulated and reinforced in the US National Security Strategy (NSS) documents released under successive presidencies, year after year since the beginning of this century. Biden has drawn from his predecessors on building and reinforcing the strategy of vigorously addressing the Chinese challenge through traditional allies and partners like India. The two latest documents released on the Indo-Pacific Strategy (February 2022) and the NSS (October 2022) clearly underline that. In these documents, the Chinese challenge has been accorded priority as China "is the only competitor with both the intent and, increasingly, the capability to reshape the international order" as against a "dangerous Russia", which has to be constrained.[6] In the Indo-Pacific strategy, the Biden administration underlined the priority of the Chinese challenge, saying that "the People's Republic of China's [PRC] coercion and aggression spans the globe, but it is most acute in the Indo-Pacific". In response to that, the US' "objective is not to change the PRC but to shape the strategic environment in which it operates, building a balance of influences in the world that is maximally favourable to the United States and its allies and partners and the interests and values we share." This, the US admitted, "cannot be accomplished alone" and, therefore, besides other things, "we support a strong India as a partner in this positive regional vision…[We] steadily advance our major defence partnership with India and support its role as a new security provider".[7] The document devotes a special paragraph to India saying:

> We will continue to build a strategic partnership in which the United States and India work together…We recognise that India is a likeminded partner and leader in South Asia and the Indian Ocean, active and connected to Southeast Asia, a driving force of the Quad and other regional fora and an engine for regional growth and development.[8]

Thus, not only is a guiding principle for the Biden administration's approach to India defined, but a roadmap for future policies is also laid out.

India, on its part, has always been keen to build a strong and cooperative relationship with the US, but the Cold War drift caused by the US could not be overcome. After the end of the Cold War, there have been clear indications that India shared the US' assessment of China's rise and assertion in Asia and was concerned about its own security interests. India's Prime Minister Atal Bihari Vajpayee sent a letter to Clinton, stating that the May 1998 nuclear explosion and declaration of India as a nuclear weapon power was prompted by China's nuclear threat. He said in that letter, "We have an overt nuclear weapon state on our borders, a state which committed armed aggression against India in 1962."[9] Days before India's nuclear declaration, its new defence minister, George Fernandes, had described China as India's potential threat number one, which had to be met through nuclear capability. The China threat was the hidden elephant in the room when US Deputy Secretary of State Strobe Talbott and India's Minister of External Affairs Jaswant Singh negotiated on nuclear and space technology issues after India's declaration of its nuclear status.[10] Vajpayee's India initiated a dialogue with the US to build understanding and a cooperative relationship by highlighting India's democratic values and character. This was a subtle contrast to China's communist system with which the US has so far had close cooperation. In a joint vision statement issued by Vajpayee and Clinton in March 2000, the two sides said:

> In the new century, India and the United States will be partners in peace, with a common interest in and complimentary responsibility for ensuring regional and international security. We will engage in regular consultations on, and work together and with others for, strategic stability in Asia and beyond.[11]

India, under Vajpayee and his successors, Manmohan Singh and Modi, has tried to stabilise relations with China and sought an amicable and peaceful resolution of their border dispute. A number of confidence-building measures (CBMs) have also been put in place since the 1990s, and economic relations have been expanded, but these have not worked. In particular, since the rise of President Xi Jinping in China in 2013, Beijing has been asserting its territorial nationalism, expanding its claims and threatening India militarily by violating the CBMs by encroaching on the disputed border in the Himalayas. China has also been expanding its naval presence in the Indian Ocean by creating new facilities like Hambantota Port in Sri Lanka and Gwadar Port in Pakistan. India is feeling increasingly encircled by China in its immediate and strategically sensitive neighbourhood. The Chinese security challenge to India has, therefore, been enhanced and has become more complicated. This has resulted in further expansion and consolidation of India's strategic convergence with the US on the China threat. At a hearing on 'Indo-Pacific Security Challenges', the Commander of the US Indo-Pacific Command, Admiral John Christopher Aquilino, endorsed the view that both India and the US were confronting the same security challenge from China.[12]

The dialogue process initiated between India and the US during the late 1990s has consistently been reinforced, diversified and institutionalised at the summit and ministerial levels concerning a host of specific issues of mutual interest. At present, there are about 50 dialogue processes operating between India and the US. Both in India and the US, there has gradually emerged a strong bi-partisan (across the Congress and the Bharatiya Janata Party in India and across the Democrats and Republicans in the US) support for close Indo-US cooperation in diverse fields.

Relations between India and the US have made impressive progress over the last two decades through extensive dialogue and discussions.[13] Some of the landmark developments in this respect may be briefly recalled. In 2005, the two countries signed a 10-year New Framework for India–US Defense Relations that opened up new areas of cooperation, including multinational operations "when they are in mutual interests". This agreement was extended and enlarged in 2015. The US accepted India as a nuclear weapon state and agreed to extend full cooperation to its civil nuclear programme under what is called the 123 Nuclear Agreement, signed in 2008. The initiative for this agreement was taken in 2005 and the Indian government had taken considerable risk in signing it as it was strongly resisted by one of the powerful Left coalition partners, the Communist Party of India (Marxist).[14] India joined the Quadrilateral Security Dialogue (Quad) in 2007 under American leadership, with two of the latter's military allies — Japan and Australia. The idea of this grouping goes back to 2004 when these four countries collectively provided humanitarian assistance to countries affected by a tsunami. The Indo-US strategic dialogue was launched in 2010 under the Obama administration, which, in 2016, designated India as a "major defence partner". This new status was to facilitate the procurement of weapon systems and transfer of technology and spares for such military platforms that are already in the Indian inventory. This also led to a process of roping in India in foundational military agreements, comprising the Logistics Exchange Memorandum of Agreement, Communications, Compatibility and Security

Agreement and Basic Exchange for Cooperation Agreement for Geospatial Cooperation. These agreements were concluded respectively in 2016, 2018 and 2020, respectively, after dealing with initial reservations and hesitation on India's part.

The Biden presidency has been carrying forward the momentum of strengthening strategic partnership with India by making its own contributions in three specific areas. The first is documenting the US' Indo-Pacific strategy and highlighting India's place in it in clear terms. Accordingly, India's leading role in ensuring regional security in South Asia, the Indian Ocean and Southeast Asia has been recognised. This has opened long-term prospects for future US collaboration with India in these areas. The previous US administrations have also been talking about long-term and extensive cooperation with India, but India's status and specific areas had not been clearly defined. Second, the Biden administration has "elevated" the strategic partnership with India by launching the initiative for Critical and Emerging Technologies (iCET) in May 2022. This will open up "opportunities for cooperation in critical and emerging technologies, co-development and co-production, and ways to deepen connectivity across our innovation ecosystems".[15] Last, but not least, has been a categorical US stand in favour of India's position on the standoff with China in the Himalayas across the Line of Actual Control (LAC). The Indo-Pacific strategy document mentions the Chinese encroachments on the LAC as one of the examples of Chinese coercion and aggression on its neighbours. Not only has a bipartisan Congressional resolution supporting "Arunachal Pradesh as an integral part of India" been adopted in the midst of Chinese claims on Arunachal Pradesh,[16] but US diplomats[17] and think tanks[18] have called upon the US to stand by India in any event of Chinese aggression on the LAC. India and the US have also had military exercises near the LAC. Of the last of these three areas listed, the US has tried to meet India's longstanding expectations.

One must also take note of the fact here that the Biden administration, in strengthening Indo-US strategic partnership, has also not allowed one of the most important divergences of its priorities with regard to India affect the relationship. This is concerning India's relations and continued cooperation with Russia despite the Russian–Ukraine war and the US' sanctions on Russia. The US' sanctions were imposed under the Countering

America's Adversaries Through Sanctions Act (CAATSA), introduced in 2017. This has been applied to Russia, Iran and several other countries. The sanctions against Russia were extended and made more stringent in the context of the war against Ukraine. Since India was a major importer of arms and oil from Russia, it came under the preview of CAATSA. In March 2022, the US warning India on this count said that India's trade with Russia "needs to be in compliance with sanctions"; otherwise, India was exposing itself to a "great risk".[19] However, this position soon changed. The US Congress adopted a waiver for India on CAATSA in July 2022. Later, American officials were quoted as saying, "[We] want to be clear that we are not looking to sanction India" and also that "...we do not believe that...our sanction policy in the energy space needs to have a universal adherence in order to be effective...we are comfortable with the approach that India has taken".[20] India has also not condemned Russian aggression like other Western nations. It is difficult to say exactly what considerations led to this change, but it seems India has persuaded the US that it was in the larger bilateral interest for India to equip itself better through diverse sources of energy and arms. The US also quietly observed that India's arms imports from Russia were gradually declining while increasing from the US. Indian oil imports from Russia, at lower prices, are also helping the US to keep global energy flows in balance when they were seriously affecting Europe. The US' strategic partnership with India has greater relevance in the Indo-Pacific region and the spillover of European conflict, where Russia was seen as a lesser and transactional challenge, should not be allowed to harm it. On its part, India has also been adjusting with the divergences on the US side, for instance, militarily bolstering of Pakistan through its alliance. The Biden administration has also kept up the tradition of not allowing India's human rights lapses to be made a factor in the growth of a strategic partnership.

Economic Interests and Social Stakes

The Indo-US strategic partnership, rooted in the convergence on China, has also been fuelling the US' economic interests in India. During the initial discussions on transforming relations, the US had made a close assessment of military sales potential in India. The *WikiLeaks* cables, released in thousands on various aspects of the US' thinking on building defence relations with India, also disclosed that India's arms procurement market that stood at more than US$14 billion was a major attraction.[21] This assessment has indeed turned out to be correct.[22] India has projected its arms purchases in the coming years at US$100 billion. It stands fourth as the global arms purchaser. Institutional arrangements to facilitate defence trade between the two countries were made through the Defense Trade and Technology Initiative (DTTI), launched in 2012, to remove "impediments by bureaucratic structures, acquisition models and budget processes". The iCET, concluded in February 2023, may be seen as an upgrade of the DTTI. The US' defence sales that were almost nil in 2008 rose to more than US$20 billion by 2022. As a result of such commercial stakes, the US strongly resented the rejection of its proposals of a sale of a medium multirole combat aircraft worth US$10.4 billion by India in 2010.[23] With India's strong lobbying for its 'Make in India' programme and the establishment of the iCET, a growing number of arms manufacturing companies are showing interest in the Indian defence market. The US is urging for "more reforms in India's defence offsets policy and higher FDI [foreign direct investment] caps in its defence sector".[24]

The US' interest in the Indian market is not confined to the defence sector alone. It is looking to expand its presence in the Indian economy as a whole. Commenting on the prospects of business in India, the New Delhi-based US embassy, in a note, said:

> The Indian market, with its one billion plus population, presents lucrative and diverse opportunities for US exporters with the right products, services, and commitment. India's requirements for equipment and services for major sectors such as energy, environment, healthcare, high-tech, infrastructure, transportation and defence will exceed tens of billions of dollars in the mid-term as the Indian economy further globalises and expands...India has potential for a sustained high growth for the next couple of years, and more and more US companies must seize the opportunities to enter the rising Indian market.[25]

The US' economic presence in India has shown considerable growth, along with the progress in strategic partnership. The coincidence of signing the iCET and a deal for 220 Boeing passenger planes worth

US$34 billion by India in February 2023, even if unintended, is a significant indicator in this respect. Bilateral trade, which stood at US$45 billion in 2010, has now reached US$157 billion, making the US India's largest trading partner, accounting for 16 percent of India's total exports. This is, however, still far off from the target of US$500 billion set by Obama and Modi in 2014. The latest International Monetary Fund assessment shows India as the third largest destination of US FDI flows,[26] at nearly US$50 billion.[27] The slow but gradual opening up and reforms in the Indian economy have attracted large US conglomerates like Amazon, Apple, Netflix and Prime Videos, among others. They are doing roaring business in India. Apple's Chief Executive Officer, Tim Cook, while opening Apple stores in Mumbai and New Delhi, claimed that India, which, at present, accounts for about 29 percent of the US$394 billion Apple market, will become one of the biggest.[28] There are a number of issues related to protectionism — tariffs, digital trade, intellectual property rights, Generalised System of Preferences and investment climate — on the part of both the US and India that are hampering the expansion of US economic presence in India. The Biden and Modi administrations are addressing the issues, but progress on them has been slow and halting.

The US has significant social stakes in building and supporting an Indo-US strategic partnership due to the presence of a 4.6 million-strong Indian diaspora.[29] In numerical strength, the Indian diaspora stands third as part of America's Asian community, after the Koreans and Chinese, but Indians are much better economically placed. The median household income of an Indo-American family is estimated to be US$119,000, which is nearly double the average national income.[30] The Indo-Americans, who constitute only about 1.4 percent of the total American population, contribute to six percent of its total tax revenue. Many Indo-Americans hold high positions in various sectors of the economy, particularly computer sciences, financial management and medicine. About 79 percent of them are college graduates as against the US national average of 34 percent.[31] A Congressman from Connecticut described the Indo-American community as the "future of US innovations". The Indian technology industry is reported to have generated US$103 billion in revenue in the US in 2021, employing 207,000 people. There are about 200,000 Indian students in US universities, contributing nearly US$8 billion to the country's educational revenue.[32] Fluency in the English language and democratic acculturation put the Indian diaspora at an added advantage in the US, as compared to the other Asian communities.

Over the years, the Indo-Americans have gathered effective political clout. They have assumed high offices of governors and diplomatic representatives in various important decision-making institutions of the US government. Under Biden, Kamala Harris, an Indo-American, has assumed one of the highest offices, that of the vice-president. The Indo-Americans will not harm US interests but would be sympathetic to India's genuine concerns. They organise themselves in various ethnic and professional organisations and also influence American elections at various levels, including the presidency. One can recall Modi addressing one of the Indian diaspora meetings in Huston on the eve of 2020 presidential elections and giving the call in Hindi of *abki bar Trump sarkar* (This time Trump government), by borrowing from his own 2014 campaign slogan in India. The Indian diaspora groups have not only promoted people-to-people relations between the two countries even at the highest political levels (*Howdy* Modi and *Namaste* Trump) but also contributed towards building a strategic partnership between the two countries. Clinton publicly admitted during his India visit that there was pressure from the Indian diaspora to lift American sanctions on India imposed in reaction to India's nuclear weapon state declaration in 1998. The diaspora groups also lobbied hard through the US Congress to facilitate the conclusion of the civil nuclear cooperation agreement in 2008. Under Biden, these groups have been active in getting restrictions relaxed with regards to the Indian H-1B visa, green card issuance and trade. India has been carefully nurturing the Indian diaspora, both as an asset as well as an instrument in its policy towards the US.

Beyond Biden

The US' approach towards India has been shaped and nursed for the past quarter of century by the convergence between the two countries on the challenge posed by a rising, assertive and aggressive China, prospects of mutually beneficial economic engagement and the strength of social stakes. We have seen that these factors have been working with Biden's predecessors and reinforced and consolidated under the Biden administration. They will most likely sustain the momentum created in Indo-US strategic partnership beyond Biden. In the security and defence sector, the upward trajectory of mutual understanding and cooperation between the two countries will continue steadily as there may be no let-up in the Chinese challenge. The 2 + 2 ministerial dialogue, held in October 2022, laid down the broad parameters of this unfolding trajectory. A statement issued by the US Department of Defense on 11 April 2022 stated:

> U.S. and Indian militaries to work more seamlessly together across all domains of potential conflict — from the seas to cyberspace. The United States and India finalized major bilateral initiatives on information-sharing, liaison exchanges and joint service engagements to support high-end, combined operations.
>
> The four leaders committed to deepening cooperation in new defence domains, such as space and cyberspace, as the U.S. and Indian militaries jointly meet the challenges of this *century*. The United States and India signed a Space Situational Awareness arrangement, which lays the groundwork for more advanced cooperation in space. They also agreed to launch an inaugural defence Artificial Intelligence Dialogue, while expanding joint cyber training and exercises.
>
> Today's 2 + 2 ministerial reaffirmed that the United States and India will continue to stand shoulder to shoulder, rooted in common democratic values as two pillars of a free and open Indo-Pacific.[33]

It is clear that the partnership is being built for this century and its thrust in defence matters will be on close operational integration between the two armies in preserving a free and open Indo-Pacific. The two sides have also decided to open up new defence domains like space, artificial intelligence and cyber while working on traditional ones like maritime security (adding underwater domain awareness), counterterrorism, climate and clean energy, education, people-to-people relations and global health, among others. The media note, issued separately, gave some more details of how these domains will be opened up.[34]

Both Biden and Modi are expecting to win their next elections in 2024 and carry forward the implementation of this agenda. Even if they (either both or any one of them) do not win, the momentum in strategic partnership in the defence and security areas between the two countries will continue upward as they have, by now, developed strong stakes in its continuation. Reversal does not seem to be an option for either of them. Whatever reservations either side had about the other partner have melted down as a result of the Cold War legacy and baggage of the past experiences of dealing with each other,[35] and the remaining are in the process of doing so under the heat of the Chinese challenge. It is least likely that China will put up a black swan posture towards the US and retreat its assertive and aggressive stance in the Indo-Pacific. At the 14th National People's Congress of the Communist Party of China, Xi said, "Western countries led by the US have implemented all round containment and suppression of China, which has brought unprecedented severe challenges to the country's development."[36] There may be a remote possibility of China putting up a softer posture towards India, if and when it decides to move militarily against Taiwan. However, any such gesture would be tactical and temporary and may not trap India into deviating from its strategic partnership with the US.

The Indo-US strategic partnership in the economic domain will also move in the upward trajectory but at a slower and tardy pace. Economic issues impeding the progress in trade and investment issues are deeply rooted in the economies of both countries. Domestic stakeholders in their respective economies cannot be easily ignored in democratic systems. Both are also displaying streaks of robust economic nationalism that does not easily submit to compromises and adjustments. Reflections of this were evident in Trump's 'America First' and can also be seen in Modi's 'Make in India' and 'Made in India' programmes. A moderating influence on the respective economic nationalisms in India and the US is emanating from the consequences of the Russia–Ukraine war as the agenda of building "resilient supply chains" has been included in the Indo-US strategic partnership. Such influence will be further stimulated if and as India and the US seriously pursue the objective of economic decoupling from China.

As noted earlier, the Russia–Ukraine war, though a part of the India–US dialogue, has not adversely affected the strategic partnership between Washington and New Delhi. The end of the war, in whatever manner it comes, will also not have any impact. However, if there is an outbreak of conflict in the Indo-Pacific, the Indo-US strategic partnership will be put to a severe test. The US, India and China are locked in a complex and delicate balance. The three powers have vowed to avoid war, but there are three sensitive hot spots in the region — the Himalayas, the Taiwan Strait and the South China Sea. China has publicly stated that it will not hesitate to use force, if need be, to integrate Taiwan with the mainland. However, the US has made it clear too that it will defend Taiwan against any use of force by China. American think tanks and strategic analysts are debating war scenarios and there are books written in the US and India on the possibilities of an open and direct military conflict.[37] China's expansionist assertiveness may also trigger a conflict either in the Himalayas or the South China Sea. In the case of China forcing a conflict either on India or the US, support would be expected from the other strategic partner. Direct military participation (putting boots on the ground or water) by the other strategic partner in such a war seems unlikely, but the strong possibility of coordinated support exists. This may also result in opening another front by India in the Himalayas or the Malacca Strait in the event of a war in the Taiwan Strait and/or in the South China Sea by the US in the event of a war in the Himalayas against China.[38] Any such war in the Indo-Pacific will be unusual and unprecedented, involving space and cyber domains, possibly even nuclear weapons. The Indo-US strategic partnership will be put under unexplainable strain in that situation.

Endnotes

1. For the text of the joint statement, see "Joint statement: The United States and India: Enduring global partners in the 21st century", The White House, 7 June 2016, https://obamawhitehouse.archives.gov/the-press-office/2016/06/07/joint-statement-united-states-and-india-enduring-global-partners-21st.
2. "2022 country reports on human rights practices: India", U.S. Department of State, https://www.state.gov/reports/2022-country-reports-on-human-rights-practices/india.
3. S. D. Muni, *Foreign Policy of India: The Democracy Dimension* (New Delhi: Cambridge University Press, 2009).
4. Condoleezza Rice, "Campaign 2000: Promoting the national interest", *Foreign Affairs*, January/February 2000, https://www.foreignaffairs.com/united-states/campaign-2000-promoting-national-interest.

5. Robert D. Blackwell and Ashley J. Tellis, "Revising US grand strategy towards China", *Council Special Report*, No. 72, March 2015, Council of on Foreign Relations, chrome-extension://efaidnbmnnnibpcajpcglclefindmkaj/ https://carnegieendowment.org/files/Tellis_Blackwill.pdf. Also see "The Indian dividend: New Delhi remains Washington's best hope in Asia", *Foreign Affairs*, Vol. 98, No. 5, September/October 2019, https://www.foreignaffairs.com/articles/india/2019-08-12/india-dividend.
6. Briefing on national security strategy in the White House. For the full document, see National Security Strategy, The White House, October 2022, https://www.whitehouse.gov/wp-content/uploads/2022/10/Biden-Harris-Administrations-National-Security-Strategy.
7. "Indo-Pacific strategy of the United States", The White House, February 2022, p. 5, https://www.whitehouse.gov/wp-content/uploads/2022/02/U.S.-Indo-Pacific-Strategy.pdf.
8. *Ibid.*, p. 16.
9. The text of the letter was leaked by the White House to *The New York Times*. See "Nuclear Anxiety; Indian's Letter to Clinton on the Nuclear Testing", *The New York Times*, 13 May 1998, https://www.nytimes.com/1998/05/13/world/nuclear-anxiety-indian-s-letter-to-clinton-on-the-nuclear-testing.html.
10. Both Jaswant Singh and Talbot have published their respective versions of these talks.
11. "U.S.–India relations: A vision for the 21st century", Joint U.S.–India statement fact sheet, US Office of the Press Secretary, The White House, 21 March 2000, https://1997-2001.state.gov/global/human_rights/democracy/fs_000321_us_india.html.
12. "India, U.S. facing same security challenge from China, says U.S. Indo-Pacific Commander Christopher Aquilino", *The Hindu*, 20 April 2023, https://www.thehindu.com/news/international/india-us-facing-same-security-challenge-from-china-says-us-indo-pacom-commander-christopher-aquilino/article66758800.ece.
13. For a detailed discussion of the evolution of strategic partnership between India and the US, see Deba R. Mohanty and Uma Purushothaman, "India–US defence relations: In search of direction", *Occasional Paper* No. 23, Observer Research Foundation, New Delhi, April 2011, https://www.orfonline.org/research/india-us-defence-relations-in-search-of-a-direction/.
14. The Communist Party of India (Marxist) refused to support Manmohan Singh's move for civil nuclear cooperation with the US and walked out of the coalition government led by the Congress under the United Progressive Alliance, threatening its survival.

15. See the White House statement released in this respect on 31 January 2023, https://www.whitehouse.gov/briefing-room/statements-releases/2023/01/31/fact-sheet-united-states-and-india-elevate-strategic-partnership-with-the-initiative-on-critical-and-emerging-technology-icet.
16. Prashant Jha, "Arunachal integral part of India, condemn China's aggression at LAC: Rare resolution in US Senate", *The Hindustan Times*, 17 February 2023, https://www.hindustantimes.com/world-news/arunachal-integral-part-of-india-condemn-china-rare-resolution-in-us-senate-101676599911594.html.
17. See statement by the US Assistant Secretary of State, David Lulu in *India Today*, 21 April 2023, https://www.indiatoday.in/world/story/little-evidence-china-is-approaching-border-dispute-talks-india-sense-of-goodwill-us-2362787-2023-04-21.
18. Lisa Curtis and Derek Grossman, "India-China border tensions and U.S. strategy in the Indo-Pacific", Centre for a new American Security, Washington DC, March 2023, https://www.cnas.org/publications/reports/india-china-border-tensions-and-u-s-strategy-in-the-indo-pacific.
19. Poulomi Ghosh, "US warns India against increasing oil imports from Russia, says 'great risk'", *The Hindustan Times*, 31 March 2022, https://www.hindustantimes.com/india-news/ukraine-russia-war-us-warns-india-against-increasing-oil-imports-from-russia-says-great-risk-101648700263308.html.
20. The officials quoted respectively are Karen Donfried, US Assistant Secretary of State for the European and Eurasian Affairs, and Geoffrey R. Pyatt, US Assistant Secretary for Energy Resources, *Deccan Herald*, 9 February 2023, https://www.deccanherald.com/national/us-makes-u-turn-on-indias-purchase-of-oil-from-russia-1189627.htm.
21. Siddharth Vardharajan, "U.S. cables show grand calculations under lying 2005 defense framework", *The Hindu*, 28 March 2011, https://www.thehindu.com/news/the-india-cables/U.S.-cables-show-grand-calculations-underlying-2005-defence-framework/article14965295.ece. Also see D. Raghunandan, "WikiLeaks and India-U.S defence agreement", *News Click*, 29 April 2011, https://www.newsclick.in/wikileaks-and-us-india-defence-agreement.
22. Sunil Dasgupta and Stephen Cohen, "Arms sales for India: How military trade could energies U.S.–India relations", *Foreign Affairs*, March–April 2011, https://www.foreignaffairs.com/articles/india/2011-02-18/arms-sales-india.
23. Deba R. Mohanty and Uma Purushothaman, *op. cit.*
24. "U.S.–India trade relations", *In Focus*, Congressional Research Service (CRS), Updated 31 March 2023, chrome-extension://efaidnbmnnnibpcajpcglclefindmkaj/https://crsreports.congress.gov/product/pdf/IF/IF10384.

25. "Doing Business in India — The second fastest growing market in Asia", US Embassies and Consulates in India, https://in.usembassy.gov/business/getting-started-india/.
26. Prashant Jha, "India third largest destination of US FDI flow: IMF", *The Hindustan Times*, 11 April 2023.
27. "U.S.–India trade relations", *op. cit.*
28. Pankaj Doval, "India's people & culture set for extraordinary journey ahead: Apple CEO Tim Cook", *The Times of India*, New Delhi, 19 April 2023, https://timesofindia.indiatimes.com/business/india-business/indias-people-culture-set-for-extraordinary-journey-ahead-apple-ceo-tim-cook/articleshow/99594350.cms?from=mdr.
29. "Douglas Todd: People of Indian descent a rising force in the U.S. and Canada", *Vancouver Sun*, 11 August 2022, https://vancouversun.com/opinion/columnists/douglas-todd-in-canada-and-u-s-people-of-indian-descent-are-a-rising-force-in-business-and-politics.
30. *Ibid.*
31. "Education attainment of Indian population in the U.S., 2019", Pew Center Research, https://www.pewresearch.org/social-trends/chart/educational-attainment-of-indian-population-in-the-u-s-2019/.
32. "These countries are the most preferred education destinations amongst Indian students", *The Economic Times*, 23 March 2023, https://economictimes.indiatimes.com/nri/study/these-countries-are-the-most-preferred-education-destination-amongst-indian-students/articleshow/98903435.cms?utm_source=contentofinterest&utm_medium=text&utm_campaign=cppst; and "Over 200,000 students went to US for higher studies in 2021–22: Report", and *Business Standard*, 14 November 2022, https://www.business-standard.com/article/education/over-2-lakh-students-went-to-us-for-higher-studies-in-2021-22-report-122111401454_1.html. Also see, Madhulika Baniwal, "Factoring Indian diaspora in the Indo-U.S relations", Indian Council of World Affairs, New Delhi, 26 October 2018, https://icwa.in/show_content.php?lang=1&level=3&ls_id=4891&lid=3480.
33. "Readout of U.S.–India 2 + 2 ministerial dialogue", US Department of Defense, 11 April 2022, https://www.defense.gov/News/Releases/Release/Article/2996350/readout-of-us-india-22-ministerial-dialogue/.
34. For the text of the media note, see "Fourth annual U.S.–India 2 + 2 ministerial dialogue", *Media Note*, U.S. Department of Defense, 11 April 2022, https://www.state.gov/fourth-annual-u-s-india-22-ministerial-dialogue/.

35. WikiLeaks disclosures brought some of India's reservations out which were not seen only as confined to the Left political spectrum but also were rooted into the Nehruvian perspective of India's strategic autonomy. News Click, no. 18.
36. Shyam Saran, "Rebalance of power", *Indian Express*, 6 April 2023, https://indianexpress.com/article/opinion/columns/former-foreign-secretary-shyam-saran-writes-china-is-firmly-in-russias-corner-india-needs-to-take-note-8540982/.
37. Max Boot, "In the US-China competition, the real 'existential danger' is nuclear war", *The Washington Post*, 17 April 2023, https://www.washingtonpost.com/opinions/2023/04/17/china-united-states-nuclear-conflict-danger/. Also see Elliot Ackerman and Admiral James Stavridis, *2034: A Novel of the Next World War* (The United States: The Daily Books, 2021). Rajiv Dogra, a senior former Indian diplomat, has written a book titled, *Wartime: The World in Danger* (New Delhi: Rupa Publications India, 2022).
38. See Harsh V. Pant and Suyash Desai, "India and the China-Taiwan conflict: The military dimension", *Commentaries*, Observer Research Foundation, 27 March 2023, https://www.orfonline.org/research/india-and-the-china-taiwan-conflict/; and Amit Kumar, "China's two-front conundrum: A perspective on the India-China border situation", *Occasional Paper*, 7 March 2023, Observer Research Foundation, https://www.orfonline.org/research/chinas-two-front-conundrum/#:~:text=Conclusion,two%2Dfront%20challenge%20to%20India.

© 2024 World Scientific Publishing Company Pte. Ltd.
https://doi.org/10.1142/9789811276439_0011

Chapter 11

United States–India Trade Relations: The IPEF and Beyond

Amitendu Palit

The Joe Biden administration in the United States (US) is more than halfway through its term in office. During this period, it has engaged constructively with India across several issues, ranging from defence, technology and climate to health, regional coalition-building and trade. One of the most notable areas of engagement between the US and India has been regional standard-setting in the Indo-Pacific region. Embodied through the Indo-Pacific Economic Framework for Prosperity (IPEF), the US and India are looking to contribute purposefully to the growth of regional standards. At the same time, both countries have been actively engaging in consultations to resolve issues that are irritants to bilateral trade.

During the last two years, bilateral trade between the US and India has increased substantially. This has happened despite both countries continuing to struggle with the episodic recurrence of the COVID-19 pandemic and a fragile geopolitical environment. This chapter attempts to capture the developments in US–India trade in the broader context of their strategic collaboration in the Indo-Pacific region through the IPEF. It is divided into five sections. The first section discusses the IPEF. The next two sections focus on the current conditions of the US–India bilateral trade and new developments in trade relations during the Biden administration, respectively. The fourth section discusses the prospects of

India being restored preferential market access through the US Generalised System of Preferences (GSP) and its connection with the IPEF. The concluding section reflects on the future of US-India trade relations.

The IPEF

Biden announced the IPEF during the Quadrilateral Security Dialogue (Quad) countries[1] heads of states meeting in Tokyo on 23 May 2022.[2] The meeting marked the president's maiden visit to Asia after assuming office. The Biden administration clearly wanted the first visit of the president to be noted for its strategic significance. The launch of the IPEF was designed to serve the purpose.

The IPEF's economic heft is noteworthy. Its 14 members — Australia, Brunei, Fiji, India, Indonesia, Japan, Korea, Malaysia, New Zealand, the Philippines, Singapore, Thailand, Vietnam and the US — account for around two-fifths of the world's gross domestic product (GDP).[3] The group includes four of the world's top 10 economies: the US, Japan, India and Korea. All major economies of Southeast Asia are a part of the group,[4] along with key Pacific economies — Australia, New Zealand and Fiji.

The strategic importance of the IPEF becomes evident by comparing it with two other prominent regional trade frameworks: the Regional Comprehensive Economic Partnership (RCEP) and the Comprehensive and Progressive Transpacific Partnership (CPTPP).

The RCEP and the CPTPP are the two overarching functional rules-based trade and economic frameworks in the Asia-Pacific region. The first, fashioned as an Association of Southeast Asian Nations (ASEAN)-plus architecture, comprises the ASEAN member economies and countries with which ASEAN has bilateral free trade agreements (FTAs). The notable exclusion from the group is India, which, despite having an FTA with ASEAN, is not a part of the RCEP.[5] The second framework — the CPTPP — comprises 11 members of the Asia-Pacific Economic Cooperation (APEC).[6] There are several members that are common to both the RCEP and the CPTPP — Australia, Brunei, Japan, Malaysia, New Zealand, Singapore and Vietnam.

All members common to the RCEP and the CPTPP figure in the IPEF. Indeed, except for China and three small ASEAN member economies — Cambodia, Laos and Myanmar — the rest of the RCEP members are in the IPEF. The overlap in membership between the three frameworks is striking.

As an economic grouping, the IPEF is the largest of the three frameworks (see Table 11.1). In addition to accounting for 40 percent of the global economy, the IPEF comprises more than a third of the global population. The RCEP accounts for a third of the global economy and nearly a third of the world population as well. The CPTPP, in comparison, is far smaller than both.

Given the overlaps in memberships between the IPEF, the RCEP and the CPTPP, the IPEF's larger size is significantly due to the presence of the US and India. Neither of the two figure in the RCEP and the CPTPP. On the other hand, China is a part of the RCEP, while being absent from the IPEF and the CPTPP.

The US and India account for 24.7 percent and 3.1 percent of the global economy, respectively, in terms of their GDPs, as proportions of the world's GDP. The corresponding share for China is 21 percent of the global economy.[7] Taken together, the US and Indian economies exceed the size of the Chinese economy by nearly seven percentage points, as a proportion of the world's GDP. The US–India economic combination is significant in raising the economic heft and strategic significance of the IPEF vis-à-vis the RCEP and the CPTPP.

From a broader regional perspective, the entry of the US and India into the regional rule-making architecture of the Indo-Pacific has far-reaching implications. Notable among these is bringing two of the world's major markets into the ambit of a cohesive rules-based arrangement with several other prominent economies. With the US and India engaged

Table 11.1: Economic dimensions of the IPEF, RCEP and CPTPP.

Agreements	GDP (US$ trillion)	GDP (% of world)	Population (billion)	Population (% of world)
IPEF	37.9	39.3	2.5	32.1
RCEP	29.6	30.7	2.3	29.1
CPTPP	11.7	12.0	0.5	6.4

Source: Compiled from World Development Indicators, World Bank.

in rule-making in the IPEF, the idea of the Indo-Pacific has acquired a comprehensive economic identity, which was missing earlier. As the largest economies of the Indian and Pacific oceans, the significance of both countries in drafting Indo-Pacific rules on trade and business implies the engagement of nearly a third of the global economy, as represented by the combined economic size of the two countries, in common standards and regulations. This is a major pull for the other members of the IPEF, as well as those outside the IPEF, to understand and align with the standards to which US and India have agreed. Over time, these standards are likely to become global standards for wider adoption. Indeed, with the US and India pioneering rule-making with several of their regional peers, the IPEF has emerged as a representative and inclusive framework for the Indo-Pacific region, distinct in identity from APEC and ASEAN.

India–US Trade: Current Trends and Characteristics

The IPEF has brought India and the US together in negotiating rules and standards on several issues that have implications for regional and bilateral trade. As they engage more closely in the IPEF, it is pertinent to examine the trends and characteristics of their bilateral trade in recent years.

Goods Trade

The Biden administration assumed office when both India and the US were struggling to cope with the COVID-19 pandemic. The top-most priority of both countries was on expanding frontline healthcare resources and facilities and ensuring the fast distribution of vaccines to their populations. It was also a time when the world economy experienced a severe economic contraction.

Global GDP growth contracted by 3.1 percent in 2020. This was a deeper contraction than the 1.3 percent in 2009 caused by the Trans-Atlantic financial crisis. Indeed, the long-term trend of annual global GDP growth highlights the contraction of 2020 as the worst in the last six decades.[8] The impact of the contraction was felt by both the US and the Indian economies, with the two countries contracting by 3.4 percent and 7.3 percent, respectively, in 2020.[9] Both economies, along with most of the rest of the world, recovered strongly in 2021 to post GDP growth of 5.7 percent and 8.7 percent, respectively.[10] The previous year, 2022, recorded relatively lower GDP growth for both, with the US and India growing by two percent and 6.8 percent, respectively.[11]

The fluctuations in the rate of economic growth have brushed off on bilateral trade, impacting its momentum. American exports to India declined from US$34.2 billion in 2019 to US$27.1 billion in 2020. The year-on-year decline in US imports from India was from US$57.9 billion in 2019 to US$51.2 billion in 2020.[12] From 2021 onwards, the pick-up in trade has been noteworthy. American exports to India increased to US$40.1 billion in 2021 and further to US$47.3 billion in 2022.[13] Compared with 2020, American exports have exhibited an increase of nearly 75 percent in 2022. American imports from India, conversely, also increased, along with the recovery in economic growth, to US$73.2 billion in 2021 and further to US$85.7 billion in 2022.[14] The increase in US imports in 2022 was more than 67 percent of their value in 2020.

The first two years of the Biden administration — 2021 and 2022 — witnessed a sharp acceleration in bilateral trade, enabled by the economic recovery in both India and the US. A notable achievement of the acceleration is the size of bilateral trade crossing the landmark of US$100 billion. In 2021 and 2022, US–India trade in goods was US$113.3 billion and US$133 billion, respectively.[15] The increase in trade has resulted in India figuring among the top 10 trade partners of the US. Conversely, for India, the US has become the largest trade partner, surpassing China.[16]

Movement of People

Along with the trade in goods, there has been a visible pick-up in the movement of people between India and the US. Indians have been migrating to the US for several decades, leading to a steady expansion in the size of the Indian diaspora in the US. With a size of 2.7 million in 2021, the Indian diaspora is the second largest immigrant group in the US, after the Mexicans, and exceeds the Chinese and Filipino diasporas.[17]

The size of the diaspora is enlarging with more Indians moving to the US. Immigration visas issued by the US for Indians increased sharply

Table 11.2: Immigration Visas issued by the US for select Asian countries (2018–2022).

Countries	2018	2019	2020	2021	2022
China (Mainland)	29,360	27,541	12,217	18,501	22,108
India	28,073	24,965	11,941	9,275	25,633
Philippines	32,123	27,460	10,067	15,862	27,401
Vietnam	28,701	32,867	20,230	10,458	22,573

Source: Immigrant Visas issued at Foreign Service Posts (by Foreign State Chargeability) (All Categories), Fiscal Years, 2013–2022, https://travel.state.gov/content/dam/visas/Statistics/AnnualReports/FY2022AnnualReport/FY22_TableXIII.pdf.

during the last year (see Table 11.2). After dropping below 10,000 in 2021, the number of immigrant visas obtained by Indians experienced a nearly three-fold increase to 25,633 in 2022. The rise has made Indians the second highest immigrant visa recipient group after the Filipinos, and bigger than the Chinese and the Vietnamese. Till 2022, India lagged behind China, the Philippines and Vietnam in receiving immigrant visas — a trend that has transformed during the second year of the Biden administration.

There has also been a sizeable increase in non-immigrant visas issued by the US to Indians. Unlike immigrant visas, where India rose to the second highest category in 2022 but remained behind the Philippines, it has been the top-most among the four highest visa recipient countries since 2020 (see Table 11.3). It is further noteworthy that 2022 was a year when the number of non-immigrant visas issued to Indians by the US more than doubled from the previous year. It is also remarkable that the number of non-immigrant visas received by Indians in 2022 was more than the combined number for China, the Philippines and Vietnam (see Table 11.3). While Indians obtained 634,670 visas that year, the corresponding combined total for the other three countries was 388,124, roughly 60 percent of the visas issued for India.

The year 2022 was, therefore, one where India achieved significant milestones in its trade relations with the US. This is observable from the sharp increase in bilateral trade and movement of people. The second year

Table 11.3: Non-Immigrant Visas issued by the US for select Asian countries (2018–2022).

Countries	2018	2019	2020	2021	2022
China (Mainland)	1,369,129	1,157,656	277,838	100,424	121,841
India	872,316	816,975	423,951	256,132	634,670
Philippines	206,137	206,504	107,037	84,374	173,371
Vietnam	123,416	131,093	64,050	35,212	92,912

Source: Non-Immigrant Visas issued by the Issuing Office (including Border Crossing Cards), Fiscal Years (2013–2022), https://travel.state.gov/content/dam/visas/Statistics/AnnualReports/FY2022AnnualReport/FY22_TableXVIII.pdf.

of the Biden administration will, therefore, be noted for its contribution in elevating US–India trade relations to a new high. It is perhaps fitting that both countries came together to embark on the IPEF in a year that pushed trade ties to a new high. However, a full flourishing of bilateral trade ties would still require more effort.

India–US Trade Relations: New Efforts and Old Issues

Over the last couple of years, particularly since the stabilisation of the COVID-19 pandemic in late 2021, the US and India have picked up momentum in engaging on a wide variety of trade issues. This latest engagement is distinct in its emphasis on extensive consultations and collaborative discussions in enabling both countries to develop an "ambitious, shared vision for the future of the trade relationship"[18] — a sentiment shared by Biden and India's Prime Minister Narendra Modi in their meeting at the White House on 24 September 2021.

US-India Trade Policy Forum

An important decision taken during the meeting between the two heads of states was to reconvene the US–India Trade Policy Forum (TPF) before the end of 2021.[19] The resurrection of the TPF to resolve issues adversely affecting the progress in bilateral trade has been a significant development with long-term implications. The initiative revives the efforts of US

President Barrack Obama's administration to create an enabling mechanism to facilitate bilateral trade and investment.

Originally created in 2010[20] as an outcome of the US–India Strategic Dialogue, the TPF lost ground during the Donald Trump administration. The forum did not meet from 2017 onwards. Its reconvening by the Biden administration has infused considerable energy in the bilateral trade and investment process through the initiative's dedicated focus on removing policy and procedural obstacles.

Co-chaired by US Trade Representative (USTR), Katherine Tai, and Indian Minister for Commerce and Industry, Piyush Goyal, the TPF has had two extensive consultations since its reconvening. These were on 23 November 2021[21] and 11 January 2023.[22] The forum's work areas are distributed across the verticals of agriculture, non-agricultural goods, services and investment and intellectual property (IP).[23]

The TPF has already begun delivering. The US' concerns over limited access to the Indian market for agricultural exports have been partly addressed through greater access obtained by US-origin cherries to the Indian market.[24] Further access to American agricultural exports has materialised, with India lowering import tariffs on pecan exports.[25] Both instances of trade liberalisation can be attributed to the efforts of the TPF. Indian garment exporter, Natchi Apparel, whose exports to the US were withheld by the customs and border protection authority on grounds of use of forced labour, was, subsequently, able to resume exports following the provision of satisfactory evidence establishing the contrary.[26] The latter facilitation is also attributable to the efforts of the TPF that is engaging on the critical issue of the relationship between trade and labour, including a deeper understanding of the use of forced labour in global supply chains.

The last meeting of the TPF on 12 January 2023 added a further working group on resilient trade.[27] Going forward, this new group, along with the rest, is expected to contribute to better bilateral understanding and communication on several major and contentious issues on trade, investments and supply chains. These include trade facilitation, labour rights, workforce development, digital trade, good regulatory practices, environmental protection and sustainability challenges. It is interesting to note that almost all these issues feature in the IPEF as well.

Intellectual Property

Along with the constructive effort to promote trade and investment through the TPF, there are some contentious issues that continue to remain as irritants in the bilateral trade space. Foremost among these is IP rights.

India continues to remain on the Priority Watch List (PWL) of the USTR's Special 301 report. The annual Special 301 report is an assessment of the global state of IP rights protection and their enforcement in various countries of the world.[28] The congressionally mandated annual review identifies a range of concerns, including the host country's IP regulations inhibiting innovation and diluting IP rights. The PWL mentions countries where these concerns are the uppermost. India figures on the list, along with Argentina, Chile, China, Indonesia, Russia and Venezuela.[29]

IP issues have traditionally been a major source of trade friction between Washington and New Delhi. India's emphasis on ensuring that IP rights do not create barriers for wider sharing of IP-intensive products (for example, pharmaceuticals) for all sections of the society at affordable rates occasionally acts against the interests of IP-holding US businesses keen on expanding market share in India. Loose IP protection is also considered a deterrent to encouraging greater innovation.

The latest TPF consultations, held on 12 January 2023, highlighted the efforts being made by both countries to overcome issues arising from India's administration of domestic IP rules and policies.[30] Given the sensitivities in India over the necessity of maintaining an economically and socially inclusive approach in managing IP regulations, it will still take considerable time before the US, arguably the world's largest exporter of IP-intensive goods and services, finds Indian policies aligned to the interests of its businesses.

Generalised System of Preferences

From an Indian perspective, the other key issue that remains a hurdle to deeper trade relations is the restoration of GSP benefits. The GSP is a trade preference programme that the US has been running for nearly five decades. The programme accords preferential access to several exports from developing countries to the US market.[31] It is administered in a non-reciprocal fashion, implying that the beneficiary countries of the programme are not required to offer similar preferences to US exports in their markets.

India's GSP benefits were terminated by the Trump administration on 4 March 2019. India was a major beneficiary of the GSP programme, with around 13 percent of its total exports to the US benefitting from preferential access.[32] The GSP termination was a major blow to Indian export prospects in the US. Notwithstanding the GSP preference programme being non-reciprocal in character, the Trump administration used "reciprocal benefits" as its argument for denying GSP benefits to India, "India's termination from [the] GSP follows its failure to provide the United States with assurances that it will provide equitable and reasonable access to its markets in numerous sectors."[33]

India's subsequent efforts to restore the GSP benefits have not yielded results. The TPF noted the issue in its first meeting on 23 November 2021, acknowledging India's "...interest in restoration of its beneficiary status under the US Generalized System of Preferences program".[34] The second meeting of the TPF on 11 January 2023 also noted India's interest in this regard. On both occasions, however, the TPF also noted the US' view that the restoration of the preference would depend upon the eligibility status determined by the US Congress.[35] The Biden administration's ability to reinstate the GSP benefits is limited since the preference programme legally expired on 31 December 2020 and has not been revived yet.[36]

India's Preferential Market Access and the IPEF

The restoration of India's GSP benefits is obviously a key variable in determining the future progress in US–India trade. While bilateral trade is increasing at a fast pace, its size and rate of growth will be enhanced if Indian exports can recover preferential access in the US market. Such access will also benefit US consumers significantly as they would be able to access several Indian products at cheap rates. There are views claiming that reinstating the GSP might also pave the way for a comprehensive bilateral FTA covering a wide range of issues.[37]

India as a 'Special Case'

For the Biden administration, however, restoring the GSP benefits for India will not be easy. Much will depend on the criteria chosen by the US Congress to decide the eligibility of beneficiary developing countries (BDC) for the GSP.

India's chances of having with the preference restored will be less if the US Congress adopts a narrow and selective criterion for determining BDCs, like limiting the preferences to least developed countries or excluding economies above a threshold size. Such conditions will not only reduce India's chances but will also result in some of the current major developing countries' emerging market economies receiving the GSP, such as Brazil, Indonesia, the Philippines, South Africa and Thailand,[38] being deprived. However, if the new criteria adopted by the US Congress allows these countries to continue as BDCs, then India would be able to press hard on its demand for restoration.

In order to restore the GSP benefits for India as a 'special case', the Biden administration must convince the US Congress on the importance of reviving the preference for India. The challenge for it in this regard will be to demonstrate that the grounds on which the Trump administration had withdrawn the preference, ostensibly for India's failure to provide 'equitable' and 'reasonable' access to its markets, is invalid. This should not be too difficult, given that US agricultural exports like cherries and pecans, as mentioned earlier, have begun to receive deeper access to the Indian market. The steady rise in US exports to India, along with efforts by the TPF to enable more access for exports on both sides, should help the Biden administration in building a convincing case for India.

The IPEF and the GSP

The issue of access to the US market has acquired a new dimension after the commencement of the negotiations on the IPEF. The IPEF is not proceeding as a traditional FTA and is not negotiating market access among its members. The negotiations in the trade pillar of the IPEF do not include exchanges of offers among the members on tariff cuts.[39] This, however, can be a major source of unhappiness among some IPEF members keenly eying preferential access in the US market, including India.

Among the ASEAN member states of the IPEF, Indonesia, the Philippines and Thailand are GSP BDCs, while Malaysia, Singapore and Vietnam are not. Singapore has a bilateral FTA with the US that enables its products to have preferential access to the American market. Such FTAs do not exist between the US and Malaysia and between the US and Vietnam. Both countries are keen to obtain preferential access to the US market. This was among the most powerful motivations that had earlier inspired them to join the US-led Trans-Pacific Partnership in the last decade.

Malaysia has already argued for a discussion on market access issues in the IPEF.[40] More countries might join the demand as the IPEF advances. American restrictions on technological exports to China (for example, semiconductors) can force leading semiconductor exporters like Korea to identify new markets for exports.[41] For these IPEF members, there cannot be a better substitute than the US market in this regard. The pressure on the US to grant the GSP or equivalent preferential access to these countries is expected to increase.

India has stayed away from the trade pillar of the IPEF, due to the absence of a 'broader consensus' among the members on several issues being discussed in the trade pillar, such as labour, environment, digital economy and public procurement.[42] The possibility of India being 'persuaded' to join the trade pillar on the assurance of it being restored with GSP benefits cannot be overlooked. Whether such assurances would be provided to the other IPEF members already engaged in the trade pillar is not clear. However, India's strategic heft with the US might go a long way in bolstering its credentials as a special case for the restoration of the GSP in the context of the IPEF.

There would, however, be conditionalities for the restoration of the GSP. In the IPEF context, this would mean India agreeing to US-drafted standards on sensitive issues, such as labour, environment and digital trade. The US would like these standards to be adopted by the IPEF as regional standards and would expect India's support in their acceptance and compliance.

India, however, should not make the restoration of the GSP a 'necessary' condition for agreeing to the standards. It is important to note that the IPEF is not proposing 'binding' standards that have implications for non-compliance. The framework does provide flexibility and India already has made use of the feature by staying away from the trade pillar. If there are regulatory pieces in other standards with which India is uncomfortable, it can always stay engaged with the overall process without committing to complying with uncomfortable rules.

The IPEF provides the opportunity for India to contribute decisively to regional rulemaking and play a role in building the economic rules-based architecture of the Indo-Pacific that is commensurate with its strategic significance. It should not shy away from doing so. Even if the GSP is not part of the deal, contributing to regional economic rules is a goal that India should stay committed to. In this regard, India should be sufficiently confident of being able to align its own standards with those of the US and the rest of the Indo-Pacific, given that it has made good progress in shaping domestic regulations on subjects like cross-border data transfer and its protection, trade facilitation, investments and competition policy.

Not the Last Word

The world's first and fifth largest economies are experiencing a robust phase of bilateral trade during the Biden administration. Bilateral trade has crossed the US$100 billion mark and is racing ahead to higher levels. Both sides are actively pursuing efforts to remove irritants in expanding bilateral trade. The TPF, reconvened after a hiatus of nearly five years, is looking closely at all possibilities of expanding access to exporters in both markets. It is also curating bilateral consultations on issues that are critical for modern trade — labour and environment standards, digital trade rules, critical and emerging technologies and greater resilience of major supply chains.

There are considerable expectations from the TPF. It will have to keep delivering meaningful outcomes to negate some of the cynicism surrounding its effectiveness.[43] However, expectations regarding the TPF facilitating a bilateral FTA need to be realistic. The most important realism in this regard is the striking contrast between the US and India on their current attitudes towards FTAs.

The Biden administration has been conspicuous in its efforts to not engage in FTAs. Indeed, the USTR and other senior functionaries of the Biden administration have completely refrained from using the phrase 'FTA'. The Biden administration has also not attempted to revive the Trade Promotion Authority that the US Congress grants to American presidents to negotiate FTAs on a 'fast-track' basis. The engagement of the US in the IPEF has been marked by the emphasis that it is not being negotiated as a traditional FTA, symbolised by the absence of negotiations on market access and tariffs.

India, conversely, is intensely engaging in FTAs. It formalised FTAs with the United Arab Emirates and Australia in 2022. It is in the advanced stages of negotiating bilateral FTAs with the United Kingdom, Canada and the European Union. It also plans to commence FTA negotiations with Israel and the Gulf Cooperation Council group of countries.[44]

It will be interesting to see how the US and India proceed with their trade relations, notwithstanding the sharp contrasts in their attitudes on engaging in FTAs. The difference, though, should not be considered a hindrance to deeper engagement in bilateral trade.

The current trajectory of overall US–India relations creates optimism over the fact that mutually wholesome appetites for consultation and bilateral strategic collaboration initiatives on a wide spectrum of issues will brush off positively on trade. These initiatives include engagement on critical and emerging technologies that include collaboration on defence, innovation, space, science, telecommunication and resilient supply chains in semiconductors;[45] the partnership on clean energy;[46] and close cooperation in three pillars of the IPEF.[47]

As the US–India strategic relationship expands, it will inevitably bring in more stakeholders and actors into the larger economic space of the relationship. Business developments like Air India's humongous purchase of new Boeings[48] and Apple making India one of its global manufacturing hubs[49] not only strengthen the bilateral economic partnership but also positively impact trade by increasing the exports of goods and services, movement of people and sharing of industrial best practices and regulations. In this regard, the US–India trade relations should not be looked at through the narrow prism of bread-and-butter issues like the GSP and tariffs but from much broader global and regional strategic perspectives.

Given the marked differences that continue to exist between the US and India on several trade-impacting regulatory issues, the work on aligning perspectives on bilateral trade will be a long-drawn out process. The current conditions of healthy consultation created by the TPF and the IPEF are encouraging signs of persisting with the process. Both the TPF and the IPEF can bridge differences in regulations between the two countries effectively. The US and India should make every effort to stay engaged with the two processes.

Endnotes

1. The Quad comprises the US, India, Japan and Australia.
2. "Fact sheet: In Asia, President Biden and a dozen Indo-Pacific partners launch the Indo-Pacific economic framework for prosperity", *The White House*, 23 May 2022, https://www.whitehouse.gov/briefing-room/statements-releases/2022/05/23/fact-sheet-in-asia-president-biden-and-a-dozen-indo-pacific-partners-launch-the-indo-pacific-economic-framework-for-prosperity/.
3. *Ibid.*
4. Cambodia, Laos and Myanmar are the three ASEAN member economies that are not part of the IPEF.
5. India opted to stay out of the RCEP due to complicated domestic reasons. See Amitendu Palit, "Domestic politics force India's withdrawal from RCEP and broader trade disengagement", *Asia Pacific Bulletin*, Number 494, East-West Center, 26 November 2019, https://www.eastwestcenter.org/publications/domestic-politics-force-india%E2%80%99s-withdrawal-rcep-and-broader-trade-disengagement.
6. The CPTPP, formerly known as the Trans-Pacific Partnership (TPP), was actively driven by the US administration under President Barrack Obama. President Donald Trump withdrew the US from the TPP upon entering office in January 2017.
7. "World development indicators", The World Bank, https://datatopics.worldbank.org/world-development-indicators/.
8. "GDP growth (annual %)", World Development Indicators, The World Bank, https://data.worldbank.org/indicator/NY.GDP.MKTP.KD.ZG.
9. "World economic outlook", International Monetary Fund, October 2021, https://www.imf.org/en/Publications/WEO/Issues/2021/10/12/world-economic-outlook-october-2021.

10. "World economic outlook", International Monetary Fund, October 2022, https://www.imf.org/en/Publications/WEO/Issues/2022/10/11/world-economic-outlook-october-2022.
11. "World economic outlook update", International Monetary Fund, January 2023, https://www.imf.org/en/Publications/WEO/Issues/2023/01/31/world-economic-outlook-update-january-2023.
12. "Trade in goods with India", United States Census Bureau, https://www.census.gov/foreign-trade/balance/c5330.html.
13. *Ibid.*
14. *Ibid.*
15. "Top trading partners — December 2022", United States Census Bureau, https://www.census.gov/foreign-trade/statistics/highlights/topcm.html.
16. "Total trade: Top countries, year 2021–22", Export-Import Data Bank, Department of Commerce, Ministry of Commerce and Industry, Government of India, https://tradestat.commerce.gov.in/eidb/iecnttopn.asp.
17. Ari Hoffman and Jeanne Batalova, "Indian immigrants in the United States", Migration Policy Institute, 7 December 2022, https://www.migrationpolicy.org/article/indian-immigrants-united-states#:~:text=Today%2C%20Indians%20represent%20the%20second,their%20numbers%20continue%20to%20grow.
18. "US–India Joint Leaders' statement: A partnership for global good", The White House, 24 September 2021, https://www.whitehouse.gov/briefing-room/statements-releases/2021/09/24/u-s-india-joint-leaders-statement-a-partnership-for-global-good/.
19. *Ibid.*
20. United States–India trade policy forum: Framework for cooperation on trade and investment", Office of the US Trade Representative, 17 March 2010, https://ustr.gov/sites/default/files/uploads/U.S.%20India%20Framework%20for%20Cooperation%20on%20Trade%20and%20Investment.pdf.
21. "Joint Statement from the United States–India trade policy forum", Office of the US States Trade Representative, 23 November 2021, https://ustr.gov/about-us/policy-offices/press-office/press-releases/2021/november/joint-statement-united-states-india-trade-policy-forum.
22. "Joint statement on India–United States trade policy forum", Ministry of Commerce & Industry, Government of India, 12 January 2023, Press Information Bureau (PIB), India, https://pib.gov.in/PressReleaseIframePage.aspx?PRID=1890606#:~:text=They%20reiterated%20the%20importance%20to,Ministers%20and%20their%20senior%20officials.
23. *Ibid.*

24. "2023 trade policy agenda and 2022 annual report", Office of the US Trade Representative, p. 139, https://ustr.gov/sites/default/files/2023-02/2023%20Trade%20Policy%20Agenda%20and%202022%20Annual%20Report%20FINAL%20(1).pdf.
25. *Ibid.*, p. 8.
26. *Ibid.*, p. 169.
27. "Joint statement on India–United States trade policy forum", Ministry of Commerce & Industry, Government of India, 12 January 2023, Press Information Bureau (PIB), India, https://pib.gov.in/PressReleaseIframePage.aspx?PRID=1890606#:~:text=They%20reiterated%20the%20importance%20to,Ministers%20and%20their%20senior%20officials.
28. "Special 301", Office of the US Trade Representative, https://ustr.gov/issue-areas/intellectual-property/special-301.
29. "2023 trade policy agenda and 2022 annual report", Office of the US Trade Representative, p. 116, https://ustr.gov/sites/default/files/2023-02/2023%20Trade%20Policy%20Agenda%20and%202022%20Annual%20Report%20FINAL%20(1).pdf
30. "Joint statement on India–United States trade policy forum", Ministry of Commerce & Industry, Government of India, 12 January 2023, Press Information Bureau (PIB), India, https://pib.gov.in/PressReleaseIframePage.aspx?PRID=1890606#:~:text=They%20reiterated%20the%20importance%20to,Ministers%20and%20their%20senior%20officials. The specific areas noted in this regard where the United States has welcomed India's domestic consultations are treatment of confidential business information for patents and streamlining copyright infringement investigations.
31. "Generalized system of preferences", Office of the US Trade Representative, https://ustr.gov/issue-areas/trade-development/preference-programs/generalized-system-preference-gsp.
32. Amitendu Palit, "Why India lost US GSP benefits", *ISAS Brief No. 642*, Institute of South Asian Studies, National University of Singapore, 19 March 2019, https://www.isas.nus.edu.sg/wp-content/uploads/2019/03/ISAS-Briefs-No.-642-Why-India-lost-US-GSP-benefits.pdf.
33. "United States will terminate GSP designation of India and Turkey", Office of the US Trade Representative, 4 March 2019, https://ustr.gov/about-us/policy-offices/press-office/press-releases/2019/march/united-states-will-terminate-gsp.
34. "Joint statement from the United States–India trade policy forum", Office of the United States Trade Representative, 23 November 2021, Press Information Bureau (PIB), India, https://pib.gov.in/PressReleaseIframePage.

aspx?PRID=1890606#:~:text=They%20reiterated%20the%20 importance%20to,Ministers%20and%20their%20senior%20officials.
35. "Joint statement on India–United States trade policy forum", Ministry of Commerce & Industry, Government of India, 12 January 2023, Press Information Bureau (PIB), India, https://pib.gov.in/PressReleaseIframePage. aspx?PRID=1890606#:~:text=They%20reiterated%20the%20 importance%20to,Ministers%20and%20their%20senior%20officials.
36. "GSP expiration: Frequently asked questions", Office of the US Trade Representative, 3 January 2021, https://ustr.gov/sites/default/files/gsp/GSP ExpirationFAQ.pdf.
37. "Experts weigh in on the 2023 US–India trade policy forum meetings", *South Asia Source*, Atlantic Council, 9 January 2023, https://www. atlanticcouncil.org/blogs/southasiasource/experts-weigh-in-on-the-2023-US–India-trade-policy-forum-meetings/.
38. "Countries eligible for GSP (as of December 2020)", GSP Program Information, Office of the US Trade Representative, https://ustr.gov/sites/default/files/gsp/countrieseligiblegsp.pdf.
39. The trade pillar, that is, Pillar 1 of the IPEF, discusses labour, environment, digital economy, agriculture, transparency, good regulatory practices, competition policy, trade facilitation, inclusivity, technical assistance and economic cooperation. "Ministerial text for trade Pillar of the Indo-Pacific economic framework for prosperity", Office of the US Trade Representative, https://ustr.gov/sites/default/files/2022-09/IPEF%20Pillar%201%20 Ministerial%20Text%20 (Trade%20Pillar)_FOR%20PUBLIC%20RELEASE %20(1).pdf.
40. "Malaysia urges IPEF to focus on market access element", *Malaysia Now*, 9 March 2023, https://www.malaysianow.com/news/2022/07/28/malaysia-urges-ipef-to-focus-on-market-access-element.
41. William Choong, "Avoiding divots in the US Pivot to Asia", *Fulcrum.sg*, 20 January 2023, https://fulcrum.sg/avoiding-divots-in-the-u-s-pivot-to-asia/.
42. "India opts out of joining IPEF trade pillar, to wait for final contours", *Business Standard*, 10 March 2023, https://www.business-standard.com/article/economy-policy/india-opts-out-of-joining-ipef-trade-pillar-to-wait-for-final-contours-122091000344_1.html.
43. "Experts weigh in on the 2023 US–India trade policy forum meetings", *South Asia Source*, Atlantic Council, 9 January 2023, https://www. atlanticcouncil.org/blogs/southasiasource/experts-weigh-in-on-the-2023-US–India-trade-policy-forum-meetings/.

44. The GCC members include Bahrain, Kuwait, Oman, Qatar, Saudi Arabia and the United Arab Emirates.
45. "Fact sheet: United States and India elevate strategic partnership with the initiative on critical and emerging technology (iCET)", The White House, 31 January 2023, https://www.whitehouse.gov/briefing-room/statements-releases/2023/01/31/fact-sheet-united-states-and-india-elevate-strategic-partnership-with-the-initiative-on-critical-and-emerging-technology-icet/#:~:text=President%20Biden%20and%20Prime%20Minister,institutions%20of%20our%20two%20countries.
46. "US–India strategic clean energy partnership ministerial joint statement", Office of International Affairs, 7 October 2022, https://www.energy.gov/ia/articles/US-India-strategic-clean-energy-partnership-ministerial-joint-statement.
47. While India has refrained from engaging in the trade pillar, it is actively engaged in the other three pillars — supply chains, clean economy and fair economy.
48. "From Apple to Boeing, India is being put to the test as China manufacturing alternative", *CNBC*, 12 March 2023, https://www.cnbc.com/2023/03/12/from-apple-to-boeing-india-is-being-put-to-the-test-as-the-new-china.html.
49. "Apple starts manufacturing iPhone 14 in India in a shift away from China", *TechCrunch*, 26 September 2022, https://techcrunch.com/2022/09/25/apple-starts-manufacturing-iphone-14-in-india/.

Chapter 12

Indian Americans: Visibility and Influence

Seema Sirohi

It is no longer an exaggeration to say that Indian Americans have "arrived" in the United States (US). A cursory look at the American society tells the story better than statistics and studies. Apart from the traditional fields associated with people of Indian origin such as medicine, science and technology, Indian faces are increasingly common in politics, on television, in comedy clubs and in culinary arts, and they are slowly showing up in American sports. In the span of one generation, Indian Americans have not only made a mark in almost every domain but have also excelled and prospered.

According to data from the Pew Research Center, while Asian Americans are better off in general, Indian Americans have the highest annual household income at US$119,000, compared to US$68,000 for all Americans.[1] Around 32 percent have a bachelor's degree and 43 percent have a post-graduate degree, compared to 20 percent and 13 percent, respectively, of all Americans.[2] Indian Americans suffer the lowest poverty rate at six percent and are the second-largest immigrant group.[3] They are often referred to as a "model minority".

Two Indian Americans — Nikki Haley and Vivek Ramaswamy — are currently competing to run for president as the Republican party candidate in 2024. Whether either procures the nomination or not, the idea that an Indian American can be in the ring for the top-most job is a measure of assimilation, acceptance and aspiration. After Bobby Jindal in 2016 and Kamala Harris in 2020, this is the third presidential election cycle with — not one this time but two — Indian American candidates.

After the 2022 mid-term Congressional elections, the number of Indian Americans in the House of Representatives has increased from four to five — a proportional representation for a population of roughly 4.5 million.[4] At the state and local levels, the list of elected Indian American office-bearers numbers 50 and is growing.[5] Jindal broke the state barrier in 2007 when he was elected governor of Louisiana, while Haley was the first Indian American woman to do the same in 2010 when she won in South Carolina. Last year, Aruna Miller became the first Indian American lieutenant governor of Maryland. "Representation matters, and there is a lot of excitement and energy in the community right now that can help determine what this country looks like going forward", according to Congressman Ro Khanna. He stressed the need to remain focused on working together and presenting "a united front" to make the Indian American community's voice stronger in all aspects of society and push for increased representation across the board.[6]

In the business world, Indian American chief executive officers (CEOs) are a plenty, heading major US companies, with Sundar Pichai (Google), Satya Nadella (Microsoft), Arvind Krishna (IBM) and Revathi Advaithi (Flex) leading the pack. At least 60 CEOs of Fortune 500 companies are of Indian origin, according to M. R. Rangaswami, founder of Indiaspora, the California-based organisation aimed at building the community's engagement with civic and social issues.

The story is the same in the world of academia, activism, literature, arts and entertainment, fashion and music. It is no wonder US President Joe Biden famously joked that Indian Americans were "taking over the country" during a congratulatory phone call with Swati Mohan, an aerospace engineer who was part of the National Aeronautics and Space Administration team that successfully landed the Perseverance rover on Mars in 2021. "You guys are incredible", he gushed as he listed other Indian Americans around him, starting with his vice president (Kamala Harris) and speech writer (Vinay Reddy).

Biden could have gone on if he wanted because he has appointed more than 130 Indian Americans in his administration — the highest number by any president.[7] Tarun Chhabra is the White House Senior Director of Technology and National Security, while Rush Doshi is Deputy Senior Director for China and Taiwan. Bharat Ramamurti is the Deputy Director of the National Economic Council. Their portfolios say it all, given the US–China strategic rivalry and the role of emerging technologies in the on-going competition. The US Surgeon General is Dr. Vivek Murthy, and the White House COVID-19 Response Coordinator is Dr. Ashish Jha. The US State Department has numerous Indian American officers.

A mile from the White House, on Capitol Hill, hundreds of Indian Americans work as staff, including at senior levels. They help members of the Congress write bills, conduct research, maintain contact with constituents and manage the media. There was a time when one could count Indian American staffers in the US Congress on one hand and when a brown face on a think tank row in Washington was seen as unusual. That is no longer the case, as Indian faces proliferate in the think tank world, heading programmes and providing inputs to the US State Department and Pentagon on a regular basis.

"Indian Americans are part of the scene of normal everyday life. We are no longer just doctors. We are literally all over the place. Diwali is celebrated in schools. Our holidays are American holidays. Indian food is American food", a long-time senior staffer on Capitol Hill said. Indian Americans have created space for themselves in policy areas, whether it is health, economics or climate issues. They have put their time in and earned their credentials, he said.

According to Rangaswami, when he started the organisation in 2012, he heard a lot about how Indian doctors and technology workers were the torch bearers. However, the community lacked influence in politics. "The question was, 'Can we be one percent of the political force and one percent of the Congress?' And, indeed, we have accomplished that pretty quickly", he said. "The community has grown in stature and influence across the board".[8]

It is important to note that much of the story is of the last 20 years because of the "numerical take-off" in 2000 when the number of Indian workers in the US surged dramatically, thanks to the technology boom. Demographic heft led to political heft as the second generation came of age. Another interesting point is that Indian American representation in the US Congress is not centred in places where Indian Americans are in majority, which means that the candidates appealed to a wider cross-section of society, according to Milan Vaishnav, Director of the South Asia Program at Carnegie Endowment.[9]

But the Picture Is Complex

Yet, the widespread success of Indian Americans does not tell the complete story. Hidden behind the narrative of a "model minority" are difficult stories of lay-offs of Indian H-1B visa holders, daily struggles of working class taxi drivers, domestic abuse of women, caste problems and discrimination by employers. Many small businesses on Chicago's Devon Street, known as a hub of Indian restaurants, and grocery stores in New York's Jackson Heights fight month-to-month to stay afloat. The impact of the COVID-19 pandemic on small entrepreneurs was devastating as stores shut down and clients stayed away. However, hardly any prominent Indian Americans were at the forefront, helping those people get loans under the Treasury Department's Paycheck Protection Program (PPP). The PPP loans were a lifeline for many COVID-19-affected businesses to help cover eight weeks of payroll costs. Data on the recipients does not show many Indian American names.[10]

Aggregate income figures for Indian Americans "mask severe inequalities within the community" with "concentrated pockets of deprivation, especially among the large number of unauthorised immigrants born in India and residing in the United States".[11] In 2019, approximately 553,000 of the estimated 11 million unauthorised immigrants in the US were from India, according to the Migration Policy Institute.[12] The latest numbers show an upward trend. In 2022, authorities reported 63,927 undocumented Indians at the US border, a sharp increase from 2,600 cases the year before.[13] With legal pathways to naturalisation becoming more difficult, more and more Indians are either overstaying their tourist visas or trying to enter illegally.

Indian Americans are also victims of discrimination and bias, a reality of life from the time they first arrived in the early 1900s as farm workers from Punjab and were deemed the least desirable of all races. Every wave of immigration resulted in some form of backlash — the earliest arrivals were not allowed to marry or own land. In the 1970s and 1980s, Indian Americans in New Jersey faced violent attacks by a hate group that called itself Dotbusters, in a reference to the traditional 'bindi' Hindu women wear on their foreheads. US Donald Trump's presidency and charged rhetoric opened the door to the latest bout of anti-immigrant sentiment. The social climate has remained volatile even after his departure and Biden is struggling to keep his promises on fair immigration policies.

According to a survey on Indian American attitudes, 31 percent of the respondents cited discrimination as a major problem, while 53 percent said it was a minor problem. One in two reported being subjected to some form of discrimination over the previous year either because of their skin colour, gender, religion or heritage.[14] The survey also showed that Indian Americans born in the US were more likely to talk about discrimination than those born abroad, revealing a generational divide on the issue.

Bias and prejudice are also present within the community, something Indian Americans do not normally like to discuss. India's caste system has followed the diaspora to workplaces in America, most notoriously in the technology world populated by hundreds of star products from India's famed Indian Institutes of Technology. In 2020, for the first time in US history, caste was at the centre of a court case when the State of California sued Cisco Systems, a software company, on the basis of a complaint by a Dalit engineer. The complainant said he was discriminated against, harassed and belittled by two upper-caste supervisors. The case is ongoing.

Over the last few years, Dalit activists have lobbied federal and local governments and university systems to take measures to specifically ban caste-based discrimination. At least six universities, including Brown and Harvard, now include caste in their non-discriminatory policy. In February 2023, Seattle became the first US city to ban caste discrimination after a tense debate between supporters and opponents. The ordinance was proposed by Kshama Sawant, a self-described socialist and the only Indian American on the city council. Dalit advocates praised the ordinance as a victory, while opponents said bringing caste into the civil rights discourse would generate more Hinduphobia and deter businesses from hiring Indian Americans. The community is deeply divided between liberals and conservatives on the issue of caste.

Difficulties of Diversity

It is evident that the Indian American community is not monolithic or homogeneous. It contains layers of class, religious and caste divisions that remain mostly in the background because of a general tendency to celebrate the achievements and highlight every "first" in the community — the first spelling bee winner, the first university president, the first CEO, the first judge or the first presidential appointee.

"Self-proclaimed community leaders who are more concerned with the "model minority" title do not want to recognise the different narratives. But it's important to validate the existence of working class people and not render them invisible", says Deepa Iyer, an activist, lawyer and former executive director of South Asian Americans Leading Together, an advocacy group.[15] "Rich Indian Americans living in silos of leafy suburbs where they mainly fraternise with people of their own faith, caste and status should have conversations with people who do not have the same advantage", Iyer added.

A 2020 study of poverty among Indian Americans prepared for Indiaspora showed that 6.5 percent of Indian Americans lived below the poverty threshold. Of them, 11 percent collected social security and 16.8 percent lived on food stamps.[16] It also showed that a majority of the affected population was not in the labour force, which could mean the people lacked proper legal status. The pockets of poor Indian Americans are concentrated in the states with the largest diaspora population such as New York, Illinois and California, and often live close to their wealthiest counterparts. The COVID-19 pandemic hit the already vulnerable segment hard, and estimates show that a quarter of poor Indian American households likely lost their principal source of income. If a full-blown recession sets in, poverty rates could increase.[17]

The Religious Divide

There is also evidence that the Hindu–Muslim divide has manifested itself among Indian Americans in recent years and more sharply since the election of Prime Minister Narendra Modi in India. The Indian American Muslim Council (IAMC), established in 2002 in direct response to violence against Muslims in the Indian state of Gujarat, has become a prominent voice against Hindu nationalism in the US. The group regularly raises questions about the treatment of minorities in India and tries to mobilise members of the US Congress against the Modi government. Its spokespersons use charged terminology such as "genocide" to describe the violence against Muslims in India.[18] The IAMC is supported by a few Christian, Arab American and left-wing groups in its efforts. Domestic politics of the Modi government has clearly become a part of domestic politics in the US, pitching Hindu Americans against Muslim Americans.

The anti-Modi feelings are so strong among Indian and Pakistani Muslims that they are willing to go to extremes and support even an anti-minority, right-wing candidate in a US election. In 2020, Sri Preston Kulkarni, a Democrat and a Hindu American, lost his second bid to be a member of the US Congress from Texas to a Trump supporter with a chequered past. Kulkarni's carefully built coalition of various Asian American groups collapsed because of Hindu–Muslim politics. A former US foreign service officer, Kulkarni was close to turning a red Republican district blue because of his formidable outreach to ethnic minorities — he campaigned in 27 languages.

Kulkarni's "sin", as it were, was to attend the '*Howdy* Modi' rally in Houston in 2019 and accept campaign donations from some pro-Modi Indian Americans. Some Indian and Pakistani Muslim Americans said he had not condemned Hindutva politics in India strongly enough even though he had condemned Islamophobia in strong terms — the new touchstones of diaspora and leftist politics. "If elections in America are decided by criteria such as who is good for India, or Indian Muslims, or Palestinians, or Israel, then who will care about what is good for America?", asked Muqtedar Khan, a professor at the University of Delaware. "Kulkarni, to my mind, is undoubtedly good for America. He is progressive, inclusive, respects science and rule of law, and understands the plight of minorities".[19] However, the charged Hindu–Muslim diaspora politics does not leave space for candidates like Kulkarni.

The Modi government's decision to revoke the special status of Kashmir in 2019 further deepened the religious divide. Indian Muslims and their supporters lobbied members of the US Congress hard, sending information on the clampdown and arrests of political leaders in Kashmir.

As a result, a public hearing in the House of Representatives in October 2019 became a contest between anti and pro-Modi groups. If an anti-Modi resolution were to be floated by a member of the US Congress today, it is almost certain that Hindu and Muslim Americans would be on opposite sides. To some extent, these cleavages dissipate the overall influence of the community in the US Congress and tarnish its image in the eyes of some.

The question of identity itself is also increasingly contested. While a majority of people identify as Indian American, many Indian-origin academics and activists prefer to use the term 'South Asian' to be more inclusive of people from other diasporas. However, it is a mismatch — how people think of their identities and how academics think their identities ought to be, according to Devesh Kapur, Director of Asia Programs at the Johns Hopkins School of Advanced International Studies. University departments, funding streams and academic conferences insist on using the term 'South Asian' even though surveys show the term is embraced only by a small minority.[20]

Community organisers insist that there is benefit in banding together with others. The inclination to call themselves South Asian rather than Indian American is generational, not one forced by academics, Iyer insisted.[21] Second-generation Indian Americans who were born and raised in the US have a different understanding and want to be inclusive. After the 9/11 attacks, when hate crimes against immigrants registered an increase, the perpetrators did not distinguish between a Bangladeshi American and an Indian American. Besides, people can have multiple identities. Iyer said, "It's important to recognise we have more political power when we band together. Even though Indian Americans are the largest group among South Asians, it's important to work in solidarity".[22]

However, first-generation Indian immigrants do not want to be associated with Pakistani Americans, especially on political issues that affect India, given the painful history of the subcontinent's partition and the continued use of terrorism against India by Pakistan's intelligence services. The agenda of Pakistani Americans, who are close to the establishment in Islamabad, remains broadly anti-India, leaving little room for real bonhomie between the two diasporas. The younger generation, however, carries less baggage on these questions and embraces the term 'South Asian' more readily. It is more willing to form issue-based alliances.

Another question of identity is tied up with a general American tendency to think of Asian Americans as largely those who come from the East and Southeast Asian countries, such as China, South Korea, Vietnam, Cambodia and others. Popular discourse on Asian Americans tends to exclude people from South Asia. Karthick Ramakrishnan, a professor of public policy at the University of California, Riverside, who tracks demographic data, has repeatedly taken the media to task for the omission. Even though South Asians are the fastest growing contingent of Asian Americans and represent more than 25 percent of the group population, news stories continue "to hold onto the outdated notion of East Asian as the archetype of what it means to be Asian in America".[23]

Wielding Influence

The fault lines along religion, caste and identity within the Indian American community make the job of working together for the betterment of the community or influencing policy on major issues more difficult. However, they can come together in some circumstances. The devastating second wave of COVID-19 in India in 2021 saw community leaders, especially Democratic party supporters, raise money and lobby the White House to send emergency aid. They also weighed in with members of the India caucus in both the House and Senate to push the administration. It was only the second time that Indian Americans had mobilised on a large scale since 2008 when prominent community members lobbied the US Congress to approve the India–US civil nuclear agreement.

Kapil Sharma, one of the first Indian American Congressional staffers on Capitol Hill, said things work when the issue is significant but of a general nature such as a major agreement between India and the US. Sharma stated, "The nuclear deal was a generational issue and older Indian Americans were active. But when the big issues are done, the community is all over the place".[24] It is hard to put a ring around the Indian American community and each segment tends to operate in its self-interest, be it doctors or hotel owners, according to Sharma, who has worked in the past on issues affecting the community.

In terms of domestic issues, something that has animated Indian Americans in recent times is the question of affirmative action in university and school admissions. Attempts by the authorities to bring diversity to the student body by including socio-economic factors, in addition to merit-based criteria, have prompted Indian American parents to push back. In 2020, changes in the admission policy at Thomas Jefferson High School for Science and Technology — often ranked as the country's number one — led to a high-octane legal fight between school authorities and a coalition of Indian and other Asian American parents.

The parents branded the new policies designed to bring in more African American students as unfair and anti-Asian. They cited statistics showing the percentage of Asian students at the school dropped from 70 to around 55 in 2021. The case went all the way to the Supreme Court, and, in April 2022, the court issued a one-sentence ruling allowing the new admission policy to continue.[25] The issue reverberated with Indian Americans across the country. A similar case challenging affirmative action policies of Harvard University and the University of North Carolina is pending in the Supreme Court.

It is noteworthy that some Indian Americans are willing to go against affirmative action policies, even though a majority identify as Democrats and racial justice is one of the most important planks of the party. Nearly 72 percent said they planned to vote for Biden in a 2020 survey. Although a slim majority (54 percent) supported the consideration of race in college admissions, a strong minority (46 percent) was against the idea.[26] As the US struggles to rectify the legacy of structural racism against African Americans, Indian Americans seem largely to subscribe to the idea of pulling oneself by the bootstraps and succeeding. Many forget their own privileged upbringing in India, about reaping the benefits of class and caste selection which, in turn, gave them the ability to come to the West where they were rewarded once again because the immigration system privileged them as skilled professionals.

The Technological Sector: H-1Bs at Great Risk

However, the tables of success can also turn quickly because of economic factors, as the most agile and dynamic group of Indian

Americans — technology workers — discovered in 2022–2023 with the downturn in the technology sector. Thousands have been laid off and face the risk of deportation because their employment-dependent visas become invalid after 60 days unless they are re-hired. The reasons behind the massive layoffs are complex but evidence shows that technology companies went on a hiring spree in 2020 as the pandemic set in and demand for their products soared. They offered high salaries to recruit and bolster their ranks; they bet that the boom would last as the other sectors of the economy were forced to work remotely. However, the demand did not last. By 2022, technology stocks plummeted amid interest rate hikes, inflation and broader worries about the economy.

A total of 140,000 technology-related jobs were lost in 2022, with Amazon alone cutting 18,000 jobs and Salesforce eliminating about 7,000 positions. By March 2023, 94,000 layoffs had already been announced.[27] Of the laid-off workers, between 30 percent and 40 percent, respectively, are believed to be Indians. Many fear deportation because finding a job within the stipulated time period is extremely difficult, even with a cut in salary. A few sympathetic members of the US Congress asked the Department of Homeland Security to double the time — from 60 to 120 days — an unemployed H-1B worker can legally remain in the country. However, they were told the regulatory changes required would take too much time. Companies such as Tech Mahindra, Tredence, Meylah and others have offered to hire H-1B workers by reaching out to community leaders.

Khanna, who represents Silicon Valley, said his office was in touch with constituents to offer help. "I am particularly concerned about what happens to children who come to the United States and age out (at 21 years) of coverage from their parents' work visas", he said. Even though they came here when they were two or three years old and have grown up here, they do not have citizenship.[28] More than 80,000 Indian American children are at risk of losing legal status.[29]

Indians have traditionally been the largest beneficiaries of the H-1B visa programme and receive 75 percent of the annual 85,000 H-1B visas issued worldwide. The phenomenon goes back to the technology boom in the US at the turn of the century and the expansion of the H-1B visas. Indian computer engineers and software developers came in large numbers to fill the demand — more than 60 percent of all Indian Americans arrived in 2000 or after. Most of them applied for permanent residency or a green card. Within a few years, they were faced with long waits because of the per-country cap.

The US Congress has a seven percent cap on the 140,000 employment-based green cards issued every year, which translates to 9,800 permits per country. The cap has resulted in a huge backlog for Indians. The backlog in 2020 was 1.2 million, of whom 68 percent were Indians, according to Cato Institute, a Washington think tank. The study used official figures from the US Citizenship and Immigration Services.[30] It said only half of the Indians will eventually get green cards. The problem worsened when Trump stopped all visa applications in 2020 during the pandemic, a decision that was reversed by Biden the following year but with little relief on the ground.

The US Congress is engaged on the issue, but if history is any guide, it is unlikely to come up with a fix. Immigration reform has eluded a solution for decades, even though both Republicans and Democrats say they want to reform the system. However, they cannot agree on how — whether to raise the per country cap or increase the number of green cards for a few years. Either way, it would create a political problem for American lawmakers because Indians would benefit the most, creating an issue for immigrants from other countries. The deep partisan divide and fear that any concession would invite a backlash make any serious immigration reform a distant prospect.

What Comes Next for Indian Americans?

In a general atmosphere of "America and Americans First", Democrats are wary of pushing for the rights of foreign workers front and centre, lest the move agitates US workers. Biden, a vocal supporter of labour unions, has stayed away from negotiating new trade agreements or opening the US market further because of potential opposition from progressive Democrats. With several economists warning of a looming recession in 2023, the plight of laid-off H-1B workers is likely to get worse. Indian American community leaders will have to step up and lobby the US Congress and the White House for some measure of relief.

Some also worry about a possible backlash against Indian Americans in general if they are seen as disproportionately reaping the fruits of society or seen as too eager to grab seats at the political high table. Over the last 20 years, many Indian American candidates have been painted as "not American enough" or simply dismissed with racial slurs during political campaigns. It is a low-cost, high-return manoeuvre. In 2010, Michael R. Pompeo, a Republican and Trump's Secretary of State, ran a nasty campaign in Kansas against Indian American Raj Goyle, a Democrat. Pompeo's staff shared a blog post on social media saying: "This Goyle character is just another "turban topper" we don't need in Congress or any political office that deals with the US Constitution, Christianity and the United States of America". The limits of participation were clearly defined.[31]

Pompeo apologised to Goyle, but the "othering" of Indian Americans in politics continues. In January 2023, when Harmeet Dhillon made a bid to become the chair of the Republican National Committee, her opponents raised concerns about her Sikh faith and used it as a "weapon" against her. The whisper campaign was damaging enough to prompt Dhillon to call out the "bigotry" of some members, while the party was trying to build links with minority communities.[32]

Khanna agrees there is a "rising fear" because of high-profile acts of discrimination and hate against minority communities. "But I am more hopeful than anxious. Our endeavour in America is to become the first multiracial, multi-ethnic democracy in the world. From Congress to Silicon Valley to fields like journalism and healthcare, the Indian American community will continue to succeed and build influence. This is the start of a new era, and we will not go backwards".[33]

Rangaswami says it is more appropriate and political to emphasise the "impact" of the Indian American community on American society rather than talking about accomplishments. One conveys the message of contribution, while the other sounds boastful. Instead of focusing on Indian American CEOs, people should focus on the number of jobs they create. At least 10 percent of Fortune 500 companies are headed by Indian Americans and, together, they account for roughly two million American jobs. Similarly, there are 200,000 Indian American doctors and around 20,000 academics who touch the lives of millions of Americans on a daily basis. "We have to shift the narrative and go up the maturity cycle. Once upon a time, the community needed role models and Americans needed to see a minority succeed. Now there are enough Indian Americans in every field and the American public sees that too", he says. "We need to go to the Congress and say, please spend on issues impacting the community and make sure regulations (such as those on H-1B visas) are changed".[34]

Some community members worry that the backlash could come not just from White Americans but from African and Hispanic Americans if Indian American success — a result of hard work as well as special circumstances — becomes a yardstick for measuring the accomplishments of other minorities. Indian information technology (IT) giants operating in the US have already faced anger as the face of "outsourcing" and for displacing better-paid American workers with lower-paid Indians. The negative image prompted IT companies to start scholarships for underprivileged students and undertake local projects to build bridges with their local communities.

Indian Americans are also increasingly trying to make an impact as philanthropists, but the fact gets obscured by the success stories of CEOs and doctors. Estimates show that Indian Americans donate about US$1 billion a year on average to various charitable organisations and non-government organisations, but most of them in India. Members of the India Philanthropy Alliance (IPA) — an organisation founded in 2019 — have raised more than US$120 million annually in the US to fund various groups in India. The IPA raised over US$1 million for its inaugural India Giving Day held in February–March 2023.[35]

Indian Americans have also begun to fund local groups, universities and national campaigns in the US. Although they lag behind Americans as a whole in hard donations, "they volunteer at double the national average: contributing 220 hours per year", compared to 137 hours for Americans overall.[36]

Most experts agree that Indian Americans have come into their own in many ways, while they are on a learning curve in some others. The community will continue to grow and remain an integral part of the American story.

Endnotes

1. "Indians in the US fact sheet", Pew Research Center, 29 April 2021, https://www.pewresearch.org/social-trends/fact-sheet/asian-americans-indians-in-the-u-s/.
2. "Education attainment of Indian population in the US, 2019", Pew Research Center, https://www.pewresearch.org/social-trends/chart/educational-attainment-of-indian-population-in-the-u-s-2019/.
3. "Indians in the US fact sheet", Pew Research Center, 29 April 2021, https://www.pewresearch.org/social-trends/fact-sheet/asian-americans-indians-in-the-u-s/.
4. *Ibid.*
5. *Ibid.*
6. Email interview with Ro Khanna by the author, 15 March 2023.
7. Press TRUST of India, "Record over 130 Indian-Americans at key positions in Biden administration", India Today, 24 August 2022, https://www.indiatoday.in/world/story/record-over-130-indian-americans-key-positions-biden-administration-1991820-2022-08-24.
8. Interview with M. R. Rangaswami by Lalit K. Jha, Chief correspondent of the *Press Trust of India*, 31 January 2023.
9. Interview with Milan Vaishnav by the author, 28 February 2023.
10. Alyssa Fowers, Andrew Van Dam, Jonathan O'Connell and Aaron Gregg, "Explore updated SBA data on businesses that received PPP loans", *The Washington Post*, 4 October 2021, https://www.washingtonpost.com/graphics/2020/business/sba-ppp-data/.
11. Sumitra Badrinathan, Devesh Kapur, Jonathan Kay and Milan Vaishnav, "Social realities of Indian Americans: results from the 2020 Indian American Attitudes Survey", Carnegie Endowment for International Peace, 2021, https://carnegieendowment.org/2021/06/09/social-realities-of-indian-americans-results-from-2020-indian-american-attitudes-survey-pub-84667.
12. Ari Hoffman and Jeanne Batalova, "Indian immigrants in the United States", *Spotlight*, Migration Policy Institute, 2022, https://www.migrationpolicy.org/article/indian-immigrants-united-states.
13. *Ibid.*
14. Sumitra Badrinathan, *et al.*, *op. cit.*
15. Interview with Deepa Iyer by the author, 8 March 2023.
16. Devesh Kapur and Jashan Bajwa, "'The invisible Indian': A study of poverty in the Indian American population", Indiaspora, October 2020, https://www.

indiaspora.org/reports/the-invisible-indian-a-study-of-poverty-in-the-indian-american-population.
17. *Ibid.*
18. Indian American Muslim Council, https://iamc.com/category/impending-genocide/.
19. Muqtedar Khan, "How Hindutva politics in the Indian Diaspora could help Trump in Texas", *The Wire*, 21 September 2020, https://thewire.in/world/hindutva-politics-indian-diaspora-donald-trump-houston-texas.
20. "The other one percent: Indians in America", Video Presentation, Carnegie Endowment for International Peace, 1 December 2016, https://carnegieendowment.org/2016/12/01/other-one-percent-indians-in-america-event-5433.
21. Interview with Deepa Iyer by the author, 8 March 2023.
22. *Ibid.*
23. Karthick Ramakrishnan, "Face the facts: South Asians need representation in Asian America", *Aapi Data*, 24 February 2023, https://aapidata.com/blog/facts-south-asians-2023/.
24. Interview with Kapil Sharma by the author, 25 February 2023.
25. Robert Barnes and Hannah Natanson, "Supreme court lets Thomas Jefferson High School admissions policy stand", *The Washington Post*, 25 April 2022, https://www.washingtonpost.com/politics/2022/04/25/supreme-court-high-school-admissions-race/.
26. Sumitra Badrinathan, Devesh Kapur and Milan Vaishnav, "How will Indian Americans vote? Results from the 2020 Indian American attitudes survey", Carnegie Endowment for International Peace, 14 October 2020, https://carnegieendowment.org/2020/10/14/how-will-indian-americans-vote-results-from-2020-indian-american-attitudes-survey-pub-82929.
27. Keethi Vedantam, "Tech layoffs: US companies that have cut jobs in 2022 and 2023", *Crunchbase News*, 2023, https://news.crunchbase.com/startups/tech-layoffs/.
28. Interview with Ro Khanna by the author, 15 March 2023.
29. David J. Bier, "1.4 million skilled immigrants in employment-based green card backlog in 2021", Cato Institute, 2022, https://www.cato.org/blog/14-million-skilled-immigrants-employment-based-green-card-backlogs-2021.
30. David J. Bier, "Employment-based green card Backlog Hits 1.2 million in 2020", Cato Institute, 2020, https://www.cato.org/blog/employment-based-green-card-backlog-hits-12-million-2020.

31. Time Carpenter, "Pompeo sorry for ethnic slur link", *The Topeka Capital-Journal*, 12 August 2010, https://www.cjonline.com/story/news/politics/state/2010/08/12/pompeo-sorry-for-ethnic-slur-link/16491931007/.
32. Natalie Allison, "Whisper campaign about RNC chair candidate's Sikh faith roils campaign", *Politico*, 11 January 2023, https://www.politico.com/news/2023/01/11/harmeet-dhillon-rnc-00077583.
33. Interview with Ro Khanna by the author, 15 March 2023.
34. Interview with M. R. Rangaswami by the author, 12 March 2023.
35. Ishani Duttagupta, "US philanthropy platform raises over $1million for 25 Indian NGOs with help of young Indian Americans", *Times of India*, 27 April 2023, https://timesofindia.indiatimes.com/nri/us-canada-news/us-philanthropy-platform-raises-over-1-million-for-25-indian-ngos-with-help-of-young-indian-americans/articleshow/99821572.cms.
36. Alex Counts, "How Indian American community is addressing social and economic issues through philanthropy", *American Kahani*, 7 February 2023, https://americankahani.com/perspectives/how-indian-american-community-is-addressing-social-and-economic-issues-through-philanthropy/.

About the Editors

C. Raja Mohan is a Visiting Research Professor at the Institute of South Asian Studies at the National University of Singapore. He was the Director of ISAS from May 2018 to December 2021.

Professor Raja Mohan was previously a Professor of South Asian Studies at Jawaharlal Nehru University, New Delhi, and the S. Rajaratnam School of International Studies, Nanyang Technological University, Singapore. He was also the founding director of Carnegie India, New Delhi — the sixth international centre of the Carnegie Endowment for International Peace, Washington DC.

Hernaikh Singh is Deputy Director at the Institute of South Asian Studies at the National University of Singapore. He has over 30 years of experience in Singapore government and non-government organisations, the business sector and academia.

Mr Singh's most recent book, *Coping with China–India Rivalry: South Asian Dilemmas,* was co-edited with C. Raja Mohan and published by World Scientific in 2023. Earlier, his co-edited book on *ASEAN and India: The Way Forward*, was published by World Scientific and launched by Singapore's Emeritus Senior Minister Goh Chok Tong in October 2022. Prior to that, his co-edited book, *India On Our Minds*, was also published by World Scientific and launched by Singapore's Prime Minister Lee Hsien Loong in December 2020.

About the Contributors

Asanga Abeyagoonasekera is an international security and geopolitics analyst and strategic advisor from Sri Lanka. He is a Senior Fellow and the Executive Director of the South Asia Foresight Network at the Millennium Project in Washington DC. He serves as a Technical Advisor to the International Monetary Fund and is an active member of the World Economic Forum.

Mr Abeyagoonasekera is the author of *Teardrop Diplomacy* (2023), *Conundrum of an Island* (2021) and *Sri Lanka at Crossroads* (2019). He was the founding Director-General of the National Security Think Tank under the Ministry of Defence until January 2020. Earlier, he served as the Executive Director of the Lakshman Kadirgamar Institute for International Relations and Strategic Studies under the Sri Lanka Ministry of External Affairs.

Javid Ahmad is a Senior Fellow with the Atlantic Council and a nonresident scholar at the Middle East Institute in Washington DC, where he focuses on counterterrorism, transregional militancy and illicit networks. From 2020 to 2021, he served as Afghanistan's Ambassador to the United Arab Emirates. Previously, he was a Fellow with the Modern War Institute at the United States (US) Military Academy at West Point and has worked with US defence contractors, including General Dynamics. He has also worked with the Pentagon's Afghanistan–Pakistan Hands, the German Marshall Fund (a Washington-based think tank) and the North Atlantic Treaty Organization headquarters in Brussels.

Mr Ahmad's writing has appeared in *The Wall Street Journal, The Washington Post, Foreign Affairs, The New York Times, Foreign Policy, The National Interest, The Hill* and *CNN*.

Devyani Chaturvedi is a Research Analyst at the Institute of South Asian Studies at the National University of Singapore (NUS). She graduated with a Master's degree in International Affairs from the Lee Kuan Yew School of Public Policy at NUS, specialising in international economics and development.

Ms Chaturvedi previously worked with the National Council of Applied Economic Research, New Delhi, where she examined India's trade, taxation and industrial policy. At the Council for Strategic and Defence Research, she was the research lead for policy analysis on the Indo-Pacific. She has also conducted research work at the Energy Studies Institute at NUS and the University of Pennsylvania's Institute of Advanced Studies.

Yogesh Joshi is a Research Fellow at the Institute of South Asian Studies (ISAS) at the National University of Singapore. His research focuses on contemporary Indian foreign and national security policy, with an emphasis on the Indo-Pacific's balance of power, evolution of India's military power and its approach to the use of force in international relations.

Before joining ISAS, Dr Joshi was a MacArthur and Stanton Nuclear Postdoctoral Fellow at the Center for International Security and Cooperation, Stanford University, United States. He is also an alumnus of the Summer Workshop on the Analysis of Military Operations and Strategy, Columbia University, and the International Nuclear History Boot Camp, Woodrow Wilson Center. He has a doctorate in International Politics from Jawaharlal Nehru University, New Delhi.

Michael Kugelman is the Director of the South Asia Institute at the Wilson Center in Washington DC. He is also a columnist for *Foreign Policy* and writes its weekly *South Asia Brief*, a newsletter featuring news and analyses from the region. His main countries of focus are Afghanistan, India and Pakistan.

Mr Kugelman's recent research projects look at the shifting geopolitics of South Asia, United States (US)–India technology cooperation, the future of US–Pakistan relations and how American strategic failures impacted the US-led war in Afghanistan.

S. D. Muni is Professor Emeritus at the School of International Studies, Jawaharlal Nehru University (JNU), and a member of the Executive Council of the Institute for Defence Studies and Analyses, New Delhi. For nearly 40 years, he taught, conducted and supervised research in international relations and South Asian studies at JNU (1974–2006), the Institute of South Asian Studies, National University of Singapore (2008–2013), Banaras Hindu University (1985–1986) and University of Rajasthan (1972–1973).

Professor Muni served as India's Ambassador to the Lao People's Democratic Republic (1997–1999) and Special Envoy to the Southeast Asian countries on United Nations Security Council Reforms (2005). He was also bestowed with Sri Lanka's highest national award for a foreigner — Sri Lanka Ratna.

Amitendu Palit is a Senior Research Fellow and Research Lead (Trade and Economics) at the Institute of South Asian Studies at the National University of Singapore. He is an economist specialising in international trade and investment policies, free trade agreements, supply chains, connectivity, cross-border data flows and the Indian economy. He sits on the World Economic Forum's Global Future Council on Trade and Investment. He is a Senior Research Fellow (Honorary) at the Wong Center for the Study of Multinational Corporations and an Adviser for Athena Infonomics.

Dr Palit has published in several peer-reviewed academic journals. He is a columnist for India's *Financial Express* and a regular contributor to the East–West Centre, *East Asia Forum* and *China Daily*.

Nishchal N. Pandey is the Director of the Centre for South Asian Studies, Kathmandu, and the Convener of the Consortium of South Asian Think Tanks. He was the Executive Director of the Institute of Foreign Affairs under the Ministry of Foreign Affairs where he worked in various capacities from 1998 to 2006.

Dr Pandey was also an Advisor to the National Planning Commission for the tourism and civil aviation sectors in 1996–1997 and was an expert at the Truth and Reconciliation Commission of Nepal in 2016. He was appointed a member of the high-level task force on foreign policy by the Nepal government in 2017. He is also currently a Non-Resident Senior Fellow at the Institute of South Asian Studies at the National University of Singapore.

Amit Ranjan is a Research Fellow at the Institute of South Asian Studies at the National University of Singapore. His latest edited books include *Migration, Regional Autonomy, and Conflicts in Eastern South Asia* (with Diotima Chattoraj, Palgrave, 2023), *Environment, Climate Change and Migration in South Asia* (with Rajesh Kharat and Pallavi Deka, 2023) and *Urban Development and Environmental History in Modern South Asia* (with Ian Talbot, 2023). He is also the author of *Contested Waters: India's Transboundary River Water Disputes in South Asia* (2021) and *India–Bangladesh Border Disputes: History and Post-LBA Dynamics* (2018). Earlier, he had also edited *India in South Asia: Challenges and Management (2019)*, *Partition of India: Postcolonial Legacies* (2019) and *Water Issues in Himalayan South Asia: Internal Challenges, Disputes and Transboundary Tensions* (2019).

Seema Sirohi is a Washington DC-based columnist and writes on foreign policy and India's place in the world for *The Economic Times*, India's largest business daily. She has covered India–United States relations for over three decades for *The Telegraph*, *Outlook*, *Anandabazar Patrika* and *FirstPost.com*. She has also reported from Italy, Austria, Israel, Slovakia, Sri Lanka and Pakistan and published opinion pieces in *The Los Angeles Times*, *The Christian Science Monitor* and *The Baltimore Sun*.

Ms Sirohi is the author of *Friends with Benefits: The India–US Story*, published by HarperCollins India in January 2023. Her first book, *Sita's Curse: Stories of Dowry Victims*, was published in 2003.

Farooq Sobhan is currently a Distinguished Fellow and Member of the Board of Governors of the Bangladesh Enterprise Institute (BEI). Established as an independent research institute in 2000, BEI focuses on research projects relating to regional cooperation in South Asia, Bangladesh's relations with India, China and the United States, private sector development, governance, and extremism and other security issues. He is the former President and founder Chief Executive Officer of the Institute.

Ambassador Sobhan was Executive Chairman of the Board of Investment and a Special Envoy to the Bangladesh Prime Minister from 1997 to 1999 and Foreign Secretary of Bangladesh from 1995 to 1997. He has also served as Ambassador/High Commissioner to India, China, Malaysia and the United Nations. Ambassador Sobhan has written extensively on international affairs and relations.

Monish Tourangbam is an Associate Professor at the Amity Institute of International Studies, Amity University (Noida), India. He is the Honorary Director at the Kalinga Institute of Indo-Pacific Studies, India. Formerly, he was a Senior Assistant Professor at the Department of Geopolitics and International Relations, Manipal Academy of Higher Education, Manipal, and an Associate Fellow at the Observer Research Foundation, New Delhi. He was a Visiting Faculty at the Department of Political Science, University of Cincinnati, Ohio, and a South Asian Voices Visiting Fellow at the Stimson Centre, Washington DC.

Dr Tourangbam was the Associate Editor of the *Indian Foreign Affairs Journal*. He has participated in several Track 2 dialogues. He was an international observer of the Russian presidential election in 2018 and has several publications to his credit.

Marvin G. Weinbaum is Professor Emeritus of Political Science at the University of Illinois at Urbana-Champaign and served as an analyst for Pakistan and Afghanistan in the United States Department of State's Bureau of Intelligence and Research from 1999 to 2003. He is currently a scholar-in-residence and Director of Afghanistan and Pakistan Studies at the Middle East Institute in Washington DC.

Professor Weinbaum has held adjunct professorships at Georgetown and George Washington Universities. He was awarded Fulbright Research Fellowships for Egypt in 1981–1982 and Afghanistan in 1989–1990. He received his doctorate from Columbia University in 1965, his Master of Arts from the University of Michigan in 1958 and his Bachelor of Arts from Brooklyn College in 1957.

Index

8th Bangladesh–US Bilateral Security Dialogue, 120–121
8th US–Bangladesh Partnership Dialogue, 119–120
9/11 attacks, 15, 36, 80, 224
9/11 terror attacks, 3
9th Bangladesh–US Defence Dialogue, 121–122

A
Afghanistan, 16–19, 53–75
Af-Pak, 33–48
Akhundzada, Mullah Haibatullah, 73
Al-Qaeda, 16, 35–36, 54, 59
al-Zawahiri, Ayman, 18
Anti-Terrorism Act, 149
Aquilino, John Christopher, 183
AUKUS, 8

B
Bajwa, Qamar Javed, 44
Belt and Road Initiative, 6, 37
beneficiary developing countries, 207
Bhutan, 97–110
Bhutto, Bilawal, 83

Biden, Joe, 1, 7–10, 13–27, 53, 113
Bilateral Communications Compatibility and the Security Agreement, 39
Birendra Peace Operations Training Centre, 100
Blinken, Antony J., 17, 119
Blome, Donald, 81
Bush, George W., 3–4, 15, 36

C
Chen Xu, 149
Chhabra, Tarun, 219
China factor, 88–89
Chinese Communist Party, 138, 145
Chollet, Derek, 83, 124, 126
Chung, Julie, 141
climate change cooperation, 89–90, 117–118
Clinton, Bill, 1, 178
Clinton, Hillary, 37
Cold War, 2–3, 20–21, 33–38, 179, 181–182
Colemen, Isobel, 121
Communications Compatibility and Security Agreement, 39

Comprehensive and Progressive Transpacific Partnership, 198–199
confidence-building measures, 182
Countering America's Adversaries Through Sanctions Act, 41, 184–185
counterterrorism, 26
COVID-19 pandemic, 13, 99, 109, 118, 197, 225

D

Dahal, Pushpa Kamal, 104
Data Protection Act (DPA), 127
Defense Trade and Technology Initiative, 186
Development Objective Agreement, 99
Dhillon, Harmeet, 219
Digital Security Act, 127

E

East Container Terminal, 151
economic cooperation, 114–115
Eisenhower, Dwight D., 177
energy cooperation, 117
European Union, 137
exclusive economic zone, 42

F

Financial Action Task Force, 86
foreign policy, 14–16
Free and Open Indo-Pacific Strategy, 39
free trade agreements, 198, 209–210

G

generalised system of preferences, 187, 198, 205–209

Global Magnitsky Human Rights Accountability Act, 125
great war on terror, 3
Gunawardena, Dinesh, 143

H

H-1Bs, 226–228
Haas, Peter D., 118
Haley, Nikki, 217
Harris, Harry B., 100
Hasina, Sheikh, 46, 124, 129
health sector, 118
Himalayas, 97–110
humanitarian, 61–63
human rights, 147–149

I

Indian American Muslim Council, 222–223
Indian Americans, 217–230
India Philanthropy Alliance, 230
India–United States relations, 177–191
India–US Defense Relations, 183
India–US trade, 200–206
Indo-Pacific, 6–7
Indo-Pacific Economic Framework for Prosperity, 123, 197–211
Indo-Pacific strategy, 184
initiative on Critical and Emerging Technology, 25, 184, 186
intellectual property, 205
Interim National Security Strategic Guidance, 15
International Labour Organization, 122
International Military Education and Training, 87–88

International Monetary Fund, 137
ISIS, 19
Islamic Movement of Uzbekistan, 59
Islamic State-Khorasan Province, 54, 59, 86–87
Iyer, Deepa, 222

J
Jaishankar, S., 148
Jaish-e-Mohammed, 80
Janata Samajbadi Party, 103
Japanese Light Rail Transit project, 151

K
Kapur, Devesh, 224
Kennedy, John F., 177
Kerry, John, 117
Khadka, Narayan, 104
Khan, Imran, 44, 82
Khan, Muqtedar, 223
Kugelman, Michael, 9

L
Laden, Osama Bin, 15
Lashkar-e-Taiba, 80
Li Zhanshu, 100
Lu, Donald, 123–124

M
Maldives, 6, 9, 34, 39, 45–48, 160–172
maritime security, 116–117
Millennium Challenge Corporation's (MCC), 47, 151
Miller, Aruna, 312
Ministry of Foreign Affairs, 103
Mizukoshi, Hideaki, 152
Modi, Narendra, 1, 23, 189, 211

Mohan, C. Raja, 40, 45
Muni, S. D., 9

N
National Defense Strategy, 14
national security approach, 18
National Security Strategy, 14, 41, 43, 141, 149
Nepal, 97–110
Nixon, Richard, 91
non-security cooperation, 86–88
North Atlantic Treaty Organization, 3, 84–85
Nuland, Victoria, 119, 142

O
Obama, Barack, 4, 85
Operation Enduring Freedom, 15
Organization of Islamic Cooperation, 92

P
Pakistan, 4
Pandey, Nishchal N., 9
Paycheck Protection Program, 220
Pentagon National Defence Strategy, 149
People's Liberation Army, 42
Pompeo, Michael R., 229
Prevention of Terrorism Act, 143

Q
Quadrilateral Security Dialogue (Quad), 6, 8, 39, 183

R
Ramakrishnan, Karthick, 225
Ramaswamy, Vivek, 217
Rangaswami, M. R., 219

Reagan, Ronald, 98
Regional Comprehensive Economic Partnership, 198–199
Rice, Condoleezza, 180
Rizvi, Gowher, 46
Russian–Ukraine war, 99, 184

S
Sawant, Kshama, 221
sea lines of communication, 142
security, 86–88
security and defence cooperation, 115–117
Sharma, Kapil, 225
Singh, Manmohan, 178
Sino-US competition, 33–34, 40
South Asia, 1–10, 13–27, 38–40, 45–47
Soviet Union, 2–3, 33
Special Immigrant Visa, 60–61
Sri Lanka and the US, 137–154
State Partnership Program, 104
Sullivan, John J., 109
Syed, Dilawar, 89

T
Taliban, 53–75
Talibanism, 57
Tehreek-e-Taliban Pakistan, 87
Tibetan refugees, 105–108
Tourangbam, Monish, 9
Trade and Investment Cooperation Forum Agreement, 114
Trudeau, Elizabeth Kennedy, 100
Trump, Donald, 1, 5–7, 221

U
United Nations Human Rights Council, 145, 148
United Nations Security Council, 6
United States, 1–10
United States and the Maldives, 159–172
United States–Bangladesh relations, 113–129
United States–Pakistan relations, 79–93
UN Security Council, 109
US Agency for International Development, 86, 98, 117, 146, 152–153
US–Bangladesh High-level Economic Consultation, 122–123
US Bilateral Assistance, 138–140
US–China rivalry, 8
US–India partnership, 2, 22–25, 85
US–India Trade Policy Forum, 203–204
US Millennium Challenge Corporation Nepal Compact, 100–105
US National Security Strategy, 180
US–Nepal development cooperation, 98–99
US–Pakistan relationship, 19–22
US South Asia policy, 34–38
US–Sri Lanka relations, 46, 137–154
US Trade Representative, 204

V
Vajpayee, Atal Bihari, 181–182
Vedanta–Foxconn deal, 49

X
Xi Jinping, 182

Printed in the United States
by Baker & Taylor Publisher Services